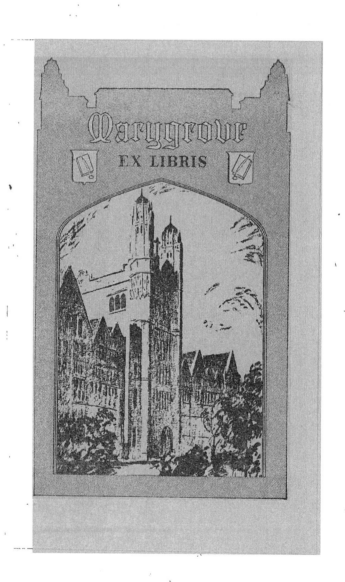

Marygrove
EX LIBRIS

FROM VIRGIL TO MILTON

Books by C. M. Bowra

THE HERITAGE OF SYMBOLISM
A BOOK OF RUSSIAN VERSE

FROM VIRGIL TO MILTON

BY

C. M. BOWRA

LONDON

MACMILLAN & CO. LTD

1948

PREFACE

This book is a study of the literary epic in four of its chief examples, and especially of certain characteristics which seem to belong to this kind of poetry. Though the epic has lost much of its old popularity, it remains one of the most remarkable expressions of the poetic art and is an important source of information for all who are interested in ideals of manhood. I have limited myself to these four authors because they seem to me greater than any of their many rivals and because they cover a wide variety of experience. Since quotations in foreign languages may cause trouble to some readers, I have given translations. Fortunately both Tasso and Camões found translators when the epic was still a living art. Sir Edward Fairfax published his version of Tasso in 1600 and Sir Richard Fanshawe his version of Camões in 1655. No modern translator can hope to rival their vigour and vitality, and if I have sometimes deserted or emended them, it is simply in the interests of greater accuracy. There is no comparable translation of Virgil, and I have done the best that I can for him, though I have occasionally used the translation by C. J. Billson and am grateful to Mr. B. H. Blackwell for permission to do so. I am also grateful to Professor W. J. Entwistle for helping me with my chapter on Camões and for making it less erroneous than it would otherwise have been.

C. M. BOWRA

Oxford, *December* 5th, 1944

CONTENTS

I

SOME CHARACTERISTICS
OF LITERARY EPIC

In the disputable and usually futile task of classifying the forms of poetry there is no great quarrel about the epic. An epic poem is by common consent a narrative of some length and deals with events which have a certain grandeur and importance and come from a life of action, especially of violent action such as war. It gives a special pleasure because its events and persons enhance our belief in the worth of human achievement and in the dignity and nobility of man. Inside this field it is easy to make distinctions, and everyone is familiar with that between "authentic" and "literary" epic. Such a distinction may invite distrust. For in the fine arts no rules are binding, and it is dangerous to be too precise in saying what a thing is or what it ought to be. And this particular distinction may well arouse other misgivings; for we may suspect that the adjectives are not chosen impartially but betray a liking for one kind of poetry and a dislike for another. While "authentic" suggests the wild wood-notes of pure poetry, the inspired, direct and unpremeditated song of the poet whom culture has not corrupted, "literary" suggests the derivative and the manufactured, the poverty of *le vers calculé* against the wealth of *le vers donné*, the reliance on books instead of on life, all that Verlaine meant when, after sketching his ideal poem, he said

> Et tout le reste est littérature.

When the innocent student is first confronted by the anti-thesis between "authentic" and "literary" epic, he must surely feel that he should admire the first and be suspicious, if not contemptuous, of the second, while those experienced in the ways of critics must no less surely feel that the distinction is prejudiced if not false, and is perhaps dictated by irrational beliefs in *Volksgeist* and *Volkspoesie* and by theories which in the interests of racial mysticism ascribe all excellences to the anonymous activities of a community rather than to the deliberate work of individual poets.

Yet though this distinction rightly arouses distrust, it would be wrong to dismiss it as worthless. There is undeniably a great difference between *Beowulf* and the *Song of Roland* on the one hand and the *Aeneid* and *Paradise Lost* on the other. But this difference is not primarily one of poetical quality. If the *Aeneid* can show nothing so stark or so sublime as Roland's refusal to blow his horn, the *Song of Roland* has nothing so intimate or so tragic as the last hours and death of Dido. Each poem succeeds in its own way; each makes its special contribution to the vision and understanding of life. We cannot say that the one kind is necessarily better than the other; we can merely mark the differences between them and enjoy the pleasure that each has to give. But though it is easy to recognise a distinction between two kinds of epic, that is not enough to justify us in calling the one " authentic " and the other " literary ". Such a division must be made on more solid grounds than a vague dissimilarity between two kinds of aesthetic enjoyment. And in fact such grounds exist. The two classes of epic are really distinct because their technique is different and because each owes its character to special methods of composition.

The distinction between *Beowulf* and *Paradise Lost*, to take two extreme examples, is mainly that between oral and written epic, between what is meant to be heard and what is meant to be read, between what is recited and what is put down in a book. Oral epic is the mature form of improvised lays such as still survive in Jugoslavia and were once popular in many parts of the world. In such countries the bard, like Homer's Demodocus, composes his poem as he recites it. He improvises impromptu, and his art requires a long and elaborate training. To tell a tale in this way he must have at his complete command a large number of lines and phrases to deal with any situation in his story; he may have stock passages for such recurring themes as the throwing of a weapon, the putting of a boat to sea, the coming of morning or evening, and all the other machinery of story-telling; he must have a rich supply of stories, for he may be called to recite any of them; he may have to be master of a traditional language which bears little relation to the vernacular of his home and has been created by generations of bards simply as the language of poetry. In his case the Greek fancy that Memory is the Mother of the Muses is true. For unless his technique is at his finger-tips, unless he can surmount with immediate and unnoticed ease whatever difficulties his theme presents, he will hesitate and stumble and fail. His task is to use as best as he can for his immediate purpose the phrases and lines which he has learned in his apprenticeship. Of such an art Homer shows a transcendent development. It is impossible to believe that the *Iliad* and the *Odyssey*, as we know them, were ever improvised, but their technique is largely that of improvisation and comes directly from it. The famous constant epithets, the repeated lines and blocks of lines, the copious store of synonyms and of alternative word-forms, are a heritage from improvisation. Homer practises on a grand scale an oral art which has grown out of improvised poetry, and this art is in many technical respects the art of *Beowulf* and the *Song of Roland*. The conditions of improvisation and of recitation have created a kind of poetry which can be recognised by its use of repetitions and formulas. And this poetry is far removed from that of Virgil or Milton. If they sometimes show traces of it, it is because they are following Homer in the conscious conviction that they ought to do so, not because their conditions compel them to use devices which are indispensable to oral poetry and make it what it is.

This difference in conditions of composition leads to a difference in the character of the poetry. Because Homer composed for recitation, his composition is in some ways freer and looser than Virgil's. Both his poems have a majestic plan ; both pass through crisis to a conclusion. But they are less closely woven than the *Aeneid* ; their episodes are more easily detached from the whole and may be enjoyed as separate poems. The Greek epic poet might compose on a grand scale, but he could not always or even often expect to recite his poem in its entirety. He must be prepared to select from it, to recite only a section which must be relatively complete in itself and not require too much explanation for its understanding. Because Homer, especially in the *Iliad*, has a loose method of composition, his art has been misjudged, and it has even been thought that his poems are collections of separate lays fastened together, as philologists of the nineteenth century fashioned the Finnish *Kalevala* from lays by different authors. But the *Iliad* is a single poem with a single plan and a remarkably consistent use of language. Its looseness of construction and of texture is the product of the circumstances in which it was composed; it might be used for piecemeal recitations and must be ready for them. Even Homer's apparent carelessness about details, which might seem a fault in a novelist, is part of his oral art. He must concentrate severely on what is really relevant, and if he were to give too much attention to small points, he would confuse his listeners and lose their attention. Modern critics, for instance, may complain that at an important crisis Achilles puts down his spear only to be found with it in his hand later, but Homer knew that the taking up of a spear is in itself of no interest, provided that Achilles has his spear when he needs it.

Between Homer's oral and Virgil's written art there is an enormous difference. The poet who writes for readers operates less with phrases and formulas than with single words. He fashions his sentences carefully and individually; he takes care to avoid omissions and contradictions, to harmonise the details of his plot, to secure an interwoven unity for his whole design. Even when he follows Homer in using the oral device of repetition, Virgil goes his own way and makes variations on a given form. For him the artifices of oral poetry are valuable for their archaic elegance; their beauty is no longer functional. Virgil is seldom wholehearted in his attempts at repetition. He prefers to vary the words and to show in how many different ways he can describe such familiar matters as the coming of dawn or of evening. Even when his characters speak to each other, they do so not with Homer's regular forms of address but with elaborate variations, no two of which are quite alike. The old formulas were of no real use to Virgil and were even a hindrance; for his aim was to compose a poem which could be read with exact and appreciative care, and for that reason he gains more by variation than by repetition.

Virgil's art is in fact akin to other modern poetry. Its aim is to pack each line with as much significance as possible, to make each word do its utmost work and to secure that careful attention which the reader, unlike the listener, can give. If the oral epic triumphs through its simplicity and strength and straightforwardness, through the unhesitating sweep of its narrative and a brilliant clarity in its main effects, the written epic appeals by its poetical texture, by its exquisite or apt or impressive choice of words, by the rich significance of phrases and lines and paragraphs. Homer sweeps us away by the irresistible movement of lines through a whole passage to a splendid climax. What counts is the singleness of his effect, the unbroken maintenance of a heroic or tragic mood, the concentration on some action vividly imagined and clearly portrayed without irrelevance or second thoughts or even those hints that lure into bypaths of fancy and suggest that there is more in the words than is obvious at first sight. But in Virgil, great though the paragraphs are, compelling though the climax is when it is reached, we are more concerned with the details, with each small effect and each deftly placed word, than with the whole. We linger over the richness of single phrases, over the " pathetic half-lines ", over the precision or potency with which a word illuminates a sentence or a happy sequence of sounds imparts an inexplicable charm to something that might otherwise have been trivial. Of course Homer has his magical phrases and Virgil his bold effects, but the distinction stands. It is a matter of composition, of art, and it marks the real difference between the two kinds of epic, which are not so much " authentic " and " literary " as oral and written.

This distinction extends far beyond a comparison of Homer and Virgil. It enables us to distinguish between one class of epic which contains the *Iliad* and *Odyssey*, *Beowulf*, the *Song of Roland* and a large mass of Jugoslav lays, and another class which contains the *Aeneid*, *Os Lusiadas*, *Gerusalemme Liberata* and *Paradise Lost*. If we call the first class oral, there is no objection to calling the second " literary " provided that we understand the word to mean " written " and to suggest that the art in such poems is not of the recited but of the written word. The distinction is of origins and character, not of quality and worth. Indeed when a class of poetry falls into two kinds in this way, each will have its champions, and it is impossible to decide between them or to say that the one is right and the other wrong. For each kind has grown in its own way and provides its own special delight. In Homer, in *Beowulf*, in the best of the mediaeval French epics, it is the story, its characters, its episodes and above all its temper that count. The very lack of precision or of insistence on detail makes the effects more impressive. What Homer does again and again, *Beowulf* does in the sinister and uncanny passages on the monster Grendel and the *Song of Roland* in such austere sublimities as Roland's death and the supernatural darkness which portends it. No written epic quite rivals these at their best on their own ground. The heroic actions in Tasso or Milton are more complex and more ingenious than their precedents in Homer. The poets have lavished care and scholarship upon them ; they have entered into the spirit of adventurous risk and caught its glamour, but there is something lacking, — the immediate and effortless ease with which Homer rises to such a topic and carries it through to its end. And this lack is inevitable. The writers of literary epic see their subject through a haze of learned associations ; they do not come to it directly as to a part of their daily lives. Their distance from it deprives them of the noble simplicity which is so natural to Homer. Moreover, because they are writing for readers and are concerned with the evocative power of every word, they demand a close attention which by its very nature excludes the immediate and direct pleasure which is given by oral poets.

A choice of examples may help to make this distinction clearer. When Roland, after an incomparable fight against insuperable odds, dies, his death is a climax in the Norman poem. Resting against a pine-tree he looks towards Spain and remembers the lands that he has conquered, remembers too his own sweet France, the men of his race, his overlord Charlemagne, all the simple elements of a life given to glory and to battle. Then he prays for the last time to God and asks for his soul to be delivered. The scene concludes :

Sun destre guant a Deu en puroffrit.
Seint Gabriel de sa man l'ad pris.
Desur sun braz teneit le chef enclin ;
Juntes ses mains est alet a sa fin.
Deus tramist sun angle Cherubin
E seint Michel del Peril ;

6

Ensembl' od els sent Gabriel i vint.
L'anme del cunte portent en pareïs.[1]
(2389-96)

The whole effect is beyond praise. Each event, so shortly and plainly told, is appropriate to the dying hero. The simple method of narration brings its own emotion, the sense of a quiet Christian end to the long and turbulent day of blood. With this, despite many differences of circumstances, we may compare another death. In the *Aeneid* Dido, herself no mean leader of men, kills herself when Aeneas deserts her. Virgil spends all his powers on her last moments and dwells upon them : ·

Illa, gravis oculos conata attollere, rursus
deficit ; infixum stridit sub pectore vulnus.
ter sese attollens cubitoque adnixa levavit ;
ter revoluta toro est, oculisque errantibus alto
quaesivit caelo lucem ingemuitque reperta.[2]
(IV, 688-92)

The art of the two passages is entirely different. The *Song of Roland* achieves an absolutely single and homogeneous effect, stirs almost a single emotion and leaves no room for reflection on remote or extraneous issues. In Virgil the poetry is more abundant, more suggestive, more intricate, but the choice of incidents is not so vivid or the actual description so significant. The words mean too much, the wavering rhythms start too many echoes, for a single picture to emerge or a single impression to dominate the mind. In return for this what a wealth of effect there is in Virgil's choice of adjectives, — the eyes first " heavy " and then " wandering ", — in the

[1] His right-hand glove, to God he offers it ;
Saint Gabriel from's hand hath taken it.
Over his arm his head bows down and slips,
He joins his hands ; and so is life finish'd.
God sent him down his Angel cherubim,
And Saint Michael, we worship in peril ;
And by their side Saint Gabriel alit ;
So the count's soul they bare to Paradis.
(C. K. Scott-Moncrieff)

[2] She tried to lift her heavy eyes, again
Fell back. The death-wound grated in her breast.
Thrice, leaning on her arm, she raised her head ;
Thrice on the bed, fell back, with wandering eyes
Sought heaven's light, and, when she found it, moaned.
(C. J. Billson)

sense of frustrated and futile effort matched by the pauses and the stops, in the long-drawn misery of the fruitless struggle and the cry of agony that sounds in the last words.

It might be argued that the difference of kind which these passages illustrate is due to a difference of temperament, that the poet of Roland saw his subject simply and clearly while Virgil saw his heavy with meaning and clouded with mystery. There is truth in this, but it is not the whole truth. For we may well doubt whether the conditions of oral epic allow a poet to express himself so elaborately as Virgil does, even if he has the wish and the capacity to do so. This may be seen from one of Homer's most sublime and most pathetic passages. When Odysseus, ignorant that his mother is dead, sees her ghost at the world's end, he asks her how she died, and in due course she tells him :

> οὔτ' ἐμέ γ' ἐν μεγάροισιν ἐΰσκοπος ἰοχέαιρα
> οἷς ἀγανοῖς βελέεσσιν ἐποιχομένη κατέπεφνεν,
> οὔτε τις οὖν μοι νοῦσος ἐπήλυθεν, ἥ τε μάλιστα
> τηκεδόνι στυγερῇ μελέων ἐξείλετο θυμόν·
> ἀλλά με σός τε πόθος σά τε μήδεα, φαίδιμ' Ὀδυσσεῦ,
> σή τ' ἀγανοφροσύνη μελιηδέα θυμὸν ἀπηύρα.[1]
>
> (Od. XI, 198-203)

In this passage the Greek language flows in its most majestical harmonies, and of course Homer's art is incomparably finer and richer and subtler than that of the *Song of Roland*. But fundamentally it is of the same kind. The single emotion of an old woman's love for her son rules the whole passage and, though poetry cannot be nobler than in these vivid, sonorous, expressive words, there is nothing in them of Virgil's play and counterplay, no half-hidden effect whose beauty is revealed only at a second or third reading, no manipulation of sounds and stops to suit the shifting pattern of a complex whole, no attempt to include a complex experience in the compass of a few lines. Homer is coherent, direct, inevitable ; he expresses a single, unqualified, sublime mood. On a first reading he overwhelms by the sheer force and majesty of his words, and

---

[1] For it was not that she, the keen-eyed Archer of Heaven,
Stole on me unperceived and painlessly smote with her arrows,
Nor did a fever attack me, and with its wasting consumption,
Such as is common with men, drain out the life from the body ;
But it was longing and care for thee, my noble Odysseus,
And for thy kindness of heart that robbed me of life and its sweetness.

on each subsequent reading we recapture our first delight. But we are unlikely to find hidden echoes and neglected hints as we know the passage better, though we shall not admire it less. The reason for this is that Homer composed for hearers and was forced to concentrate his powers on his main theme, to make it pre-eminently vivid and significant, and to neglect subsidiary or extraneous associations which might have been brought into it.

The difference in the methods of epic composition coincides on the whole with another difference which is social and even spiritual. For most oral epics display what is commonly and rightly called a heroic spirit and come from societies which hold heroic standards of conduct, while literary epics, though they have their " heroes ", have a different conception of heroism and of human greatness and come from societies which cannot really be called heroic. The heroic world holds nothing so important as the prowess and fame of the individual hero. The single man, Achilles or Beowulf or Roland, surpasses others in strength and courage. His chief, almost his only, aim is to win honour and renown through his achievements and to be remembered for them after his death. He is ruthless to any who frustrate or deride him. In his more than human strength he seems to be cut off from the intercourse of common men and consorts with a few companions only less noble than himself. He lacks allegiance, except in a modified sense, to suzerain or cause. What matters is his prowess. Even morality hardly concerns him ; for he lives in a world where what counts is not morality but honour. Historically, this ideal seems to have grown in societies which have burst through the stiff forms of primitive life. It is the reflection of men's desire to be in the last degree themselves, to satisfy their ambitions in lives of abundant adventure, to be greater than other men in their superior gifts, and to be bound by no obligation except to do their uttermost in valour and endurance. If they succeeded, such men were thought to be comparable almost to gods. This ideal, outmoded though it has long been in most parts of the world and intolerable as it is in civilised society, had its uses when peoples were on the move, as the Greeks were in the dawn of their history or the Angles and Saxons were when they came to England from their continental homes.

In such times the hero, the superman, is the leader who inspires and commands others in the work of war which precedes the establishment of a new order.

The claim of this heroic ideal is that after all it is an ideal and that its adherents are ready to make any sacrifice for it. Even though Achilles lives mainly to win glory and assumes that it is his right, his life is darkened by suffering and at the end he dies for his belief in his heroic manhood. His aim is not ease but glory, and glory makes exacting demands. A man who is willing to give his life for it wins the respect of his fellows, and when he makes his last sacrifice, they honour him. Even Roland, who ostensibly fights for Charlemagne and for Christendom, comes to his heroic end simply because his honour has been wounded and he feels that he must make amends by facing incalculable odds. In fact, what counts in the high estimate in which such men are held is not so much their power to destroy as their readiness to die. Their heroism is the greater because they sacrifice pre-eminent gifts of strength or beauty or eloquence or counsel. The doom of a short and glorious life which hangs over Achilles is tragic in its menace that he, the noblest and most gifted of men, is soon to go down to the dust and be made equal to the humblest servant. The memory of Roland haunted the Middle Ages because he, the greatest of soldiers, was willing to give his life for something that he valued above everything else, — his honour. It is because they are ready to make this last annihilating sacrifice that heroes are honoured. Compared with this even their courage and prowess are of secondary importance.

The truly heroic ideal and standards of conduct did not exist for the writers of literary epic. Though Virgil was a devoted student of Homer and owed much to him, he had quite a different conception of human worth and lived in a society from which Homer's heroes were remote and alien. When he took the traditional epic form, he had to adapt it to the changed conditions of his own day. Between him and his heroic models lay a vast tract of history. He looked to the past for inspiration, but his work was inevitably shaped by the present. His epic has rightly been called " secondary "; for, it was an attempt to use again in new circumstances what had already been a complete and satisfactory form of poetry.

Virgil differs from Homer in at least two essential points. First, his method of composition, as we have seen, is meant for readers, and in consequence the whole texture of his poetry is different. Secondly, his conception of heroism is equally different. He has one, but it is not Homer's, or indeed that of any heroic age. The whole temper of the *Aeneid* is far from that of the *Iliad*. Virgil created a poetry which was epic in its scope and nobility and sense of human worth but was unlike any other epic before it. So great was his success that other poets have followed his example, and their performance is such that we can mark a whole class of literary epic, discern its special characteristics and consider it as a whole.

It may seem artificial to class the work of such men as Camões, Tasso and Milton with that of Virgil, — for the good reason that not only did they write after him but they knew his work well and consciously imitated it in many ways. Indeed the whole theory of epic in the Renaissance was built upon Virgil's practice. When the " immortal " Vida wrote his *Ars Poetica*, he laid down rules for epic of an exact and exacting kind, and insisted that any modern epic must closely follow a Virgilian model. To these rules the epic poets of the Renaissance were in their different ways obedient. Epic had become almost a standard form, and the poets competed in the new turns which they gave to a traditional theme or device. It might therefore be claimed that these poets model themselves on Virgil and are his successors and imitators but not his peers in the same kind of poetry. This might well be true, but the facts suggest a different conclusion. The epic poets of the Renaissance were indeed Virgilians both in their desire to rival him and in their dependence on him, but they were also his peers because they did in their own way what he had done in his and because the conditions in which they worked were often like his and led to independent results which are comparable to his. Literary epic is the work of a real class of poets who resemble each other in aim and outlook, and it is widely separated from heroic epic both ancient and modern.

The fundamental difference between literary and oral epic is in the circumstances of origin. The writers of literary epic lived in highly organised societies where unfettered individualism had no place. Neither Virgil under the all-pervading influence of Augustus Caesar, nor Camões under the Catholic monarchy of Portugal, nor Tasso under the Counter-Reformation, nor Milton under Cromwell and the Puritans, was likely to praise the virtues of a noble barbarian. Even their lords and patrons did not claim to be heroes in the old sense. Augustus liked to be thought the first citizen of Rome, bound by all the decencies of conventional morality ; the potentates and prelates of the Renaissance, Reformation and Counter-Reformation were Christian rulers who believed that they were at least subordinate to God. Man had changed his place in the universe. His life was no longer a short span of light in the encompassing darkness, his duty no longer towards himself. From the eminence of his own glory he had been reduced to a subordinate position where he was much inferior to the state or the church to which he belonged. Cosmogonies and theologies had arisen which displayed his insignificance before the vast abyss of time, the claims of empire, or the will of God. The very qualities for which the old heroes had been honoured were themselves suspect or barely understood. That Achilles or Roland should harm their sovereign lieges from motives of injured pride was not a notion to appeal to the potentates of imperial Rome or Renaissance Europe. Nor in such times could individual prowess have the significance that it had for Homer. The great prince was not the warrior who defeated his enemies in hand-to-hand encounter but the organiser of victory and the administrator who imposed his will upon other men. It was impossible for the epic poet to treat his subject in the old heroic spirit. If he wished to present a heroic theme, he must create a new type of hero and a new ideal of heroism.

It is certainly paradoxical that civilised societies and their poets should claim for those whom they admire names and titles which belong to ages very unlike their own, and that the conception of heroic man should appeal as it did to the Augustan age and the Renaissance. In such a quest different forces were at work. Both at Rome and in the Renaissance the epic was thought to be the grandest and noblest form of poetry and the right means to celebrate great achievements. No doubt its scale was felt to be appropriate to such subjects. Its mere size appealed to a love of grandeur and magnificence. But more important was the spirit of the epic, its attempt to

find significance in the achievements of man and to show
him in his essential nobility. The writers of literary epic
held new and different conceptions of human greatness, but
such was their concern for it that epic alone could suffice to
portray it. Moreover they were particularly impressed by
the special form which the old heroic outlook took. The
great hero, Achilles or Roland, appeals to two deep impulses
of the human heart, the desire for glory and the respect for
sacrifice. Through the second the first is satisfied ; the hero
sacrifices his life and wins thereby an immortal glory. When
this happens, the human state gains in dignity, and the value
of its efforts is triumphantly affirmed. It must have been for
this reason more than for any other that Virgil and his
successors believed that only through epic could they say all
that they wished. It was the right means for them to assert
their belief in human greatness and to show the special form
of it which they honoured.

Virgil revealed a new field both for glory and for sacrifice.
The cause which deserves the one and inspires the other was
for him not an ideal of individual prowess but of service to
Rome. It is Rome to whom in the last resort the glory of
her sons belongs, and it is for her that they make their sacrifices
not merely of life but of happiness and personal ambitions
and all that the old heroic type took for granted as its right.
Virgil abandons the scheme of life by which the hero lives and
dies for his own glory, and replaces a personal by a social
ideal. The old concept of a man's honour is merged in a
scheme of morality where duties are laid down with precision
and must be fulfilled if the gods' will is to be done. Virgil
revealed an entirely new use for epic to an age for which the
old heroic outlook was too anarchic and anti-social. With him
the epic became national, and though later it was to extend
its scope beyond the boundaries of nations and of continents,
his was the first step in a new direction. Moreover, because
he had a new outlook on human greatness, he brought into
the epic much that earlier poets denied or neglected. Above
all he made it contain almost a philosophy of life and death,
a view of the universe which answered many desires in the
heart of man and provided an impressive background to the
new ideal. Virgil's epic is still epic because it treats of what
is greatest and noblest in man ; it is of a new kind because

this greatness and this nobility are themselves new.

When the poets of the Renaissance followed Virgil's example, they were moved by more than one reason. His pre-eminent prestige was of course largely due to the magic of his poetry. He exerted a powerful spell on men to whom Latin was a second tongue and the classical past almost an ideal world. For Vida he is the greatest of all poets and the most worthy of study and imitation. He was studied in every school and became the chief model of the many Renaissance poets who wrote in Latin. From him young poets learned the elements of their art, and there was no serious doubt about his perfection. But he was more than a poet and a model. He kept in the Renaissance some of the special appeal which had been his in the Middle Ages. The poet whom Dante made the voice of earthly wisdom was held in even greater honour when classical learning revived, and the Renaissance saw in Virgil much that had meant little or nothing to Dante. For him Virgil expounds one part, and only one part, of man's ambiguous existence between earth and heaven. For the Renaissance Virgil might not be an oracle on all earthly matters, but he was something that mattered more. He had tried to interpret the spiritual significance of the Roman Empire and to cast the light of heroic glory on its achievements. His admirers wished to do the like for their own times, to make the most of the secular glory which their age valued so highly and to see in it symbols and signs of something spiritual and eternal. Just as Virgil created a poetical philosophy for Rome, so in their different ways Camões, Tasso and Milton wished to pierce the surface of things to their real and abiding significance, to explain the duty and the magnificence of man, and to create works of art which should take note of all that was most important in the world. The wide sweep of Virgil's poem, his inclusion of so much history and religion and philosophy, was an enlivening example to poets who wished their own work to survey the universe and to present a comprehensive vision of reality in the light of their new knowledge.

In Virgil the poets of the Renaissance found a poet after their own hearts, and their admiration for him explains why the literary epic took its most notable form. The poets wished to rival him by his own means and in his own way;

they were his fellows in a special kind of poetry. For not only did they do in their way what he had done in his, but their situations resembled his and called for a poetry like his. Neither he nor they could do again what Homer had done. The epic was faced with a new task, and Virgil defined its character. Because he wished to write a poem about something much larger than the destinies of individual heroes, he created a type of epic in which the characters represent something outside themselves, and the events displayed have other interests than their immediate excitement in the context. He sought to provide a poem on the Roman character by linking his fabulous hero Aeneas to his living patron Augustus, to bracket past and present in a single whole, and to give a metaphysical unity to Rome by displaying the abilities which had made it great in his own day and had existed in it from the beginning. His first aim is to praise the present, but the present is too actual, too complex and too familiar to provide the material of his poem. So he joins it to the past and exalts it as the fulfilment of a long, divinely ordained process. Augustus gains in glory by being associated with Aeneas, Rome by being traced back to its humble origins. The plan was bold, but there were no limits to its possibilities.

Camões, Tasso and Milton were equally eager to celebrate the great issues and the powerful experiences of their own times, but none of them found a purely contemporary subject to suit him. Camões came nearest in the Portuguese discoverers and governors of India, but none of these could carry on his own shoulders all that Camões had to say. Even his avowed hero, Vasco da Gama, is one man among many, the representative of some but not of all the qualities which have made Portugal. Camões' subject is Portugal, as Virgil's is Rome, and he uses Virgil's devices of narrative and prophecy to give his complex picture of the Portuguese character. Tasso also was moved by a contemporary issue, by the need for chivalrous and heroic virtues in the battle against the heathen. He found such in his own patron, Alfonso II of Ferrara, but they were not sufficient to fill an epic. So he displayed them ideally in a poem about the First Crusade, in which Alfonso's ancestor shows the hereditary qualities of the family and other warriors complete the round of soldierly

virtues and chivalrous magnificence. Milton in his prime of
life felt a warm regard for Cromwell and for the English
triumphs of the Commonwealth. He had paid his special
tributes in sonnets to the chief leaders, but that was not
enough. *Paradise Lost* is a transcendental dramatisation of
the Puritan spirit. Milton transposes to a vast stage, to the
whole of space and the whole of time, the qualities, the
conflicts and the ideals which stirred him in the high hopes
of the Commonwealth and in the disillusionment of the
Restoration. To give a proper scale to his subject, to show
how important and universal it is, he goes back to the begin-
ning of time and connects the Fall of the Angels and of Man
with the difficulties which met him in his own days. These
poets add grandeur and complexity to their contemporary
themes by relating them to the past and producing a scheme
which explains the present through its remote origins and
creates a unity which can be called metaphysical because it
shows how through the varied events of a long historical pro-
cess certain fundamental facts remain unchanged.

From this an important result followed. The literary
epics, unlike those of Homer, are not content to present
individuals as such. They present something that is more
like a symbol or even an ideal, a person who represents some-
thing else. As Aeneas stands for Rome, so Gama stands for
Portugal, Goffredo for Christian chivalry, and Adam for all
mankind. This means that enormous issues, not immediately
relevant to the story, are sooner or later introduced, and the
poet attempts to convey almost the whole duty and the whole
circumstances of man. In consequence his work is instructive
as Homer's never is. Homer may have wished to present
one noble type in Achilles and another in Hector; he may
have felt a strong predilection for his astute Odysseus. But
these heroes are not set out as ideals to be followed, and
they convey no direct or immediate lessons. But the writers
of literary epic are almost forced to point a moral. Their
heroes are examples of what men ought to be or types of
human destiny whose very mistakes must be marked and
remembered. In themselves they may be misty and even
characterless, but they are not meant to be characters so
much as examples. The writers of literary epic would all
agree with Dryden's account of a heroic poem : " The design

16

of it is to form the mind to heroic virtue by example; 'tis conveyed in verse that it may delight, while it instructs ". This didactic intention is never far away, though it need not have an immediate or contemporary reference. While Camões and Tasso wished Europe to prosecute a crusade against Islam, Virgil wished to explain the destiny of Rome and Milton the workings of Eternal Providence. Nor need this didactic purpose be explicit. A poet can teach by indirect means, by appealing to the hearts and imaginations and consciences of his readers. But if he is anxious that they should really believe what he says, he can hardly avoid being to some degree didactic. So these poets wished to inspire, to elevate, to instruct. They did not share the common belief that poetry merely beguiles hours of leisure or stimulates to a refined enjoyment. They believed that their calling was extremely serious and that its object was to make men better.

Yet despite this noble resolve, they were also poets, and their poems must succeed as poetry. Too copious or too obvious instruction is by common admission hostile to the Muses, and even if it is skilfully and imaginatively disguised, the result may still be too austere to win readers or to have any practical effect. Epic poetry must appeal to the imagination and do much more than present types and symbols of human nobility. The poets themselves were all men so trained in poetry and so devoted to it, so responsive to the beauties of life and of literature, that even if they had wished to confine themselves to instruction, they would hardly have been able to do so; their natural impulses would have broken out and taken control of their work. The stern moral task of the new epic, as Tasso saw, needed additional attractions to make it palatable:

> Così a l' egro fanciul porgiamo aspersi
> Di soave licor gli orli del vaso :
> Succhi amari ingannato intanto ei beve,
> E da l' inganno suo vita riceve.[1]
>
> (I, 3, 5-8)

[1] So we, if children young diseased we find,
Anoint with sweets the vessel's foremost parts
To make them taste the potions sharp we give;
They drink deceived, and so deceived, they live.
(Fairfax)

17

Fortunately this natural desire was fortified by an excellent literary precedent. Heroic epic had left other descendants than its conscious heir in literary epic. There was another kind of narrative poetry which told of high adventures and martial prowess. This poetry is usefully classed as romance, and its main characteristic is that though it resembles heroic epic in telling a story for its own sake and having no instructive purpose, it differs because it lacks anything that can be called a heroic ideal. What matters is the story, and the poet's aim is to make this as lively and as fantastic as possible without much regard either to probability or to morals. In the ancient world Homer's language and metre were used by Apollonius of Rhodes in his *Argonautica* to tell of great adventures in the Euxine Sea, and from him sprang other poems which dealt with violent passions and improbable situations. Something similar occurred in the early Renaissance when, by a strange paradox, the austere old story of Roland was retold and refashioned until it became a peg on which to hang every kind of adventure. This art, which had its roots in popular taste, was taken up by courts and given a new polish and refinement. Its skill is often beyond praise; it opens up wonderful worlds of fancy whose magic enthrals any lover of poetry. It is fundamentally different in spirit both from heroic and from literary epic, but it sprung from the first and it had a great influence on the second. Just as Virgil fell under the spell of Apollonius, so Camões and Tasso could not free themselves from the enchantment of Ariosto, and there are times when even Milton's poetical genius is drawn to Italian fancies which his intellect and conscience rejected.

The influence of romantic epic is strongest in an ancient subject of poetry, — the marvellous. This is common enough in heroic epic. Just as the *Odyssey* has its elements of fairy-tale, of what Longinus calls "a fancy roving in the fabulous and the incredible", so there are great supernatural moments in the fight with Grendel's dam in *Beowulf* and in the unearthly darkness of the *Song of Roland*. In early societies these marvels are no doubt accepted as true in the sense that they might in certain conditions happen. They do not belong to a separate world of pure imagination but are assumed to be at least possible in a real world. It is quite different with romantic epics like the *Orlando Innamorato* of Boiardo

or the *Orlando Furioso* of Ariosto. These poets know well
that many of their episodes are impossible, and their claim is
that they are simply delightful. In their wonder-world
anything may happen. Warriors ride in the air on hippo-
griffs and continue to fight after they have been sliced to
pieces ; magicians and sorceresses work their fantastic and
fell designs ; warriors travel quickly and easily to China or
the Orkneys or the moon or Paradise. The poet's chief aim
is to give delight, and he lives in a world where ordinary
rules do not apply. He has his serious moments, and Ariosto
not only informs his characters with a glowing humanity but
rises to an impressive grandeur when he calls upon Italy
to shake off the Spanish dominion or the Pope to defend his
flock. But this art makes no claim to interpret reality and
may even surrender when reality becomes too strong for it,
as it was for Boiardo, who abruptly broke off his poem when
the French invaded Italy in 1494. It is in the highest sense
a poetry of escape, of pure delight and gaiety. It was written
for a cultivated, aristocratic society and made no claims to
be national or universal. But the marvellous appeals even to
the most serious poets, and the writers of literary epic could
not be deaf to it. They had to find out what their own atti-
tude was and make it clear.

While Boiardo and Ariosto frankly admit that their work
is pure fancy, Camões, Tasso and Milton claim to tell the
truth. We have only to open the *Orlando Innamorato* to see
that Boiardo is not concerned with ordinary facts. When he
playfully announces his theme,

> Questa novella è nota a poca gente,[1]   (I, 3, 1)

he hints that what is to come is his own invention, and his
subsequent pretence that he gets his story from the record of
Archbishop Turpin deceives no one. The marvels begin at
once, and the plot proceeds through ingenious and delightful
impossibilities. When Ariosto says at the beginning of
Orlando Furioso,

> Dirò d' Orlando in un medesmo tratto
> Cosa non detta in prosa mai, nè in rima,[2]
>   (I, 2, 1-2)

---

[1] This tale of mine is known to very few.

[2] In the same strain of Roland will I tell
What never yet was said in prose or rhyme.

he admits that he is inventing. This light-hearted confession of fancy is very different from the epic spirit as Virgil conceived it or as his followers obeyed it. He opens the *Aeneid* with a paragraph whose seriousness compels us to believe that we are concerned with the real truth about Rome. So the writers of the Renaissance were at pains to stress their difference from the chivalrous poets. Camões calls on the King of Portugal to hear the true story of his country :

> Ouvi : que não vercis com vãs façanhas,
> Fantásticas, fingidas, mentirosas,
> Louvar os vossos, como nas estranhas
> Musas, de engrandecer-se desejosas : [1]
>
> (I, II, I-4)

and goes on to say that the Portuguese achievements, though historical, are greater than all the fables about Rodomonte and Orlando. Ariosto is put in his place by the champion of truth and history. Tasso, who was by tradition and temperament much closer to Ariosto, is uneasy about the element of fiction in his poem and apologises for it with a prayer to his heavenly Muse :

> Tu rischiara il mio canto, e tu perdona
> S' intesso fregi al ver, se adorno in parte
> D' altri diletti, che de' tuoi, le carte.[2]
>
> (I, 2, 6-8)

Milton is more emphatic and speaks with contempt of

> Warrs, hitherto the onely Argument
> Heroic deem'd, chief maistrie to dissect
> With long and tedious havoc fabl'd Knights
> In Battels feign'd,   (*P.L.* IX, 28-31)

and picks up Ariosto's own words to turn them against him as he uses them for a new purpose :

> Things unattempted yet in Prose or Rhime.   (*P.L.* I, 16)

[1] Hear me, I say, for not for actions vain,
Fantastic, fabulous, shall you behold
Yours prais'd, though foreign Muses, to obtain
Name to themselves, have ev'n feign'd names extolled.
(Fanshawe)

[2] My verse ennoble, and forgive the thing
If fictions light I mix with truth divine,
And fill these lines with other praise than thine.
(Fairfax)

The writers of literary epic were determined to show that they differed from the writers of romantic epic in their attitude to the truth. Mere fancy and mere delight were not enough for them. They sought something more serious and closer to life.

These austere claims do not mean that everything in these poems is true or that their authors believed it to be. All of them owed a great debt to the inventions of romantic epic and found in it material for some of their finest flights. All of them introduced episodes which defied the historical knowledge of their times. Virgil's association of Dido with Aeneas ran counter to the views of Roman historians and called forth complaints from the learned; even Milton put into his war in Heaven much that has no authority in the Book of Revelation. But though these poets indulge in much pure fancy, they know that they are doing so and they believe that it does not affect the essential truth of their poems. They placate their consciences by making their romantic and chivalrous themes serve ulterior purposes and become the means for presenting important truths indirectly. Most of Virgil's story is invention, and at times, as when Aeneas' ships are turned into nymphs, he writes pure romance, but his narrative is almost a myth of great indefinite forces. Behind each episode we can see what important issue is involved and what it means to his age. The Renaissance poets felt a greater discord between fact and fancy than he did and found it harder to resolve. Camões follows history with some care and keeps his flights of fancy for his symbolical divinities or for episodes which turn out in the end to be allegorical. Tasso, deeply imbued with the spirit of Ariosto, introduced many marvellous episodes into his poem. Later he was driven by his critics and his own too sensitive conscience to explain that they were allegorical, and though this is hard to accept, yet his marvels are told not only for their own sake but because they illustrate situations in human life or the human soul. They have a secondary, subordinate significance and help to convey Tasso's complex view of existence. Milton makes great claims to truthfulness, and though he too has his grand moments of invention, they are seldom essential to his main theme. Indeed he seems to have felt that his high task called on him to discard many subjects which had appealed to earlier poets

and had not quite lost their appeal for him. So he introduces
them by indirect means as a kind of incidental decoration, as
when he pays a majestic tribute to Boiardo and Ariosto by
comparing the numbers of the fallen angels to the hosts of
chivalry :

> And all who since, Baptiz'd or Infidel,
> Jousted in *Aspramont* or *Montalban*,
> *Damasco*, or *Marocco*, or *Trebisond*,
> Or whom *Biserta* sent from *Afric* shore
> When *Charlemain* with all his Peerage fell
> By *Fontarabbia*. (*P.L.* I, 582-7)

In reading this poetry we are entitled and expected to distin-
guish between the essential truth and the poet's decoration
of it. The chivalrous poets made no such distinction, and
though the writers of literary epic despised them for it, they
felt the claims of that wonderful imaginary world and could
not do entirely without it.

There is a great difference between a poem which admits
that it is fiction and one which claims, even with reservations,
to tell the truth. The difference does not really touch the
question of poetical value, but it concerns the reader's feelings.
especially if his own age or country or beliefs are involved.
The admirers of Boiardo and Ariosto read about Orlando for,
sheer pleasure in the poetry. Although the poems might
incidentally contain a serious " criticism of life ", they were
not on the whole taken seriously; it was enough that they
were delightful. But with poets who claimed to tell important
truths it was different. To us such a claim may seem un-
important. Camões' history and Milton's theology are not
so urgent as they once were. Yet if a poet is earnestly con-
cerned with the reality of his subject, he may enjoy at least
one great advantage. He is in an excellent position to give
weight to what he says and to make his lessons impressive ;
he can strengthen his case with real examples and give to it
the solidity of something rooted in fact. It is because Virgil
wrote about historical Rome that we pay attention to his
shadowy hero who embodies so many Roman ideals. Because
we can never quite dissociate the matter of the *Aeneid* from
the world in which it was written or from the contemporary
issues embedded in it, it has something else than its aesthetic
appeal, something which undeniably claims and wins atten-

tion. It is the product of a religious and moral revival. Augustus claimed that he wished to re-establish old Roman standards of simplicity and devotion. For this purpose he used the propaganda most suited to his times, — poetry. Somehow this cold-blooded Caesar inspired such poets as Virgil and Horace with his ideals and with a desire to write about them. Virgil saw that if morality is to make a persuasive appeal, it must be related to facts and embodied in human characters. He proclaimed the wisdom of the Augustan creed by identifying its ideals with the forces that had made Rome. In consequence his poem had an enormous influence and was treated as a record of history. He might have taken some plot which did not even pretend to be historical and filled it with all the lessons that he wished to teach, but then his appeal would have been much weaker. It is the association of moral ideals with Roman history that makes his poem unlike others, more serious and more worthy of study. In so doing he shows his difference from the romantic Alexandrian poets who had been so popular in his youth and to whom he himself owed so much.

In the sixteenth and seventeenth centuries moral reform was again in the air. What Augustus was to Virgil, the Catholic Church was to Tasso and Puritanism to Milton, while the Christian imperialism of the Portuguese monarchy appealed to Camões and made considerable demands of him. The Jesuits were pained by the degree to which a love for Pagan antiquity had fouled the wells of Catholic truth. They could not entirely eradicate the taste for heathen stories, but they could reduce them to a subordinate place or insist that at least they were allegorical. The Reformers were no less insistent that poets should tell the truth. Spenser found that his world of delightful fancy was attacked for being untrue :

> Right well I wote most mighty Soueraine,
> That all this famous antique history
> Of some th' aboundance of an idle braine
> Will iudged be, and painted forgery
> Rather then matter of iust memory ;
>
> (*F.Q.* II, Int. 1, 1-5)

and rather disingenuously argued that just as new places had recently been found in America, so perhaps his "Faerie lond" might one day be placed on the map. With Milton the desire for truth becomes a passion. Despite the obvious inventions which make some of the best parts of *Paradise Lost* he still claims to be telling the truth and proudly contrasts the divine source of his own inspiration with the Muse of antiquity :

> For thou art Heav'nlie, shee an empty dreame. (VII, 39).

Indeed he owes some of his posthumous renown to the common belief that he is only less canonical than Holy Writ. No wonder that he cast scorn on Italian inventions and claimed the superior merits of his own poem.

A second characteristic of literary epic, comparable to its emphasis on truth and in strong contrast to the ways of chivalrous romance, is its attitude to sensual pleasures. Such were on the whole alien to the real heroic spirit. Homer's heroes enjoy their food and drink, but their amours are conducted with a perfunctory detachment which suggests that they must not be treated too seriously. Odysseus does not enjoy his year with Circe or his enforced sojourn with Calypso,

ἐν σπέσσι γλαφυροῖσι παρ' οὐκ ἐθέλων ἐθελούσῃ.[1] (*Od.* v, 155)

The gay or fantastic aspects of love-making are confined to the gods who are free from the limitations of human life and from its obligation to live nobly. They belong to a different order of beings and have their own rules and their own license. But by heroic standards men do not so indulge their passions and appetites ; they keep them under control or at least do not make too much ado about them. This attitude is common in heroic epic and belongs to the heroic view of life. It was not shared by the writers of chivalrous romance. Into the martial story of Roland Boiardo and Ariosto brought a whole series of amorous adventures until their epics really deserved their titles. Love had played no less a part in Alexandrian poetry and was the dominating subject of the small epics which were the smart literature of Virgil's youth. In that luscious air the cultivated aristocrats of republican Rome seem to have found something that supplied a need in their lives. When Virgil set out to create a new kind of epic, he followed neither Homer nor the Alexandrians. The Homeric precedent was too austere for

[1] 'There in the depth of a cave, he unwilling by her who was willing.

him, the Alexandrian too frivolous. Since Augustus held views on sexual morality and embodied them in legislation, for Virgil to write in any spirit other than caution or warning would have run counter to his patron's desires. In consequence the one great love episode of the *Aeneid*, Dido's passion for Aeneas, is treated in a tragic spirit and takes its place in the poem as a fearful obstacle which the hero has to overcome in his moral progress and as the prelude of disasters to come in the relations of Rome and Carthage.

In this respect the position of Camões and Tasso was like that of Virgil. Behind both lay a tradition of fine literature, popular and courtly, in which love held a paramount place and was not presented as anything to be deplored. To this spirit they felt no natural repugnance. Both of them had passionate Latin natures and highly romantic conceptions of love. But they were uneasy. They knew that their patrons would not approve of too much frankness about love, and they felt that perhaps this was right. Camões indeed goes as far as he dares in the agreeable rewards which Venus and her Nymphs give to his sailors, — only to announce that the goddesses and their pleasures are allegorical. Tasso follows Ariosto by making his knights peculiarly susceptible to female charms, but his finest flight of fancy, the enchanted palace of Armida, is an abode of sin, and Armida herself, the mistress of seductive wiles, is converted to Christianity and united to Rinaldo whom she has corrupted. The Counter-Reformation viewed sensual delights with no small disapproval and shed its inhibiting gloom on the arts. The freedom of the fifteenth century was lost, and good Catholics like Bellarmine felt a more than Puritan horror of the nude even in stone. The Reformation agreed with its opponents on this point if on no other. Spenser, thrown among Protestant reformers, tried to circumvent the difficulty by claiming that he sang of ideal love, but his defence was hardly satisfactory to such grave spirits as Burleigh who criticised his voluptuousness. Milton, despite his advocacy of divorce, did not approve of any looseness in sexual matters and would no doubt have condemned many heroines of romance as wicked creatures bred only

To dress, and troule the Tongue, and roule the Eye.

(*P.L.* xi, 616)

C

He made Adam and Eve an example of connubial bliss and
displayed in them that happiness which he had failed to find
in his own first marriage. He contrasts their unstained affec-
tions with the alleged pleasures which assumed so glamorous
an air in chivalrous poetry or at the Court of Charles II :

> Here Love his golden shafts imploies, here lights
> His constant Lamp, and waves his purple wings,
> Reigns here, and revels ; not in the bought smile
> Of Harlots, loveless, joyless, unindeard,
> Casual fruition, nor in Court Amours,
> Mixt Dance, or wanton Mask, or Midnight Bal.
>
> (*P.L.* IV, 763-8)

In these words a whole world of real or imagined indulgence
is dismissed. Milton condemns with all the stern disapproval
of the Puritan conscience, and his condemnation is perfectly
appropriate to his epic task which is too serious to allow the
intrusion of such frivolities.

The earnestness which his times and his task laid on the
writer of literary epic led inevitably to the exclusion of another
quality notable both in heroic and in chivalrous epic, — the
ludicrous and the absurd. Homer varies his heroic stories
with moments of comic relief. Most of them come in his
accounts of the gods, but he sometimes obtrudes a sly note of
friendly fun into his accounts of men and women. In the
mediaeval epic a man of so great eminence as Raynouart,
whom Dante places in Paradise, becomes a humorous, if not
an entirely comic, figure. Russian and Jugoslav lays have a
strong element of playful mockery which is exerted at the
expense even of such popular heroes as Ilya of Murom or
Marko Kraljević. Such laughter is not scornful or malicious ;
it is the laughter of love and affection, open only to those
whose beliefs are so strong that they can occasionally be
treated as absurd. This spirit, which appears in much
mediaeval sculpture and stained glass, grows from an intimate
familiarity with its subject and is possible only when that
subject is accepted so naturally that it does not need to be
exalted with solemn effort. With this spirit Boiardo and
Ariosto have much in common. They have their grave
moments, but the imaginary society which they depict is so
well founded that they can laugh at it. The ideals of chivalry
transposed to a purely fantastic sphere provide matter for

much genial mockery. To this delightful outlook the Reformation and the Counter-Reformation put an end. The later writers of epic could not and would not laugh at the ideals which they proclaimed. There is no laughter in Tasso, who seems to regard it as particularly pernicious ; for when his knights prepare to rescue Rinaldo from Armida, they are warned against a fountain which makes men laugh :

> Un fonte sorge in lei che vaghe e monde
> Ha l' acque sì che i riguardanti asseta,
> Ma dentro ai freddi suoi cristalli asconde
> Di tosco estran malvagità secreta ;
> Chè un picciol sorso di sue lucide onde
> Inebria l' alma tosto e la fa lieta :
> Indi a rider uom move ; e tanto il riso
> S' avanza alfin, ch' ei ne rimane ucciso.[1]
>
> (XIV, 74, 1-8)

Camões has perhaps a smiling indulgence for one or two characters like the unsuccessful lover Lionardo, but on the whole he treats his figures with serious respect. In Milton there are traces of a bitter, sardonic humour, notably in his Limbo of Vanity. But this is not turned against his main characters or his chief subject ; it is a weapon of controversy and of contempt, similar to the amusement which the Almighty finds in the confusion of tongues at Babel or in the eccentricities of the Ptolemaic astronomy :

> if they list to try
> Conjecture, he his Fabric of the Heav'ns
> Hath left to thir disputes, perhaps to move
> His laughter at thir quaint Opinions wide
> Hereafter.   (VIII, 75-9)

The central theme, august and remote, is not touched by laughter ; there is nothing ludicrous in Heaven or in Hell. Even Virgil, who in early life had shown traces of a delicate humour, almost excludes the comic aspects of life from the

---

[1] There welleth out a fair, clear, bubbling spring,
Whose waters pure the thirsty guests entice,
But in those liquors cold the secret sting
Of strange and deadly poison closed lies,
One sup thereof the drinker's heart doth bring
To sudden joy, whence laughter vain doth rise,
Nor that strange merriment once stops and stays
Till, with his laughter's end, he end his days.
(Fairfax)

Aeneid, and his indulgence in it over unsuccessful athletes is hardly to be counted among his successes. These poets were busy building new worlds of the mind and could not allow mockery to upset their dignity or detract from their ethical purpose.

Literary epic, if we may judge by its best examples, flourishes not in the heyday of a nation or of a cause but in its last days or in its aftermath. At such a time a man surveys the recent past with its record of dazzling successes and asks if they can last; he analyses its strength, announces its importance, urges its continuance. Such a detachment does not belong to poets who write in the middle of a great struggle when the outcome is still dim and the issues are undecided. Periclean Athens, Elizabethan England, France under Louis XIV, had their own superb literatures but no literary epic. They looked not back but forward; they dwelt with pride and excitement on the brilliant present and saw it big with promise for the future. But the epic poets show a different spirit. They are melancholy and laden with responsibilities. It is as if success were already too burdensome for them, as if, in trying to assess its worth, they saw how great a price it exacted. It may even be true that men do not begin to understand a great achievement or to look carefully at it until it is almost finished. In any case when these poets set out to proclaim the greatness of a people or a cause or a system of life, their praise of it suggests that all is not so great or so glorious as it looks. If this occurred only in one case, we might ascribe it to the poet's temperament and leave it at that. But it occurs more than once and demands some other explanation. We are forced to conclude that the full force of literary epic comes at the end of some great historical process and that the poet tries to sum up all that the process has meant.

Of this Virgil is an eminent example. Such are his doubts, his hesitations, his melancholy that he has often been regarded as the poet of *lacrimae rerum*, of the misgivings and uncertainties which prey upon the human spirit. Such a reputation is curious in the poet of imperial Rome, but it is not undeserved. His melancholy is an essential part of his endowment and greatly affects his poetry. He wrote at a time when the Roman world turned with weariness and relief from the vaulting ambitions of the Caesarean age to the rest and quiet promised by Augustus. Virgil marks the transition from the restless years of the Republic, with its strong personalities and violent struggles, to the long peace when few men mattered except the *princeps*, and intellectual and artistic life passed into an even, unadventurous quietude. He himself bears the marks of both ages; he honours the great past and he longs for peace. He is the poet of transition, and his attempt to glorify the conquering Roman spirit is tempered by a sense of weariness and futility, by a feeling that perhaps after all the struggle is not worth while. His mighty structure, built to contain the history, the theology and the ethics of his age, was his protest against these misgivings, but none the less they found their way into it and are responsible for half his fame.

Camões, like Virgil, lived at the end of great adventures and on the eve of great changes. When he published *Os Lusiadas* in 1572, the prodigious effort which the Portuguese had put forth for nearly a century was almost over. The empire which he knew from his own experience was soon to pass under the dominion of Spain and never again reached its former eminence or satisfied the hopes once held of it. Camões saw the threatening dangers, knew the cost of all the effort to Portugal, and had misgivings about its continuance. Yet he set out to sing of its greatness and of the greatness of those who had made it. His poem surveys the history of his country and sums up the qualities which have produced its astonishing triumphs. He treats the past as a store of examples and of inspiration for the future, tries to stir the sluggish Europe of his own day to join in the mighty work and presents fine figures of adventurous manhood in his Portuguese leaders. Yet great though his picture of the past is, and stirring though his call is to fresh efforts and sacrifices, his poem is tinged with melancholy. He saw the corrupting effects of empire, the prodigious demands that it made of its servants, the ugly contrast between the brutality of life in Asia or Africa and the delightful pastoral pleasures of home. He decided that the effort was worth the cost and nobly proclaimed his decision, but through his work there runs a note of doubt and melancholy, the cry of the exiled Portuguese, destined to suffer every humiliation and deprivation, for the simple pleasures of peace and quiet at home.

The Italian epic of Tasso was not written in circumstances so grandiose as *Os Lusiadas*. Italy could boast of no imperial splendours since the fall of the Roman Empire. Even such slight unity as it had known in the fifteenth century had been gravely impaired by French invasion and Spanish rule, by intestine quarrels of Pope and princes. The background to Tasso is not an empire but a spiritual movement. It is the Renaissance, of which he is the last belated singer. The great men of the *Quattrocento* had conceived an ideal of self-realisation on the fullest scale. It had liberated their spirits in an astounding spate of creative energy ; then it had fallen almost through the excess of its genius. The world does not allow men to be themselves on such a scale. Foreign conquerors and a resurgent priesthood checked and depressed them, and the Counter-Reformation brought princes and poets to order. Tasso, writing at the enlightened court of Ferrara, breathed the old magical air and put much of it into his poetry. He wished his warriors to be real heroes, his lovers to give everything for love ; he created landscapes in the spirit of Giorgione and adventures in the spirit of Ariosto ; he dwelt tenderly on physical beauty and on all the sentiments of romantic love ; he liked style and chivalry and courtesy and display. But the discords of his time entered into his soul. His painful life was as much the fruit of his own tortured character as of unsympathetic circumstances.. He tried to harmonise his natural love of pleasure with an ideal of obedience, to find in the vision of a united Christendom a sphere for true heroism, to adjust the most brilliant fancies to an exacting morality and to his own haunting sense of guilt. His effort was entirely sincere, even when he forced himself to alter or explain away the chief beauties of his *Gerusalemme Liberata* and to recast his poem in the vastly inferior form of the *Gerusalemme Conquistata*. But the conflict to which Tasso was a martyr was that of his time. The high glory of the Renaissance was past, and sterner powers were in command. Tasso's poem springs from the great days, but he has trimmed and shaped it to suit the more exacting spirit of his own age.

Milton was the chief poet of the Reformation, in a sense its only poet ; for he alone gave voice to its whole temper. He did for it what Dante did for the Middle Ages, passing judgment on all history in the light of his theology. He

wrote the greater part of *Paradise Lost* when his great hopes
for the Commonwealth and for the Rule of the Saints had
foundered in reaction and failure. He felt that the world had
become unfamiliar and hostile. He continued to write

> though fall'n on evil dayes,
> On evil dayes though fall'n, and evil tongues,
>   (VII, 25-6)

and to create in his art that order which he had not found in
life. His epic is the record of his high Puritan hopes, of a
universe thoroughly mapped and explained, with every main
question settled to his satisfaction. Yet in his poetry we cannot
fail to mark a contrast between the triumphant pride of his
earlier Puritanism and the defeats of his old age. It is because
his world has fallen on evil days that he sees more clearly the
worth of his beliefs. His gloom made the blind old poet more
determined to portray the ultimate harmony of the universe
and the true nature of human virtue. His knowledge that in
his own day the human race had failed to find the millennium
made him more conscious that it was worth finding and more
eager to show how partial evil contributes to universal good.

In their different ways these poets wrote because their
times stressed an ideal to them and stirred them to spend
their great powers on presenting it. The ideal seems always
to have reached or to have passed its prime and to have lost
its hold on the mass of mankind. Only so could it be seen in
its fullness and displayed in its true worth. So, because they
were to some degree fighting against the flow of history, the
poets had to face hostile elements in their circumstances or
in themselves. But from this some of their finest effects arise.
The struggle not only makes their work more human and
more imaginative but it widens their scope and enriches their
subject. In Homer there is no such discord. He has no
purpose like Virgil's, no doubts and no mission. But once
we begin to grasp the various elements which make the
complex art of literary epic, we are on the way to appreciate
poetry of a special kind, which, though it claims to deal with
a single subject, attacks it from different angles and at
different levels. The mere story is less important than what
it represents in the poet's vision of life. It is for this that we
go to him, in this that we find his special contribution to our

experience. The writers of literary epic set themselves a task of uncommon difficulty when they tried to adapt the heroic ideal to unheroic times and to proclaim in poetry a new conception of man's grandeur and nobility. Each had his own approach, his own solution, and his own doubts and reservations, but because all were concerned with ultimately the same issues and used the same kind of poetical form, their labours belong to a single chapter in the history of the human spirit.

II

VIRGIL AND THE IDEAL
OF ROME

When Virgil lay on his death-bed at Brundisium in 19 B.C.
he called for his manuscript of the *Aeneid* with the intention
of destroying it, and his will directed that his executors
should publish nothing but what he himself had already edited.
But on Augustus' instructions these last wishes were over-
ridden, and the *Aeneid* was given to the world to win an
immediate success and a continuous renown without parallel
in history. More than any other book it dominated Roman
education and literature. It became a " set book " for cen-
turies of schoolboys and was admired by almost every writer
from Petronius to St. Augustine. Servius composed his
massive commentary on its interpretation, text, grammar and
mythology ; Donatus expatiated on the moral lessons to be
drawn from it ; Macrobius devoted his *Saturnalia* to a
discussion of its problems. It survived both the rise of
Christianity and the fall of Rome. In the Dark Ages it kept
a special prestige and was studied successively by Bede, by
Alcuin and by Anselm. In the Middle Ages Dante exalted
Virgil to the highest place among all poets and saw in him the
embodiment of earthly knowledge :

> tu duca, tu segnore e tu maestro,[1]   (*Inf.* II, 140)

while Chaucer regarded him as the perfect master whom
others should honour and follow :

> Glory and honour, Virgil Mantuan,
> Be to thy name ! and I shal as I can
> Folow thy lantern as thou gost biforn.

In the Renaissance the *Aeneid* became the great poem which
many poets tried forlornly to rival. It kept its pre-eminence
and became in turn a school of good manners for the seven-
teenth century and of noble style for the eighteenth, while
doubting spirits of the nineteenth found in it anticipations of

---

[1] Thou art my guide, my master and my lord.

their own hesitant misgivings before the problems of life and death. In two thousand years of history the *Aeneid* has kept a central place in European literature and survived vast changes both secular and religious. It has shown an unparalleled variety of appeal and has been admired at different times for very different reasons. Whatever faults the dying Virgil found in it, it has succeeded in doing something that no epic has done before or since, and helped many generations of men to formulate their views on the chief problems of existence.

Virgil was not the first to write the epic of Rome. In the third century B.C. Naevius had used the old Saturnian measure for his *Punic War* and in the next century Ennius' *Annals* traced the Roman story from Romulus to his own day. The first of these poems must have had many similarities to oral epic or even to ballad ; the second, despite its use of the hexameter and many effective adaptations of the Homeric manner, was built on the annalistic plan which is always liable to appear when poetry annexes history. Virgil knew both works, and his own poem must have been meant to supersede them and to give in a more satisfactory form the truth about Rome as it had been revealed to his own generation. To do this he adopted a remarkable method. He abandoned the annalistic scheme and instead of versifying history presented the Roman character and destiny through a poem about a legendary and largely imaginary past. His concern was less with historical events than with their meaning, less with Rome at this or at that time than as it was from the beginning and for ever, less with individual Romans than with a single, symbolical hero who stands for the qualities and the experience which are typically Roman. By skilful literary devices, such as prophecies spoken by gods or visions seen in Elysium or scenes depicted on works of art, Virgil links up the mythical past with recorded history and his own time. But such excursions are exceptional and take up less than 300 lines in a total of nearly 10,000. The main action of the *Aeneid* takes place some three hundred years before the foundation of Rome ; the leading hero and his followers are not Romans nor even Italians but Trojans whose ancestral connection with Italy is dim and remote ; much of the action takes place outside Italy, and when it moves there, is confined to a small

area around the Tiber; Aeneas himself is a homeless wanderer who asks for no more than a few acres for himself and his company. This remote past is connected with the present by many ingenious ties. The Trojan heroes are the ancestors of famous Roman families and bear names honoured in Roman history; their ceremonies, their habits, their games, forecast what are later to be characteristic of Rome; they touch at places familiar to every Roman; into their story local legends and traditions are woven; the gods who support and sustain them are those whose cults formed the official religion of the Roman people. And more significant than these external connections are the Roman spirit, virtues and outlook which the Trojans display. The difficulties encountered by these first ancestors, their relations to the gods, their emotions and their ideals, their family loyalties, their behaviour in peace and war, their attitude to the divine task laid upon them, are somehow typical and representative of the Romans as they were believed to have always been. Virgil is less concerned with origins than with a permanent reality as it was displayed from the first and is still being displayed in his own time.

Such a plan and such a purpose demanded a new kind of poetry, and when we turn from the *Iliad* to the *Aeneid*, it is clear that the whole outlook is different and that Virgil has a new vision of human nature and of heroic virtue. Homer concentrates on individuals and their destinies. The dooms of Achilles and Hector dominate his design; their characters determine the action. But from the start Virgil shows that his special concern is the destiny not of a man but of a nation, not of Aeneas but of Rome. Though he opens with " Arms and the man " and suggests that his hero is another Achilles or Odysseus, he has, before his first paragraph is finished, shown that he reaches beyond Aeneas to the long history that followed from him :

genus unde Latinum
Albanique patres atque altae moenia Romae.[1]
(I, 6-7)

Soon afterwards, when he has noted the obstacles which the

1 . whence came the Latin race,
The Alban sires and lofty walls of Rome.

Trojans meet in their wanderings, he again ends a period on a similar note :

tantae molis erat Romanam condere gentem.[1] (I, 33)

Then, when Venus complains that her son, Aeneas, is unjustly treated, Jupiter replies not only by promising that all will be well with Aeneas but by giving a prophetic sketch of Roman history to Julius Caesar. The reward which the ancestor of the Roman race is to receive is much more than his own success or glory, more even than his settlement in Italy ; it is the assurance of Rome's destiny, of universal and unending dominion :

his ego nec metas rerum nec tempora pono :
imperium sine fine dedi.[2] (I, 278-9)

At the outset Virgil shows what kind of destiny is the subject of his poem. The wanderings and sufferings and ultimate success of Aeneas and his followers are but a preliminary and a preparation for a much vaster theme. It was with reason that Petronius, like Tennyson, called the poet " Roman Virgil ".

The fundamental theme of the *Aeneid* is the destiny of Rome as it was revealed in this mythical dawn of history before Rome itself existed. This destiny is presented in the person of Aeneas who not only struggles and suffers for the Rome that is to be but is already a typical Roman. If his individual fortune is subordinate to the fortune of Rome, his character shows what Romans are. He is Virgil's hero in a new kind of heroic poem, and in him we see how different Virgil's epic vision is from Homer's. Aeneas is Virgil's own creation, conceived with the special purpose of showing what a Roman hero is. Unlike Homer, Virgil owes little in his hero's character to tradition. Whereas Homer had to conform to established notions and make his Achilles " swift of foot ", his Agamemnon " king of men " and his Odysseus " of many wiles ", Virgil was bound by no such obligations. He could find his characters where he chose and shape them to suit his own purpose. His Aeneas owes something to Homeric precedent in being a great warrior and a devout servant of the gods, but he has taken on a new personality and

---

[1] So vast a task to found the Roman race.

[2] To them I give no bounds in space or time
But empire without end.

36

is the true child of Virgil's brooding meditation and imaginative vision. The persons of the *Aeneid* are created and fashioned for a special purpose. They contribute to the main design, and everything that they say or do may be considered in the light of Rome's destiny. For this reason it is wrong to treat them as if they were dramatic characters like Homer's. They are more, and they are less. They are more, because they stand for something outside themselves, for something typically and essentially Roman ; they are types, examples, symbols. And they are less, because any typical character will lack the lineaments and idiosyncrasies, the personal appeal and the intimate claims, of a character who is created for his own sake and for the poet's pleasure in him. Moreover, because Aeneas is typical of Rome, the events through which he passes are equally so. The difficulties which he has to surmount, the burden which the gods have laid on him, the human beings who ensnare or hinder him, the obstacles which he finds in his circumstances or in his followers or in himself, represent what may happen to any Roman. Aeneas behaves as a Roman would in conditions familiar to Roman experience. Therefore though the action takes place in a kind of historical past, it transcends history in a way that the Trojan War does not for Homer. Each action in the *Aeneid* may be interesting for its own sake, but its special claim is that it typifies a class of actions and situations in which great questions are raised and great issues are at stake. That is partly why Virgil tells a story less well than Homer. His task prevents him from really enjoying a tale for its own sake, from concentrating entirely on the excitement of what happens. Beyond the actual events there is always something else, a problem or a principle or a hint that what occurs has some other claim than its immediate interest.

Virgil worked at the *Aeneid* for twelve years, and was at the end profoundly discontented with it. It seems unlikely that what moved him to demand its destruction was its incomplete state. For even the unfinished lines have often a beauty of their own, and the artistry of his language and versification has won him centuries of devoted admiration. It seems more likely that he felt something wrong in his whole conception, as if he had undertaken a task for which after much work he still did not feel properly qualified. Before his

37

death he wrote to Augustus that he had begun the poem, *paene vitio mentis,* almost in a perversion of mind, and this suggests that what discouraged and depressed him was some failure in his main plan. Whether this is so or not, most readers of the *Aeneid* would agree that in deciding to write a heroic epic on his Roman theme Virgil embarked on a task of extraordinary difficulty. On the one hand his epic was to be in some ways a rival to the *Iliad* and the *Odyssey*; it was to present a hero comparable to Achilles and Odysseus; it was to have all the Homeric accoutrements. So much his time demanded of him. The Augustan age felt that anything less than Homeric epic was unworthy of its great achievements. Just as Alexander had lamented that he had no Homer to sing of his conquests, so Augustus seems to have determined that Virgil should be a second Homer. But this new epic was also to be something else. It was to present an ideal of Roman *virtus* quite unlike the Homeric ideal of manhood, and it must somehow make this conform to the old-fashioned epic plan. Such a task was not entirely suited to Virgil's gifts. In his self-depreciatory way he seems to have felt this. Fortunately others saw that his successes quite outweighed his failures, and saved his poem for posterity.

Virgil's first obstacle in writing a heroic poem was his own temperament. He was enormously impressed by Homer and felt that many of his effects should be Homeric. At the same time he recognised the portentous nature of such a task and said that it was as easy to take his club from Hercules as a line from Homer. None the less he persevered and often competed with Homer on his own ground. It is in such passages that Virgil is most open to criticism. He had little of Homer's understanding of the fury and frenzy of war. So far from feeling that war was exciting, he felt that it was odious and horrible. He had to make Aeneas a great warrior and to depict scenes of carnage, but he seems to have postponed them as long as possible, and his first attempt at heroic battle comes in Book X. Then laboriously and conscientiously he tries to recreate in his own sensitive and melodious language what Homer had done so naturally and so brilliantly. Virgil tries his utmost to make his battles interesting. He varies them with contemporary devices of warfare such as cavalry, siege-engines and battering rams. But these are not enough, and over his battles there hangs a sense of effort, as if the poet's heart were not in them. The slayings of men in Homer are not to modern taste, but they have their own vitality and certainly much more poetry than a passage like this from Virgil :

> Caedicus Alcathoum obtruncat, Sacrator Hydaspen
> Partheniumque Rapo et praedurum viribus Orsen,
> Messapus Cloniumque Lycaoniumque Erichaeten.[1]
>
> (x, 747-9)

The faint ghostly figures behind the resounding names have no part in the story ; their fates are without pathos or interest. Such a passage bears no relation to experience and is purely literary. Virgil wrote it because he felt that his poem demanded it, but he did not give life to it or make it really his own.

Even when Virgil is more successful than here, his meditative, literary, highly educated self seems to impose barriers between his Homeric original and his attempt to reproduce it in new circumstances. For instance, when Homer tells of the fatal pursuit of Hector by Achilles and says that the two did not run for a sacrificial ox or a tripod such as are given for prizes in foot-races,

> ἀλλὰ περὶ ψυχῆς θέον Ἕκτορος ἱπποδάμοιο,[2] (Il. XXII, 161)

the point is true and magnificently made. It comes straight from the heroic world where the qualities needed for athletic prowess are needed also for war, and all that differs between the two kinds of race is the stake for which each is run. Virgil tries to copy this effect when Aeneas pursues Turnus :

> neque enim levia aut ludicra petuntur
> praemia, sed Turni de vita et sanguine certant.[3]
>
> (XII, 764-5)

The Latin eloquence makes its point clearly enough, but it hardly arouses our pity and horror as Homer's direct approach

[1] Caedicus kills Alcathous, Sacrator
Hydaspes, Rapo kills Parthenius
And mighty Orses, and Messapus kills
Clonius and Erichaetes, Lycaon's son.

[2] But they ran for the life-blood of Hector, the tamer of horses.

[3]   No light or worthless prize
They seek, but fight for Turnus' life and blood.

does. The imagery of the race, so real and so true for Homer, is somehow not so real for Virgil. He did not look on physical and athletic prowess with an expert soldierly eye and he can hardly have enjoyed the excitement of racing as Homer did. Something of freshness and truth has gone from the comparison.

Virgil's inability to rival Homer on his own ground and his distrust of himself in trying to do so were partly due to his circumstances and reflected the temper of his time. The generation to which Augustus appealed so deeply with his promises of peace and order had known too much of war to believe that it was really exciting or enjoyable. No one was more conscious of this than Augustus himself, and he took care that one of his chief claims to power was the restoration of peace. In his own account of his actions he laid great emphasis on it; peace was indissolubly connected with his name in the prayers offered for his protection; the Temple of Janus was closed, as a sign that peace reigned by land and sea. The Augustan world was weary of war and was ready to sacrifice its liberty that it might enjoy peace. Virgil shared this feeling. In his youth he had known the confiscation of his lands by soldiers of the Civil War, and he joined in the chorus of praise for the man who had brought peace to Rome and to the world. His Jupiter prophesies the coming of Augustus who shall make an end of war :

> aspera tum positis mitescent saecula bellis.[1] (I, 291)

In this Virgil was at one with most Romans. The sight of embattled legions which Lucretius was able to bear with a philosophic equanimity was too much for Virgil's war-worn generation. Yet into this world, with its longing and admiration for peace, he had to introduce his epic with its inevitable accounts of battle and of the heroic spirit. He could not, even if he had the right gifts, present war as Homer had presented it. He could not even re-echo the tramp of armies and the confident spirit of victory which still sound in the fragments of Ennius. If he was to write an epic which was really significant for his time, he must treat of war in a way that appealed to contemporary experience of it and show what

[1] Then wars shall cease, and the rude age grow mild.
(C. J. Billson)

40

part it played in the Roman conception of life.

In this Virgil was not entirely successful, but he was more successful than is often allowed, and at certain places he created a new poetry, which his contemporaries understood and appreciated, about the tragedy and confusion of war. It is significant that Book II, his most sustained and most finished scene of battle, did not meet with the approval of Napoleon, who said that Virgil was " nothing but the regent of a college, who had never gone outside his doors and did not know what an army was ". By the austere standards of a Staff College this is true. Virgil does not write as a general nor even as an old soldier. He sees war from the standpoint of a suffering civilian as a chaos of horror and muddle. This standpoint is perfectly human, and there is much tragic beauty as well as eternal truth in Virgil's Sack of Troy. In war horror and muddle inevitably play a large part, and Virgil added a new realm to poetry when he wrote about them. No ordinary soldier will deny the reality and the realism of this famous narrative, from the simple but cunning device of the Wooden Horse, which brings the invaders inside the beleaguered city, to the final scene where the conquerors collect the booty and place a guard over it, while the prisoners wait in a long row by them. There are aspects of war which mean little to the hero or to the general but are well known to the common man. Of these Virgil is the poet.

Virgil's Sack of Troy gives the poetry of defeat from the point of view of the defeated. Such a theme is familiar to heroic epic, but Virgil works differently. The defeat which he describes is not heroic and glorious as in the *Battle of Maldon* or the *Song of Roland*. In them the defeated almost choose to die when they might escape, and their choice is a sign of their heroic natures, of their belief that death is better than dishonour. Virgil's Troy has no such choice; it is doomed from the beginning, when Laocoön is devoured by Neptune's serpents for doubting the honest intentions of the Wooden Horse, and at the end the predestined character of its fall is marked by the menacing vision of revengeful gods :

> apparent dirae facies inimicaque Troiae
> numina magna deum.[1]   (II, 622-3)

[1] The dreadful faces throng, and, hating Troy,
Great presences of gods.

All through the events of the capture this inevitable doom is clear. When the ghost of Hector appears to Aeneas in a dream, it makes no appeal for a fight ; — all is lost, the fate of Troy is sealed, and the only wise course is to flee. The Greeks fall on Troy like some irresistible natural force, like fire upon corn-fields or a mountain stream upon tilth and woodland. The Trojans are entirely unprepared and peacefully asleep when the attack comes. They are caught unawares, have no leadership and no plan, and are trapped by the enemies in their midst. They fight with the courage of despair, as Aeneas shows when he calls upon his comrades :

> moriamur et in media arma ruamus.
> una salus victis nullam sperare salutem.[1]
>
> (II, 353-4)

This is not the authentic spirit of heroism. When the Old Companion in the *Battle of Maldon* calls on his men to fight to the last, he knows what he is doing, and his decisions rise from his belief that in such a desperate resistance manhood really reaches its heights. The Trojans have no such belief. Their disaster is tragic but not heroic. The old conception of a fight to the finish has been replaced by something nearer to life and in its way more painful and more appalling.

Poetry like Virgil's Sack of Troy almost inevitably raises great questions about the nature of heroism and the worth of the old heroic ideal. If war is really like this, Homer can hardly have been right in treating warriors as if they were supermen. Virgil does not shirk any of the questions raised by his story and implicitly criticises the heroic ideal by showing to what baseness it can degenerate. His Trojans are noble enough, but they lack the qualities necessary to victory and cannot be called heroes. His Greeks, whose names and actions come from the Homeric and post-Homeric epics, are not redeemed by nobility or mercy or chivalry. The agent, Sinon, who secures the introduction of the Wooden Horse into Troy, is a master of perjured falsehood who does not shrink from invoking the most holy powers to confirm his lies, or from winning his way by playing on the Trojans' noble compassion and sense of justice for a man

---

[1] Forward to death in battle's midst !
One chance the conquered have, to hope for none.

whom they think grievously misused. The guilefulness which
Homer portrayed so humanly and attractively in Odysseus has
become sinister and bestial and alien to decency and truth.
Sinon is the corruption of one heroic type, the clever soldier
as a later, disillusioned age saw him. Equally unattractive is
the type of relentless fighter, as Virgil presents it in Neopto-
lemus. The son of Achilles inherits his father's proud
temper and martial fury, but he is brutal and bloodthirsty.
He is compared to a poisonous snake, and with remorseless
cruelty he kills the boy Polites in front of his old father,
Priam, and then kills Priam himself. The hideous horror of
such a death is conveyed in Virgil's words :

> iacet ingens litore truncus,
> avulsumque umeris caput et sine nomine corpus.[1]
> (II, 557-8)

The hateful brutality of the Greeks increases the helpless
appeal of the Trojans, of Cassandra dragged by the hair from
the sanctuary of Pallas, of Hecuba and her daughters cluster-
ing like frightened doves about the sacred hearth, of Priam
girding on his useless sword and throwing his pathetic,
ineffectual spear at Neoptolemus. In such a fight it is the
best who perish, like Rhipeus

> iustissimus unus
> qui fuit in Teucris et servantissimus aequi
> (dis aliter visum).[2]   (II, 426-8)

Such a victory has no glamour and no glory. It is won by
treachery and cruelty. To this Homer's Achaeans have
degenerated.

The criticism of the heroic type which Virgil gives in his
Sack of Troy is not his only approach to it. It shows one side
of the question as he saw it, but only one side. It was as clear
to him, as to others, that an ideal which had in its time exerted
so great an influence on the world, could not be entirely like
this, though at times it might degenerate to this. Indeed his
task almost forced him to take another, more favourable view

[1]   The great corpse lies upon the shore,
   A severed head, a trunk without a name.

[2]   Of the Trojans he
   Most just and most observant of the right, —
   The gods thought otherwise.

43

of it ; for if the Augustan Romans sought to be compared with heroes, the heroic ideal must have some dignity and appeal. Virgil's more friendly feelings about it may be seen in his characterisation of Turnus. The Rutulian prince who defends Latium against Aeneas and his Trojans is one of Virgil's most convincing creations. He has the vitality and nobility of a Homeric hero, and we are forced to admire him and even to sympathise with him. Virgil delineates him with care and love, and in him, much more than in the degenerate Neoptolemus, we learn the poet's feelings about a hero. Turnus is a second Achilles, as the Cumaean Sibyl tells Aeneas :

> alius Latio iam partus Achilles,
> natus et ipse dea,[1] (VI, 89-90)

and such his actions prove him to be. Like Achilles, he lives for honour and for renown, especially in war. When he hears that the stranger has landed in Latium and is destined to take his affianced bride from him, his immediate impulse is to fight for his rights and his honour. Feeling that his pride has been insulted, he turns furiously to his weapons. Virgil's similes show the strength and energy of Turnus. When he attacks the Trojan camp, he is like a hungry wolf circling round a sheepfold (IX, 59-64) ; when he is driven slowly and reluctantly from the battlefield, he is like a lion that refuses to turn and fly (IX, 79-6) ; he falls on Pallas as a lion falls on a bull (X, 454-6) ; he is again like a wounded lion when he sees the failing spirit of his companions and refuses to admit defeat (XII, 4-8). These comparisons are based on the *Iliad* and show Turnus in his heroic magnificence as a peer of Achilles and Ajax. Virgil takes pains to make Turnus live up to the old heroic standards and shows how in the best traditions of his type he rallies his troops, attacks the Trojan camp, deals deadly blows to all who come in his way, and fights with heroic courage in his last encounter against hopeless odds. He is a true hero by Homeric standards and finds in battle proper scope for his great gifts.

Turnus is more than a great warrior. He believes, not entirely without reason, that he is fighting for his country. He calls on his countrymen to see the issues at stake, and

[1] In Latium is a new Achilles born,
Himself a goddess' son.

44

there is something of Hector in him when he appeals to the Latin Council :

> nunc coniugis esto
> quisque suae tectique memor, nunc magna referte
> facta, patrum laudes.[1]   (x, 280-82)

Unlike Achilles, he does not exult over his fallen enemies, and though the slaying of Pallas is to cost him his own life in the end, he does not maltreat the body nor gloat in triumph over it, but with a generous gesture gives it back for burial. Nor is his confidence of the kind that collapses with the first signs of failure. He takes heavy blows, the defeat of his troops, the failure of his diplomatic overtures to Diomedes, the half-hearted support of his colleagues and the ill-concealed envy of his rivals, and he still retains a proud trust in his Latin allies (xi, 428 ff.). He is eager to devote his own life in single combat for his country, no matter against how powerful an enemy, and even when his hopes grow dim and death is all but certain, he is still ready to shoulder his burden, though the gods are against him, and he keeps his honour untainted to the last. Since he may not live, he will die like a man and worthily of his race :

> usque adeone mori miserum est ? vos o mihi, Manes,
> este boni quoniam superis aversa voluntas.
> sancta ad vos anima atque istius inscia culpae
> descendam magnorum haud unquam indignus avorum.[2]
>   (xii, 646-9)

In the final fight he is not afraid of his antagonist, but only of the gods ; he refuses to abase himself before the triumphant Aeneas and says proudly :

> non me tua fervida terrent
> dicta, ferox ; di me terrent et Iuppiter hostis.[3]
>   (xii, 894-5)

---

[1]   Let each remember now
His wife, his home. Recall your fathers' acts,
Great deeds that brought them praise.

[2] Is death a sorrow ? Spirits of the dead,
Be kind to me, since Heav'n has turned away.
A soul unstained, unblamed, I shall go down,
In naught unworthy of my mighty sires.

[3]   Thy hot words daunt me not,
Proud man, — Heav'n daunts me and Jove's enmity.

Though he begs Aeneas to spare his life, it is because he thinks of his old father, and because he cannot believe that Aeneas will pursue hatred and revenge when he has won all that he desires. In Turnus there is much of Achilles, much too of Hector; there is nothing of Sinon or of Neoptolemus. He is the hero who fights for honour and for home. In him the heroic qualities have lost none of their grandeur or their fascination, and we may be sure that Virgil admired him as much as we do.

Virgil does more than admire Turnus; he feels deeply for him, especially in the final fight with Aeneas. Turnus has no hope of victory; for the gods have abandoned him. But he does not give up the struggle. There is a tragic pathos in his frustration when he lifts his last weapon, a huge stone, and throws it, in vain, against his enemy. Nowhere in the *Aeneid* are lines so intimate and so tender as the simile which shows the futility of Turnus' efforts:

> ac velut in somnis, oculos ubi languida pressit
> nocte quies, nequiquam avidos extendere cursus
> velle videmur et in mediis conatibus aegri
> succidimus — non lingua valet, non corpore notae
> sufficiunt vires nec vox aut verba sequuntur:
> sic Turno, quacunque viam virtute petivit,
> successum dea dira negat.[1]   (XII, 908-14)

This is something quite outside Homer. Though the bare outlines of the simile come from the *Iliad* where the pursuit of Hector by Achilles is compared to the pursuit of one man by another in a dream:

> ὡς δ' ἐν ὀνείρῳ οὐ δύναται φεύγοντα διώκειν,
> οὔτ' ἄρ' ὁ τὸν δύναται ὑποφεύγειν οὔθ' ὁ διώκειν·
> ὡς ὁ τὸν οὐ δύνατο μάρψαι ποσίν, οὐδ' ὃς ἀλύξαι,[2]
> (*Il.* XXII, 199-201)

[1] And as in sleep, when night has sealed the eyes
In drooping rest, in some long race we seem
To strive in vain, and in our striving fail
And fall; our tongue fails, our familiar strength
Is useless, and our words and voice fail too;
So wheresoever Turnus sought a way,
That goddess dread denied success.

[2] As in a dream a man cannot catch whom he pursueth,
Neither the one can escape in flight, nor the other pursue him,
So the one could not surpass in the race, nor the other elude him.

46

the Homeric simile is much less pathetic, much less concerned with the feelings of the defeated than Virgil's is. Homer sees the struggle from outside while Virgil sees it in all the horror and despair and frustration that it means to Turnus. The climax comes, and Turnus is killed, and with his death the poem ends, not on a note of success or triumph or even of duty done, but almost with a lamentation for this great spirit sent to an untimely doom. In the *Aeneid* it is not of Aeneas but of Turnus that we are made to think at the finish :

ast illi solvuntur frigore membra
vitaque cum gemitu fugit indignata sub umbras.[1]
(XII, 951-2)

The poem of imperial Rome closes not with a patriotic paean or a hope of high national achievements but with the pathos of a young man's death. We cannot doubt that Virgil meant us to feel that Turnus was a noble and heroic figure and that his death was not a mere incident in the foundation of Rome nor a punishment for resisting the divine plan. He stresses the nobility and the pathos of Turnus, and both must have had some relevance to his general plan.

Turnus is a tragic figure and his death is a tragic event. He dies because he opposes the inevitable and predestined rise of Rome, but that does not mean that we should rejoice in his death or condemn him in all that he does. The rise of such a power as Rome demands sacrifices of this kind. They are inescapable, but they are not necessarily matter for rejoicing. Virgil treats Turnus as a tragic hero, as a great man who is highly gifted and in many ways admirable but falls through a single fault. The scheme is more Sophoclean than Homeric. For the fault which ruins Turnus is also the source of his greatness ; it is his heroic pride and sense of his own worth. Such a scheme fits naturally into the epic pattern and gives depth and significance to the story. Turnus opposes the divine mission of Aeneas because the gods decide that he shall and Juno, who herself opposes it, uses him as her instrument. But this does not mean that Turnus is an unwilling victim or puppet in the hands of the gods. He acts like this because he is the kind of man to set his own pride

---

[1]   His limbs grow faint and cold,
And, wailing, his indignant life takes flight.

47

before any other consideration. He fails to see how great are
the powers that fight for Aeneas and believes that his own
destiny can match them. He is therefore blind to the portents
and deaf to the prophecies which reveal the meaning of
Aeneas' arrival in Italy and affects to believe that the mere
arrival of Aeneas is all that matters and that with it the
oracles are fulfilled. For this reason he is not afraid of them :

> nil me fatalia terrent,
> si qua Phryges prae se iactant, responsa deorum :
> sat fatis Venerique datum, tetigere quod arva
> fertilis Ausoniae Troes.[1]   (IX, 133-6)

So confident is he of his own destiny and in his own judgment
that he makes fatal mistakes, first when he gladly and con-
fidently takes up arms against the Trojans and secondly when
there is a good chance of peace but, instead of taking it,
he follows his own wild ambition and decides to renew the
battle and display his own prowess. His love of battle and
of glory blinds him to the wrong that has been committed.
The result is that he is forced to fight Aeneas alone and is
killed. His high temper impairs his judgment, and he does
not know where to stop. He is an example of that tragic $\ddot{v}\beta\rho\iota\varsigma$,
or pride which leads a man too far and works his destruction.
In the end he dies because he attempts what is beyond his
powers. Virgil conveys this in a significant way. When
Turnus kills Pallas, he takes an embossed belt off the body,
and Virgil comments :

> nescia mens hominum fati sortisque futurae
> et servare modum rebus sublata secundis ![2]
>   (X, 501-2)

Turnus shows his exultant spirit by taking the belt ; at the
end, when he himself lies helpless before Aeneas and begs for
his life, there is a chance that he will be spared until Aeneas,
on the point of yielding, sees the belt and is inflamed by the
sight to kill him. Turnus is not, strictly speaking, punished

---

[1]   They daunt me not, these dooms
And oracles of which the Phrygians boast.
Enough for Fate and Venus that they touched
Ausonia's rich fields.

[2] Blind heart of man, blind to its coming doom,
That keeps no bounds in arrogant success.

for killing Pallas ; for that is a legitimate act of war. He is killed because he lives a life of war and inevitably resorts to war when his will is crossed. He represents that heroic world which contains in its ideals the seeds of its own destruction, and in him Virgil shows that he understood the heroic type and even admired it but knew that it was no longer what the world needed.

Turnus is not Virgil's only presentation of a heroic type. With him we may in many ways compare Dido, Virgil's most complete and most successful woman in the *Aeneid*. Just as Turnus obstructs Aeneas in the course of his destiny, so in her own way does Dido. She too is an instrument of Juno ; she too evokes our admiration and our sympathy. Dido does not come from Homer and has no roots in heroic story. Virgil has given her a heroic status in his own manner and for his own reasons. She is an example of what a woman can be if her character is like that of a heroic man. In her case too Virgil conceives the story in a tragic spirit and shapes it almost like an Attic tragedy. It opens with a conversation between Dido and her confidante, like that between Phaedra and the Nurse in Euripides' *Hippolytus* ; it marches inevitably to a crisis and a catastrophe, but the poetry is put more into speeches than into accounts of action ; the injured woman decides to kill herself, but first lays a hideous curse on the man who has, as she believes, wronged her ; then the end comes peacefully with a *deus ex machina*, when Iris releases Dido from her dying agony. There are even passages, like the account of Atlas or of Rumour, which are like choral odes and provide lyrical interludes in the grim story. The tone and construction of Book IV come from Greek tragedy, and we are right to respond to Dido's catastrophe as to a tragic disaster. The tears which St. Augustine deplored that he had wasted on her in his misguided youth show that at least his literary judgment was not at fault. Behind this external resemblance to tragedy we can see also a tragic vision and intention, a scheme which relates Dido to other great women whose character is their doom.

Dido, like Turnus, has a tragic fault. She has taken a vow to be faithful to the spirit of her dead husband, Sychaeus, but she breaks it when she unites herself to Aeneas. This is the *culpa* which eventually proves her undoing. But for it

49

she would never have fallen so much in love with him or have
felt his desertion so deeply. While Dido still hesitates to
yield to her passion, she says :

> si non pertaesum thalami taedaeque fuisset,
> huic uni forsan potui succumbere culpae.[1]
>
> (IV, 18-19)

and later when she has yielded, Virgil repeats the word *culpa*
to set his meaning beyond doubt :

> nec iam furtivum Dido meditatur amorem :
> coniugium vocat, hoc praetexit nomine culpam.[2]
>
> (IV, 171-2)

The fault would seem more grave to a Roman than to us.
Not only would he feel a special sanctity in an oath taken to
a dead husband, but in theory at least he would hold that a
woman ought not to have more than one husband in her life-
time. So when Dido yields to her passion, she is not entirely
blameless. On the other hand her punishment is far beyond
her deserts. Virgil is explicit about the source of her sorrows,
but he does not say that she deserves them all, and the judg-
ment of posterity has been that she suffers unjustly. It is she
and not Aeneas who wins our sympathy, she whose suffer-
ings call out Virgil's most splendid poetry. Like Turnus she
is built on a heroic scale. She has conducted a great and
hazardous enterprise in founding Carthage, and until Aeneas
arrives she is a great ruler. For this reason the catastrophe is
all the greater when it comes. In her dying hours we forget
her initial fault, and we appreciate the justice with which in
the Underworld, where she is united again to her dead
husband, she turns scornfully away from Aeneas' apologetic
attempts to make his peace with her.

The modern world sympathises with Dido against Aeneas,
and on the whole the Romans seem to have done the same.
Perhaps Ovid is partly responsible for this ; for in his *Letter
of Dido to Aeneas* he wholeheartedly took her side and set an
example which others followed. But even without Ovid's
example, it seems likely that the Romans would have sup-

---

[1] Were I not tired of bridal torch and bower,
I might perhaps give in to this one fault.

[2] Nor longer dreams of secret love, but calls
It wedlock, and with this name decks her fault.

ported Dido. St. Augustine shed tears over her in his youth, and in later life noticed Aeneas' hardness of heart in his treatment of her. Once Virgil had presented her as he did there was almost no alternative to accepting her as a much-injured woman. Yet to Virgil's first readers Dido might not have been expected to make so immediate and so powerful an appeal. In reading about her they might well have felt suspicion and distrust. Virgil must have been conscious of this, and his presentation of Dido shows how he was able to make his Roman public rise above national passions to a more impartial outlook. For his Dido must inevitably have called to mind the influence of another foreign queen on Roman history and her fatal hold on a great Roman. The episode of Antony and Cleopatra proved how dangerous the East was to the West, and the general relief over Cleopatra's death may be seen in Horace's almost hysterical outburst of joy over it. That Virgil shared the common view of her is clear from her place on the Shield of Aeneas:

> sequiturque, nefas, Aegyptia coniunx.[1]   (VIII, 688)

The damning word *nefas* leaves no doubt about the wicked-ness of Antony's relations with Cleopatra. It is against this background of hatred, fear and horror that we must set Virgil's Dido. She is not Cleopatra. Yet the two women have enough in common for Dido to suggest the lures and perils which the Romans knew to have lurked in Egypt. The two queens have certain superficial and accidental resemblances. Each reigns in Africa, and has in youth been driven from her heritage by a brother; each falls in love with a famous Roman, if so Aeneas may be called, and each ends by killing herself. More important are resemblances of character. Each is imperious and self-willed, capable of desperate action and able to promote great enterprises and to rule a people surrounded by enemies; each has the passionate temperament of a woman who is bound by no Roman proprieties and has all the forceful independence of one born to rule. There was in Cleopatra, as in Dido, much to compel respect and admiration. In a Roman world these great figures stand remarkably apart. Virgil must have seen that, when he created Dido, his readers would remember Cleopatra and

[1] And follows, shame on it! th' Egyptian bride.

would, consciously or unconsciously, revive for Dido much of their old feeling for the Egyptian queen and see yet another example of the dangers which the East held for the West. Such doubts would need all Virgil's art to allay them, and yet he seems to have succeeded in doing so.

Dido might be equally suspect for another reason. She was a Carthaginian, a ruler of the people which had been the greatest menace known to Rome and of which little good was said long after the destruction of Carthage. The official and no doubt popular view of Carthage is clear from Livy's judgment on the great Hannibal. In this soldier, whose achievements still stir the imagination, he sees the exemplar of cruelty, unscrupulousness and "more than Punic treachery".[1] The same spirit breathes in some of Horace's odes, when he dwells on the treachery of Carthage and regards its ruin as a proper punishment for its impiety. Similar feelings had been held by Cicero who made an exception to the honourable enemies of Rome in the "treaty-breaking Carthaginians and cruel Hannibal".[2] Virgil knew these suspicions and to some degree shared them; he saw that Dido, as the foundress of Carthage, would invite distrust. He adopts a bold solution. When Dido finds that she has been abandoned by Aeneas, she curses him and his descendants, and her curse forecasts the hideous struggles of the Punic Wars, and the rise of Hannibal :

> exoriare aliquis nostris ex ossibus ultor
> qui face Dardanios ferroque sequare colonos,
> nunc, olim, quocumque dabunt se tempore vires.[3]
>
> (IV, 625-7)

In her death-hour Dido invokes vengeance on Rome, and for the moment seems to be responsible for the Punic Wars. Yet she does this because Aeneas has deserted her, and so Aeneas is hardly less responsible than she. It is true that this might well cause Roman readers to dislike or condemn Dido as the enemy of their race, yet such is the power of Virgil's poetry that he makes us sympathise even with Dido's curse. He seems to take her side so wholeheartedly that the Romans

---

[1] XXI, 4, 17.   [2] *De Off.* I, 38.

[3] Let some avenger rise up from my bones
To chase Troy's wanderers with fire and sword,
Now, afterwards, whenever strength is ours.

must almost have been forced to forget their national griev-
ances in their sympathy with her tragic destiny.

Virgil in fact makes Dido's misfortunes awake a compas-
sion and a sympathy which outweigh and even obliterate
legitimate considerations of what such a woman might mean
to Rome. He uses every means to make her majestic, human
and tragic. He dwells on her greatness of character and of
heart. When she first appears, she is a great queen and a
great woman. She has founded and built Carthage; she has
led a large company from Tyre to the waste shores of Africa
where she is building a city so splendid that it must have
recalled the temples and palaces which Augustus was building
in Rome; the welcome which she gives to Aeneas and his
Trojans is as warm as it is sincere. She makes no reservations
in her offers of hospitality, invites the Trojans to stay in
Carthage and promises to make no discrimination against
them :

> Tros Tyriusque mihi nullo discrimine agetur.[1] (I, 574)

She recalls the ancient ties between her own house and that of
Aeneas, and shows what the ancient world would have thought
a becoming modesty when she says that her own sufferings
have taught her to succour the distressed :

> me quoque per multos similis fortuna labores
> iactatam hac demum voluit consistere terra.
> non ignara mali miseris succurrere disco.[2]
> (I, 628-30)

Her regal style displays itself in her feasts and her gifts, in
her ceremonies for the gods, in her court with its attendants
and minstrels and its talks prolonged into the night, in the
kindness which she lavishes on the boy Ascanius. More even
than Turnus she is a ruler of men who carries out her duties
with a fine conscience and a high style. It was not like this
that the Romans saw Cleopatra. Dido appeals to deep-seated
Roman feelings such as their respect for power and hospitality

---

[1] Trojans and Tyrians — I shall deem them one.
(C. J. Billson)

[2] Me, too, like fortune through a world of woe
Hath tossed, and in this land late rest hath given.
My own wounds teach me to salve others' pain.
(C. J. Billson)

and generosity. She is a true heroine in her great gifts and her noble instincts.

Even in her relations with Aeneas Dido is presented in an unexpectedly favourable light. She is wrong to break her oath to her first husband, but after this it is not easy to condemn her conduct. She is in love with Aeneas, and Virgil never says that he is in love with her. In her love she believes that their union is a real marriage. Nor is she entirely wrong. The two first consummate their love in a cave into which a storm has driven them, and Virgil describes the circumstances :

> prima et Tellus et pronuba Iuno
> dant signum ; fulsere ignes et conscius aether
> conubiis, summoque ulularunt vertice Nymphae.[1]
> (IV, 166-8)

The events are less simple than they look. What happens is that powers of earth and sky carry out in their own way the ceremony of an ancient marriage. Mother Earth and Juno, goddess of wedlock, give the signal for the rites to begin ; the lightning-flashes correspond to the marriage torches ; the air is a witness, and the Nymphs raise the nuptial cry. All is in order and correct for a marriage, but it is carried out not by human beings but by natural powers. The conclusion is inevitable that the marriage is in some sense valid. Dido does not wed Aeneas as a Roman woman weds a Roman man, but she weds him with the approval of nature and believes that the marriage is real. In this belief she never falters, and to it she appeals when she begs Aeneas not to leave her :

> per conubia nostra, per inceptos hymenaeos.[2] (IV, 316)

But it is precisely in this that the tragic discord lies. Aeneas, already a typical Roman, does not share her belief. In his answer to her he denies that they were ever married :

> nec coniugis unquam
> praetendi taedas aut haec in foedera veni.[3]
> (IV, 338-9)

[1]   Old Earth and spousal Juno give
A sign ; bickering fires and conscious sky
Witness the rite, and mountain Nymphs cry hail.

[2] By wedlock that is ours, by rites begun.

[3]   I never lit
A bridal torch or entered on this pact.

He knows that, since his destiny calls him to Italy, no ties with Dido can be binding. Between the two points of view there is an irreconcilable conflict. Dido has committed her whole life to her love for Aeneas, and when he rejects it, there is nothing else for her but death ; for life has no meaning for her without it. This conflict rises from a deeper discord. Different in origin and in destiny, she and Aeneas cannot be united in any real or abiding way. Each believes that she or he is right, and each has good reason for it. By giving in to her original fault and indulging her passion for Aeneas, Dido opens the way to her own doom. The consummation in the cave is the beginning of the end :

> ille dies primus leti primusque malorum
> causa fuit.[1]   ,   (IV, 169-70)

Once she believes that Aeneas is hers, she is determined to keep him at all costs and forgets everything else in her love for him. The result is that, when he leaves her, she kills herself.

The parallel between Dido and Turnus is close. Each comes to a tragic end through a relatively small fault, and each wins compassion and sympathy. Just as Turnus' last hours set him beyond all condemning or critical judgments, so we forget that Dido is partly responsible for her own catastrophe and take her side when she invokes the powers of heaven and hell to carry out her curse :

> Sol, qui terrarum flammis opera omnia lustras,
> tuque harum interpres curarum et conscia Iuno,
> nocturnisque Hecate triviis ululata per urbes
> et Dirae ultrices et di morientis Elissae. . . .[2]
> (IV, 607-10)

Virgil is more than fair to her. He allows his poetic imagination full rein in his treatment of her and presents her case with great pity and understanding. Yet she too, like Turnus, illustrates the limitations and the dangers of the heroic outlook. Her high spirit makes her act in defiance of her better

---

[1] That day the first of woe and first of death
Was cause.

[2] Thou Sun, whose beams survey all works of earth,
And Juno, witness of my agony,
Hecate, at the cross-roads wailed at night,
Avenging Curses, and my gods of death. . . .

nature and brings her to her doom. She lives in the last resort for herself, for her own emotions and passions and pride. Once her love for Aeneas dominates her nature and engages her vanity, nothing else matters to her. When she first falls in love, she forgets about Carthage and neglects the great task which she has begun :

> pendent opera interrupta minaeque
> murorum ingentes aequataque machina caelo.[1]
> (IV, 88-9)

So when she knows that Aeneas is leaving her, she thinks only of herself and her injured pride, and turns on him ; if he will not stay with her, let him perish in a hideous death and let the world of their descendants be convulsed in war. Her heroic nature, despite all its great qualities, lives for itself. When it is frustrated and injured, it can only turn to destroy others and itself. Virgil seems to have felt that the heroic type, which he understood and in many ways admired, had this fatal fault, that, because it lives for its own glory and satisfaction, it is bound to cause destruction. It is a just comment, and Virgil was entitled to make it. It shows why the old heroic and Homeric outlook was inadequate either to him or to Augustan Rome. His world had enough experience of this reckless self-assertion to know what harm it can cause.

Against these imperfect types Virgil had to set his own reformed and Roman ideal of manhood. His task was indeed difficult. He had to create a man who should on the one hand be comparable to the noblest Homeric heroes in such universally honoured qualities as courage and endurance and on the other hand should present in himself the qualities which the Augustan age admired beyond all others but which had meant nothing to Homer. Virgil's treatment of Dido and Turnus shows that his new hero could not be ruled by the self-assertive spirit and cult of honour which inspired the heroic outlook ; he must be based on some other principle more suited to an age of peace and order. But if he was to rival Achilles and Odysseus, he must be a great man and a ruler of men. Virgil had to present a hero who appealed both by his

Half-built the works hang, and the great
Menacing walls and cranes that touch the sky.

greatness and by his goodness, by his superior gifts and by his Roman *virtus*. On the one hand he must be a fitting member of the heroic age to which legend assigned him, and on the other he must represent in its fullness and variety the new idea of manhood which Augustus advocated and proclaimed as characteristically Roman. The result was Aeneas, a character so compounded of different elements that he has often been derided even by those who love Virgil. Yet to him Virgil gave his deepest meditations and some of his finest poetry. To understand him we must try to recapture some of the ideas and sentiments of the Augustan age.

Aeneas comes from Homer, and in the *Aeneid* he is presented as a great warrior who is almost the equal of Hector. To him Hector appears after death, as to his legitimate successor in the defence of Troy. Andromache associates him with Hector when she asks if the boy Ascanius has the courage and spirit of his father Aeneas and his uncle Hector. Aeneas' fame has spread through the whole world, and Dido knows all about him before she sees him, while in Italy Pallas is amazed that so renowned a man should appear before him on the Tiber. He has the heroic qualities of divine blood, prowess in war, personal beauty and power to command men. But he has something more than this. His essential quality, as his distinguishing epithet of *pius* shows, is his *pietas*, his devotion to the gods and to all their demands. When Ilioneus speaks of him to Dido, he shows the combination of qualities in Aeneas :

> rex erat Aeneas nobis, quo iustior alter
> nec pietate fuit, nec bello maior et armis.[1]
>
> (I, 544-5)

Aeneas is not only a great soldier ; he is a good man. So, to some degree, Homer had made him when he told of his many sacrifices to Poseidon, but Virgil enlarges the concept of this goodness until it covers much more than the performance of religious rites. Aeneas' *pietas* is shown in his devotion to his country, to his father, to his wife, to his child, to his followers and above all to the many duties and the special task which the gods lay on him. He is *pius* because he does what a good man should. The epithet which Virgil gives him is unlike

---

[1] A king we had, Aeneas : none more just,
More righteous, more renowned in war and arms.

the epithets which Homer gives to his heroes. For while these denote physical characteristics or qualities useful in war, *pius* indicates a spiritual quality which has nothing to do with war and is specially concerned with the relations between Aeneas and the gods. Thus at the start Virgil's hero is set in a different order of things and claims a different kind of attention. In this unprecedented epithet for an epic hero and in all that it implies is the clue to Virgil's conception of Aeneas.

Aeneas is *pius*, but he is not a perfect and ideal man throughout the poem. The indignation which he has excited in more than one critic for his obvious faults shows not that Virgil's idea of goodness was singularly unlike our own but that he chose to show a good man in the making and the means by which he is made. To understand Aeneas we must understand the scheme by which Virgil presents him, a scheme based on the moral views of the Augustan age but modified by Virgil's own beliefs and admirations. The clue to Aeneas is that he is built on a Stoic plan. St. Augustine hints at this when he touches on Aeneas' treatment of Dido and treats it as being typically Stoic because while he sheds tears for her, his purpose is not shaken by her sufferings :

mens immota manet, lacrimae volvuntur inanes.[1]   (IV, 449)

It is not certain that St. Augustine interprets the line correctly, but his main conclusion is right. Aeneas has undeniably something Stoic about him which accounts for the alleged paradoxes and contradictions of his character. There is nothing strange in this. In the moral reforms which Augustus preached and planned a revived Stoicism took a prominent place. It breathes through the patriotic odes of Horace, and it survived through the first two centuries A.D. Originally Stoicism was a creed to meet the horrors of an age in which there was no political or personal security. Against this disorder it set the citadel of a man's soul in which he could live at peace with himself and with the universe and by subduing his emotions be undismayed at whatever might happen. The Augustan Romans took over this creed and gave it a new reference. It suited them because it disapproved of self-assertion and ambition and laid great emphasis on social duties. It was well suited to an age which hoped to

---

[1] His mind unmoved, his tears fall down in vain.

recover from the excesses of unfettered individualism. The quiet, self-denying, self-sacrificing citizen who was prepared to do what he was told was a type dear to Augustus. Virgil knew the theory and the doctrine, and though in his youth he had leaned towards Epicurus, he was deeply affected by them.

The Stoics believed that a man is not born good, or as they called it "wise", but becomes so through testing, *exercitatio*, by which his natural qualities are brought into practice and his character is strengthened and developed. If he responds rightly to this process, he will in the end find that wisdom which is the same as goodness. What matters is the result, the final state of a man. It does not matter if he makes mistakes provided that he learns from them and becomes wise. The great exemplars of Stoic virtue were Hercules and the Dioscuri, men who spent their lives in performing hard tasks and were in the end exalted to deity by their success in them. Into such a scheme the career and character of Aeneas may be fitted. In the first five books of the *Aeneid* he is tested ; in the later books he has become wise and good and is a complete man. Since the result is good, it does not matter that in the past he should sometimes have failed ; what counts is his ultimate character, and this Virgil sets before us after showing his failings. That this was Virgil's intention is shown by his use of Stoic language at certain important points. The process of testing is revealed twice. The first occasion is when Aeneas is in despair over his failure to settle in Crete, the second when he has seen four of his ships burned in Sicily and thinks of giving up his quest altogether. Both occasions find him at his least confident, and on both he is saved by his father, Anchises, first in the flesh and later as a ghost in a dream, who addresses him with the words

nate Iliacis exercite fatis.[1]   (III, 182 ; V, 725)

The word *exercite* is technical and means " tested " and almost " tested by ordeal ". Seneca says that God tests those whom he loves.[2] So the gods love Aeneas and test him. Nearly half the *Aeneid* is concerned with this process, and it explains why Aeneas acts as he does. The naturally good man, who is faithful to his gods and to his family, has been chosen for a special task, and to fit himself for it he must pass

[1] Son, tested by the fates of Troy.   [2] *Dial.* I, 4.

through ordeals. He makes mistakes in them, but he learns from his mistakes, and in the end he finds his true self.

The faults of Aeneas are an ancient topic of derision. They may perhaps have been stressed in a lost work by Carvilius Pictor called *Aeneomastix* (*The Scourge of Aeneas*), and they received full attention from the Fathers of the Church who felt that one of their chief opponents was this mythical hero held up to the admiration of Roman youth. Many of the charges against Aeneas are frivolous, but there remain three cases when by the highest standards he fails, in the Sack of Troy, in his relations with Dido, and at the burning of his ships in Sicily. On each of these occasions he allows his emotions to get the better of him and make him act unwisely or wrongly. The Stoics held that the emotions must be entirely subordinated to the reason, and Virgil made use of this belief. Aeneas, for all his natural nobility, begins by being emotional in the wrong way and fails to understand what his duty is or what actions he ought to take. The tests to which he is subjected reveal this weakness in him and in due course teach him how to counter it.

In the Sack of Troy Aeneas behaves courageously enough, but his courage is useless. The Stoics would explain this by saying that real courage is not of a physical or animal kind but a moral quality directed by the reason and that it lies largely in knowing what to do in any given circumstances. This Aeneas lacks. He believes the lying tale of Sinon, though experience should have taught him to distrust the Greeks, and helps to bring the Wooden Horse into Troy, an action in which, as he himself says, he and his friends are

immemores caecique furore.[1] (II, 244)

They are excited and forgetful, not reasonable and foreseeing; they lack that courage which Cicero calls " memory of the past and foresight for the future "[2] and they allow their emotions to subdue their reason. Even in the actual fighting they do not act as rational beings, but fight in a mad, blind fury, without clear purpose or plan. Again Aeneas condemns himself: when he prepares to fight,

arma amens capio, nec sat rationis in armis,[3] (II, 314)

[1] Unmindful, blind with rage.   [2] *De Sen.* 78.
[3] Mad, I take arms, but have not plan enough.

and when he rushes with his companions into the fray,

> furor iraque mentem
> praecipitant.[1]   (II, 316-17)

Any foresight that he may possess is subdued by passion and fury. The mood in which the Trojans fight shows that they are a doomed people. Their aimless courage is useless against the far-sighted plans of the Greeks, and it is symptomatic that at one point they kill their own comrades in error. In his excitement and anxiety Aeneas still manages to take his father and son from Troy, but on the way he loses his wife, Creusa, and never sees her again in the flesh. On this failure the Christian Fathers dwelt with some satisfaction, but Virgil showed them the way. He makes Aeneas admit that at the time his mind was confused and that is why he lost Creusa :

> hic mihi nescio quod trepido male numen amicum
> confusam eripuit mentem.[2]   (II, 735-6)

Aeneas is at this stage still at the mercy of his instincts and emotions ; he has not learned to be master of himself or of his circumstances.

In his relations with Dido Aeneas fails again, though not quite in the way that modern critics find so deplorable. What is wrong is not his desertion of her, which is ordered by the gods and necessary for the fulfilment of his task in Italy, but his surrender in the first place to her love and his subsequent neglect of his real duty which lies away from Carthage. Virgil does not show clearly what Aeneas' motives are ; they seem at least not to be love for Dido, for whom he shows little more than grateful affection. But of his fault there is no question ; it is neglect and forgetfulness of duty. Mercury, sent by Jupiter, makes it quite clear :

> heu, regni rerumque oblite tuarum ![3]   (IV, 267)

This forgetfulness, due perhaps to sloth and love of ease, is

[1] Frenzy and anger drive
My mind headlong.

[2] Then in my fear some unkind spirit stole
My frenzied wits.

[3] Forgetful of thy realm and fate !

a kind of intemperance, a failure in moderation, a state of false pleasure in which a temporary advantage is mistaken for a real good. Aeneas' duty, as Mercury tells him, is owed to his son, and he must do it. This is precisely what he tells Dido, and though her furious reception of his defence makes it look feeble, it is all that he can say, and it is right. Nor would it perhaps have seemed so weak to a Roman. For his duty is concerned with the foundation of Rome, and it cannot be right to set a woman's feelings before that destiny. Aeneas is fond of Dido and feels pity for her, but his conscience is stronger than his emotions and wins in the end. When he leaves her, he acts as a Stoic should, and undoes, so far as he can, the evil which he has committed by allowing himself to forget his task in her company.

In Book V Aeneas is faced with another crisis. During the Funeral Games of his father, the women of his company, stirred up by Juno's agent, begin to burn his ships with the purpose of keeping him in Sicily. Aeneas sees the havoc that they have started and prays to Jupiter to stop it. Jupiter sends rain and the fire is quenched. But even after this display of divine help, Aeneas is full of misgivings :

> At pater Aeneas casu concussus acerbo
> nunc huc ingentis, nunc illuc pectore curas
> mutabat versans, Siculisque resideret arvis
> oblitus fatorum, Italasne capesseret oras.[1]
>
> (v, 700-703)

It seems almost incredible that Aeneas should at this juncture think of abandoning his quest. Yet he does, and it shows how deeply his emotions still rule him. The catastrophe of the burned ships has filled him with such despair that for the moment he ceases to believe in his destiny. Fortunately he is saved by the old sailor Nautes, who not only gives him sensible advice about leaving the women in Sicily and sailing with the rest of his company, but sums up the situation in a way that must have appealed to every Roman conscience :

---

[1] But prince Aeneas, by that sad mischance
Sore stricken, rolls the burden of his thoughts
This way and that. There should he make his home,
Heedless of fate, or grasp Italian shores ?

(C. J. Billson)

nate dea, quo fata trahunt retrahuntque sequamur ;
quidquid erit, superanda omnis fortuna ferendo est.[1]

(v, 709-10)

The fate which Aeneas should follow is the destiny which the
gods have given him, and he should be master enough of
himself to know this. Nautes brings him to his senses, and
when this advice is fortified by words from the spirit of
Anchises, Aeneas recovers his confidence and sets sail for
Italy. He never again allows his feelings to obscure his
knowledge of his duty.

Once he lands in Italy Aeneas is a new man. He makes
no more mistakes, and always does what is right in the
circumstances. He is never again assailed by doubt or despair ;
his only hesitations are about the right means to the known end,
and these after due consideration he finds. The change in
him is clear when he visits the Cumaean Sibyl and says to her:

omnia praecepi atque animo mecum ante peregi.[2] (vi, 105)

The word *praecepi* comes from the technical language of
Stoicism. The duty of the wise and brave man is to foresee,
praecipere, all possible emergencies and to be ready for them.
Cicero uses the word when he says that the duty of a great
nature is to foresee what can happen, whether good or bad,[3]
and Seneca quotes Virgil's actual words to illustrate his view
of a good man, — " Whatever happens, he says ' I foresaw
it ' ".[4] When Aeneas touches the fated soil of Italy, he has
learned his lessons and found that self-control and wisdom
which the Stoics regarded as the mark of a good man. His
earlier adventures and mistakes have not been in vain. For
they have made him surer of himself and more confident of
the divine destiny which leads him.

The Stoic ideas which inform Virgil's conception of
Aeneas' ordeal and development persist to some degree in
the later books of the *Aeneid*, but with a different purpose.
Aeneas is the just and wise prince, and he must not act
unjustly, particularly in such important matters as peace and
war, about which the Augustan age had been taught by bitter

---

[1] Go, goddess' son, where fate drives — back or on.
Endurance conquers fortune, come what may.

[2] I have foreseen and thought all in my soul.

[3] *De Off.* I, 80.   [4] *Ep.* 76, 33.

experience to hold strong views. Aeneas is very like an invader, and he lives in a heroic past, but he must not be allowed to make war as Homer's heroes make it, simply to indulge his own desire for glory. For this reason Virgil makes Aeneas face war with a consciousness of grave responsibilities and of nice distinctions between moral issues. Just as Cicero says that the only right reason for declaring war is that " life may be lived in peace without wrong ",[1] so Virgil is careful to put Aeneas in the right when war is forced upon him by the Latins. Earlier versions of the story said that the Trojans began the attack and were resisted by the Latins ; Virgil reverses the situation and makes Aeneas do everything to secure his aims by peaceful negotiations. His envoy makes the most modest demands of King Latinus, and the king is perfectly willing to accede to them. When war is begun by the Latins, Aeneas conducts it in the spirit which Cicero advocates, "that nothing should be sought but peace ".[2] Even after the aggression of the Latins, Aeneas tells their envoys, who ask for leave to bury the dead, that he is willing to grant much more than that :

> pacem me exanimis et Martis sorte peremptis
> oratis ? equidem et vivis concedere vellem.[3]
>
> (XI, 110-11)

When the truce is broken, his chief thought is to have it restored. He tries to avert a general slaughter and offers to settle the issue by a single combat between himself and Turnus. He cries out to the excited armies :

> o cohibete iras ! ictum iam foedus et omnes
> compositae leges, mihi ius concurrerre soli.[4]
>
> (XII, 314-15)

In this we hear the spirit of the Augustan age as its master proclaimed it when he said that he himself had never made war " without just and necessary reasons " and that he always pardoned his enemies when the general safety allowed. Such an attitude towards war bears no resemblance to anything

---

[1] De Off. I, 34.   [2] Ib. I, 83.

[3] Peace for the dead and slain in war you ask.
I'd grant it gladly to the living too.

[4] Oh stay your wrath ! The pact is made, and all
The rules are fixt. My right to fight alone !

heroic or Homeric. War has become an evil which may be undertaken only when there is no alternative, and it must be conducted in a spirit of chivalry and clemency.

Though Aeneas is built largely on a Stoic plan and conforms in some important respects to the Stoic ideal of the wise man, he is not only this. He has other qualities which lie outside the Stoic purview and are even hostile to it. This is not hard to understand. The Stoic ideal, interesting though it is as an attempt to set a man above his troubles and his failings and to provide him with a feeling of security in a disordered society, failed to conquer mankind because it denied the worth of much that the human heart thinks holy and will not willingly forgo. St. Augustine was not alone in feeling that the Stoics were inhuman in their attempt to suppress all emotions, no matter how reputable. Many other men felt that such an exaltation of reason is wrong in so far as it dries up the natural springs of many excellent actions. Though Virgil used Stoic conceptions for the development of Aeneas' character, his warm-hearted, compassionate temperament was not satisfied with an ideal so cold and so remote. If Stoicism provides a scheme by which Aeneas is tested and matured, it does not explain much else in him. Aeneas, with all his faults and contradictions, is essentially a creature of emotions. It is true that at first these are the cause of his failures and may be condemned, but Virgil did not believe that his ideal Roman should lack emotions altogether. His confident Aeneas of the later books is still highly emotional, but his emotions are now in harmony with his appointed purpose and help him in his pursuit of it.

The most important of these divagations from the Stoic norm is the part played by pity in the character of Aeneas. For many readers this is the most Virgilian of all qualities, the most typical and most essential feature of the *Aeneid*. When Aeneas sees the episodes of the Trojan War depicted in stone at Carthage, he utters the famous words which have so often been quoted as the centre of Virgil's outlook and message :

> sunt hic etiam sua praemia laudi ;
> sunt lacrimae rerum et mentem mortalia tangunt.[1]
> (1, 461-2)

[1]   Here praise has its rewards,
Fortune its tears, and man's fate stirs the heart.

The words do not mean all that is sometimes claimed for them ; they are certainly not a declaration that human life is nothing but tears. But they show that Aeneas on arriving in a strange land feels that here too is not only the glory but the pathos of life. In his mind the two are equally important, and such a view is far removed from Stoic detachment. The same quality comes out when Aeneas sees the ghosts of the unburied dead wandering in the underworld and halts his steps :

> multa putans sortemque animo miseratus iniquam.[1] (VI, 332)

He allows his compassion here to assert itself at the expense of a divine ordinance and to criticise the government of the universe. No correct Stoic would dream of doing such a thing, and it shows how strong pity is in Aeneas and what importance Virgil attaches to it. It makes a remarkable appearance when Aeneas is fighting in Italy. When he kills the young Lausus, he is deeply affected :

> at vero ut vultum vidit morientis et ora,
> ora modis Anchisiades pallentia miris,
> ingemuit miserans graviter dextramque tetendit,
> et mentem patriae subiit pietatis imago.[2]
> (x, 821-4)

Aeneas is not merely sorry for the dying boy ; his pity is deeply rooted in his own domestic affections and sanctities. He feels pity for Lausus' father, and he thinks of his own father, Anchises, who might so easily have lost his son in this way. The great patronymic *Anchisiades* helps to convey this sense of a tie between father and son and gives reality and depth to what might otherwise be a stray, unfounded emotion.

Behaviour of this kind is alien to Stoic principles. For the Stoics pity was as wrong as any other emotion and was condemned, in the words of their founder, Zeno, as a sickness of the soul. They believed that it was caused by the mistaken notion that a man's sufferings are really evils and claimed that more could be done by a reasonable act of clemency than by

---

[1] With thought and pity for their unjust lot.

[2] But when Anchises' son looked on the face
And dying eyes, so marvellously pale,
He groaned aloud with pity, stretched his hand,
And saw the semblance of his filial love.

66

the emotion of pity. With this theory few Romans agreed completely. It is true that Seneca calls pity " the vice of a feeble mind which succumbs at the sight of the sufferings of others ",[1] but more often the Romans tended to accept the Aristotelian view that pity was useful for helping others to endure calamity and that liberality was impossible without it. Yet Aeneas' pity is not even of this utilitarian kind. He cannot help the ghosts of the unburied dead ; he does not spare Lausus. His pity is part of his nature and must be valued, as it has been, for its own sake. Virgil follows no doctrine and no theory in giving this quality to his hero and seems rather to obey the dictates of his own sensitive and compassionate soul.

More surprising than Aeneas' outbursts of pity are his outbursts of anger and fury, which continue after he has arrived in Italy and are evidently essential to his mature personality. The Stoics would have disapproved of them without qualification. They defined anger as the desire for revenge and thought it odious because it makes deliberate and considered action impossible. Seneca says that it is the result not of goodness but of weakness, often frivolous or flippant, and that any good it may do in the way of punishment or correction can be better done from a sense of duty. Even Marcus Aurelius, who in many ways resembles Aeneas and seems to embody the ideal Roman in his historical self, condemns anger with majestic austerity. In anger, he says, the soul wrongs itself ; it is senseless against wrongdoers because they act unwillingly through ignorance, and it is not a proper function of man. Yet Virgil made anger part of Aeneas' character and a potent force in his warlike doings. It rises at the death of Pallas and takes the form of a violent desire to punish Turnus, though for a time it is exercised at the expense of others like Magus, Tarquitus and Lucagus, who do not share Turnus' responsibility for killing Pallas. In the second part of Book X Aeneas is driven by a wild fury against all his opponents. He takes the four sons of Sulmo to be a human sacrifice at Pallas' pyre, and not all the admiration of Donatus, — " how great Aeneas' virtue is shown to be, how great his devotion in honouring the memory of the dead ", — can make us feel that he is acting humanly or even

1. *De Clem.* II, 5, 1.

rationally. When Magus makes a pitiful appeal for mercy, Aeneas refuses with heartless irony and tells him that his death is demanded by the dead Anchises and the boy Iulus. He throws Tarquitus to the fishes and denies him the decencies of burial with the derisive taunt that his mother will not bury him nor lay his limbs in the ancestral tomb. When Lucagus appeals for mercy in the name of a father's love for his son, Aeneas kills him without a qualm. When Turnus lies helpless before him and asks for his life, Aeneas remembers the death of Pallas and kills him

> furiis accensus et ira
> terribilis.[1] (XII, 946-7)

When Aeneas acts like this, he is indeed formidable and strangely unlike the man who pities the dying Lausus.

The combination of such qualities in a single hero demands some explanation. It is sometimes said that in it Virgil modelled Aeneas on Achilles and did not reconcile the obvious discords. It is true that these episodes have their parallels in the furious revenge which Achilles exacts for the death of Patroclus. But if so, Virgil has failed to make his hero convincing or consistent. These outbursts of heroic fury ill suit the exponent of Roman virtues with his strong distaste for war. But another explanation is possible. Virgil liked and admired Augustus, and at the same time knew that Augustus' dominion was based on force. In his youth he had risen to power by a series of violent acts, which he justified as the vengeance for the death of Julius. Legends had gathered round this vengeance and portrayed Augustus as moved by violent and angry feelings. They may not be true, but they were circulated and known and had become part of Augustus' myth. After Philippi Augustus was said to have behaved much as Aeneas behaves after the death of Pallas. Aeneas refuses burial to Tarquitus and tells him that the birds and fishes will lick his wounds ; when a dying man asked Augustus for burial, he said that the birds would soon settle that question. Aeneas is so angry that no appeal to the names of his father and his son moves him to spare Lucagus ; Augustus is said to have made a father play a game with his sons to

[1]   With fury flamed, and wrath
Most fearful.

decide which should live and then looked on while both were killed. Aeneas sacrifices the sons of Sulmo at Pallas' pyre; Augustus was said to have sacrificed three hundred prisoners of war after Perusia on the Ides of March at the altar of Julius. Whether these tales are true or not, Augustus undoubtedly took a fierce revenge for the murder of his adopted father, and it is possible that Virgil modelled Aeneas' revenge for Pallas on it. He seems to have felt that there are times when it is right even for a compassionate man like Aeneas to lose control of himself and to be carried away by anger. This anger is thought to be good not only in its cause but in its results. It helps Aeneas to secure his destiny and to overcome those who resist it. Normally considerate and compassionate, he is slow to anger, but some things so shock him that they awake it, and, when it comes, it is terrible. At the back of his mind Virgil seems to have had a conception of a great man whose natural instincts are all for reason and agreement, but who, when he finds that these are useless, shows how powerful his passions can be. Aeneas, who has to subdue so much of himself, has also at times to subdue his gentler feelings and to allow full liberty to more primitive elements which are normally alien to him.

Virgil has put so much into Aeneas that he has hardly made him a living man. But though he lacks human solidity, he is important as an ideal and a symbol. So far from acting for his own pleasure or glory, he does what the gods demand of him. In the performance of this duty he finds little happiness. He would rather at times give up his task, and he envies the Trojans who have settled in Sicily and have no such labours as his. His stay in Carthage shows how easily his natural instincts can conquer his sense of duty, and there is a pathetic sincerity in his words to Dido :

> Italiam non sponte sequor.[1] (IV, 361)

He takes no pride in his adventures, no satisfaction in their successful conclusion. His whole life is dictated by the gods. They tell him what to do and make him do it, and he obeys in an uncomplaining but certainly not a joyful spirit of acceptance. He is aptly symbolised by Virgil's picture of him

---

[1] I seek not Italy by choice.
(C. J. Billson)

shouldering the great shield on which Vulcan has depicted the deeds of his descendants :

attollens umero famamque et fata nepotum.[1] (VIII, 731)

On Aeneas the whole burden of Rome seems to lie, and it is not surprising that he lacks the instinctive vigour and vitality of Homer's heroes. The new world which Virgil sought to interpret needed men like this, not heroes like Turnus whose individual ambitions lead to destruction.

The significance of Virgil's contrast between Aeneas and Turnus, between the new and the old ideals of manhood, is strengthened by his treatment of the gods who control and take part in the action. Their presence was demanded equally by Homer's precedent and by Virgil's conception of what Rome meant in the scheme of things. The contrast between Aeneas and Turnus is matched by a contrast between Venus and Juno. Venus supports the Trojans, Juno the Italians. So far Virgil follows the Homeric plan by which gods take sides in war, and his goddesses keep their Homeric attachments. For Homer such a proceeding was quite natural. His deities are embodiments of power, who, being free from the limitations of men, follow their own whims and exert their influence as they choose. With Virgil it is different. The identification of the old Roman goddesses, Juno and Venus, with the Greek Here and Aphrodite, meant little to the religious consciousness. Juno and Venus gained little by their new attributes, and a poet could make of them very much what he pleased. Just as the materialist Lucretius makes Venus a principle of life and procreation, so Virgil makes his goddesses symbolical of natural powers. Perhaps he owed something to Empedocles' conception of Νεῖκος and Φιλία, Strife and Love, as the two chief powers of existence, and formed his Juno and Venus on similar lines. In any case his two goddesses have important parts to play, and help to explain the central meaning of the *Aeneid*.

Juno is the patroness of Turnus and the Italians, and she resembles Turnus in one important way. She is exceedingly jealous for her honour and for the respect in which she claims to be held. Old injuries, such as Paris' failure to give her the prize of beauty, rankle in her mind and make her indulge

[1] His shoulder bears his grandsons' fame and fate.

hatred and pursue revenge. She is a goddess with a grievance. She imagines that the Trojans have so ruined her reputation that no one any longer pays honour to her. Therefore she tries to prevent Aeneas from reaching Italy, and when, despite her, he arrives, she makes things as difficult as she can for him by stirring the Italians to resist. Her character and her motives are clearly revealed in her monologue after his arrival and summed up in a famous line :

flectere si nequeo superos, Acheronta movebo.[1] (VII, 312)

For this fell purpose she uses the fury Allecto, who instils hatred, fear and jealousy into the Latins and provokes the war which is to prove so disastrous for Turnus. Just as Juno herself is moved by injured pride, so her agent appeals to it in others, to a mother's feeling that her son is wrongly treated, and to the enraged vanity of a frustrated suitor in Turnus himself. Juno shows a spirit and motives very like Turnus' own. She is in some sense a divine counterpart to him and an embodiment of that self-assertive spirit which knows no bounds and will accept no compromise once it feels itself to be wronged. Just as this spirit may in the right circumstances be noble and admirable, so in other circumstances it may be dangerous and destructive. Juno stands for it and represents that element of θυμός or spirit, of pride and desire for honour, which Plato made so important an element in the soul and regarded as the spring of the active life. So long as it consorts with reason, all is well, but if it is dominated by passion, it overrules reasonable considerations, destroys harmony and works harm. We cannot say that Juno is nothing but a presentation of such a power, but such is undeniably her spirit, and she shows it in heaven as Turnus shows it on earth.

Venus stands in strong contrast to Juno. She does more than support Aeneas ; she is concerned almost entirely for his safety and happiness. She stands for a principle of affection which is so strong that it limits its own outlook and is sometimes blind to important considerations. Thus though her plans for Aeneas agree often enough with his appointed destiny, there are times when she almost opposes it because she is more concerned with his happiness than with his duty. When he is shipwrecked at Carthage, Venus is so anxious

---

[1] If Heaven stirs not, I shall summon Hell.

about his safety that she makes a pact with Juno to let Dido
fall in love with him and so keep him in Africa. This is
directly against what Jupiter wills and has to be set straight
by his interposition through Mercury and the whole tragic
disaster of Dido's death. Venus even believes that Aeneas
and Dido will unite their peoples in a single city in Africa,
though Jupiter has told her that Aeneas must go to Italy. In
her own way she is here almost as great an obstacle to Aeneas'
mission as Juno is in hers. Again, in the debate on Olympus
in Book X, though Aeneas has already landed in Italy, Venus
is so dispirited by the dangers that he runs that she is prepared
to give up all ambitions for him provided that he can live in
safety. She offers to take his son Ascanius to some place
under her protection and to let him spend the rest of his days
there in inglorious peace :

> est Amathus, est celsa mihi Paphus atque Cythera
> Idaliaeque domus : positis inglorius armis
> exigat hic aevum.[1]   (x, 51-3)

Venus stands in the same relation to Aeneas as Juno to Turnus.
Just as Aeneas himself is hampered by doubts and uncer-
tainties and is at times anxious to give up his task and to enjoy
peace and quiet, so Venus is no less ready to secure his ease
at the cost of his glory. She embodies maternal love and
affection, qualities in themselves highly admirable, but not
to be reckoned against the hard life of sacrifice which Jupiter
demands of Aeneas. Like Juno, Venus is incomplete and
one-sided and in certain circumstances wrong. Neither the
self-assertive principle in Juno nor the principle of tenderness
in Venus offers a complete or satisfactory way of life. Each
must be set in its proper place and subordinated to some wider
scheme of things.

The conflict of Venus and Juno represents on a celestial
plane the conflict on earth and helps to make Virgil's meaning
clearer. The destiny of Rome is hampered by two forces,
each of which is excellent in its own place, the old heroic self-
asserting spirit and the civilised love of peace which is based
on the affections. Just as the one makes Turnus obstruct

---

[1] Cythera, Paphus, Amathus, are mine,
The Idalian courts are mine : there let him live
Disarmed, inglorious.

(C. J. Billson)

the divine plan, so the other at times prevents Aeneas from going straight to his destiny. The conflict may even be observed in Aeneas himself when his natural instinct for pity turns to angry fury. The future Roman character, it seems evident, must partake both of Venus and of Juno, of Aeneas and of Turnus ; it must have the proud strength of the one and the humane qualities of the other, but each must be kept in its proper bounds and made subservient to a new view of manhood. Such a solution is in fact found. When at last Juno abandons her futile struggle and consents that Aeneas shall vanquish Turnus, she asks for terms, for a clear and practical compromise : the Trojans and the Latins are to live in peace with each other in Italy, side by side as equals. Her words are of great importance :

> ne vetus indigenas nomen mutare Latinos
> neu Troas fieri iubeas Teucrosque vocari
> aut vocem mutare viros aut vertere vestem.
> sit Latium, sint Albani per saecula reges,
> sit Romana potens Itala virtute propago :
> occidit occideritque sinas cum nomine Troia.[1]
>
> (XII, 823-8)

Juno's request, which Jupiter grants, is that the Latins shall keep their name and customs and that Rome shall be strong with an Italian breed : Troy and all that it stands for are to be forgotten. This is a surprising conclusion. The cause for which Juno has striven is to triumph once its leaders are dead, and the human material of which Turnus is made is to make the future race of Rome. So Virgil widens his Latin and Trojan scene until it becomes Italian and contains a new mixture and harmony of races. The fine fighting qualities of the Latins are to be kept, and there is a place for a modified and reformed heroism. The principles which Juno and Turnus embody have their great uses and are to help the creation of this new society. From this combination of Latin and Trojan something new, Roman and Italian, will arise, as Jupiter promises :

[1] Bid not the native Latins change their name,
Nor become Trojans and be called from Troy,
Nor change their speech nor take on other dress.
Let Latium be, and Alban kings through years,
Let Latin valour make the Roman strong ;
And fallen Troy be nameless where she fell.

F

hinc genus Ausonio mixtum quod sanguine surget,
supra homines, supra ire deos pietate videbis.[1]

(XII, 838-9)

Juno sacrifices Turnus that she may save the Latins, and the sacrifice is right and appropriate; for Turnus shows the heroic spirit in excess, while the new race will have it in due proportion.

In this compromise Venus too makes a sacrifice : Troy is to be forgotten and its name is to perish with it. In this Virgil takes up an idea which had some currency in the Augustan age. In one of his odes Horace makes Juno deliver a speech against rebuilding Troy on the grounds that it has deserved its end and that Rome has taken its place. This has with some reason been connected with a long speech which Livy gives to Camillus in 390 B.C. when Rome was recovering from the Gaulish invasion and a proposal was made to move the government from Rome to Veii. Livy's Camillus opposes this with much eloquence on the grounds that it is impious. It is quite possible that Livy and Horace, no doubt in reply to imperial instructions, were really concerned with a proposal to transfer the seat of government from Rome and opposed it. Virgil may have had this in mind, but he gives it a wider and different meaning. His Troy is not a seat of government but a disused way of life which is not to be revived. The new Rome is to have no connection with a world which perished largely through its own faults. Rome is to contain all that is best in Latin and in Trojan without their characteristic defects, and in it a new spirit will rise from what have been conflicting ideals. The struggle between Venus and Juno, between Aeneas and Turnus, is to end in a new harmony and strength. By this solution Virgil reconciles the warring issues which he found in his own time. The high spirit of Turnus and of Juno is to be modified and turned to better ends than personal aggrandisement ; the occasional weakness shown by Aeneas and by Venus is to be counteracted by the stout qualities of the Italian stock. For such a result the price to be paid is the old heroic spirit as Turnus shows it, but this is worth paying since it secures the dominion of Rome.

A conclusion of this kind implies something like a philo-

[1] The race that rises from Ausonian blood
Shall pass all men in goodness, and all gods.

74

sophy of history, at least of Roman history, and Virgil's three main excursions into the historical past of Rome show how he related it to the general ideas of his poem. The first is Jupiter's prophecy to Venus in Book I and is concerned with the fortune of Rome. When Venus complains of the way in which her son, Aeneas, is treated, she is told that he is to be the father of Rome and to start a glorious process which will culminate in the universal dominion of Augustus. This process has been determined by Fate, and in revealing it Jupiter reveals " the secrets of the Fates ". Throughout the poem the destiny of Aeneas and of Rome is regarded as predestined in this way ; it may be postponed but it cannot be averted. Even Juno recognises it :

> hinc populum late regem belloque superbum
> venturum excidio Libyae : sic volvere Parcas,[1]
> (I, 21-2)

This idea of a Roman destiny was nothing new. In the second century B.C. the sage historian Polybius wrote " Fortune has caused the whole world and its history to tend towards one purpose — the empire of Rome ",[2] and the same belief may be seen in a quaint little poem by the Greek poetess Melinno of Locri, who says that Fate has given to Rome " the royal glory of unbroken rule ". The idea may have grown up in the Punic Wars, when the triumph of Rome over Carthage seemed to indicate the possession of something else than human qualities. Virgil adopted it and applied it not only to Rome but to Aeneas, who is himself a man of destiny, foretold in prophecies and recognised by signs, as Latinus and his Latins know to their cost :

> fatalem Aeneas manifesto numine ferri
> admonet ira deum tumulique ante ora recentes.[3]
> (XI, 232-3)

Just as Aeneas, despite hindrances and temporary defeats, eventually reaches his goal because he is fated to do so, so too

[1] Whose warlike people, king o'er regions wide,
Would strike at Libya's heart : so rolled the doom.
(C. J. Billson)

[2] I. 4, 5.

[3] God's anger warns him, and those new-made graves,
That Fate's clear purpose leads Aeneas on.
(C. J. Billson)

does Rome, as her whole history bears witness.

The second excursion is the vision of great Romans which the spirit of Anchises shows to Aeneas in Elysium. It falls into five sections, of which Augustus occupies the third and central. Before him come the Alban kings and Romulus, and after him the kings of Rome and the leaders of the republic. Each man has done something to promote the growth and power of Rome, and the fruit of their labours is to be seen in the Roman dominion of the world under Augustus:

> en huius, nate, auspiciis, illa incluta Roma
> imperium terris, animos aequabit Olympo.[1]
>
> (VI, 781-2)

The pageant is remarkable because it includes figures whose memory was not universally honoured in Rome. The memory of her kings was not always sweet to the republic which had ejected them; the Etruscan Tarquin was usually considered a bloodthirsty tyrant; even Pompey and Caesar had darkened Virgil's youth with bloodshed and were largely responsible for the disastrous years of civil war. Yet these too are named, because, like more honoured figures, they have enhanced Rome's power. They stand for that ability to command which is Rome's characteristic quality:

> tu regere imperio populos, Romane, memento.[2]   (VI, 851)

Such a power belongs also to Aeneas, as Evander, the type of ripe wisdom and experience, recognises when he addresses him as one under whose leadership Troy can never be finally conquered:

> maxime Teucrorum ductor, quo sospite numquam
> res equidem Troiae victas aut regna fatebor.[3]
>
> (VIII, 470-1)

The descendants and successors of Aeneas have shown this same unflinching devotion to their cause and the same capacity to rule.

The third excursion is on the Shield of Aeneas, where the

---

[1] Beneath his auspices great Rome shall reach
Earth's bounds with rule, and heaven with her prowess.

[2] Thine, Roman, be the empire of the world.

[3] Great Trojan leader, while thou art alive
Never shall I confess Troy's kingdom lost.

76

scenes depicted show those occasions when the existence of Rome seemed to be imperilled, either physically or morally, and yet somehow it survived. The series begins with Romulus and Remus and suggests on how slender a thread the future of Rome hung when its founders were nursed by a wolf. Then follow six different escapes, from the Romans' own mistake when they made a treaty with the Sabines, from the attempt of Mettus of Alba to destroy Rome by treachery, from the Etruscan dominion of Tarquin, from the Gaulish invaders, from the revolutionary Catiline, and from the oriental dominion of Antony and Cleopatra. The last is presented in the greatest detail and is the culmination of the whole series ; for it is both a moral and a physical escape, an escape from foreign rule and from the corrupting influences of the East. The escapes vary in character, but in all of them Rome, when she seems to be all but lost, is saved either by some person or by what looks like luck and is really divine protection, like the geese on the Capitol who give warning of the Gauls' approach. The parallel of Aeneas is close. He has his narrow escapes from Troy, from the Cyclops, and from the results of his own bad judgment in Carthage and in Sicily. Even in Italy he suffers from acts of treachery such as later imperilled Rome. Virgil's excursions into Roman history show the process that he saw behind it and suggest that this process has been symbolised in the career of Aeneas.

From ethics and history Virgil inevitably moves into theology. Indeed his conception of Rome and of mankind would be incomplete if it were not based on religious beliefs. Like other men of his time, he neither inherited nor adopted a dogmatic theology and was content to make his own choice from current beliefs and to give his own meaning to familiar myths and symbols. Just as his Juno and his Venus stand for powers and tendencies of the spirit and are none the less divine for that reason, so his Jupiter provides a central point in his theological system, and is specially connected with the Fates and the destiny of Rome. Much ado has been made about the ambiguity of Jupiter's relation to the Fates, and Virgil sometimes seems to indicate that they are more powerful than he, but that is his mythological way of presenting drama in Heaven. In the last analysis Jupiter and the Fates are one ; for what Jupiter wills is fate, as he himself says :

> sua cuique exorsa laborem
> fortunamque ferent. rex Iuppiter omnibus idem ;
> fata viam invenient.[1]   (X, 111-13)

The idea was not new. The Fate, which is called Zeus by
Cleanthes, is Divine Providence, the πρόνοια, which directs
events in the world and is now called Jupiter, now Fate, now
the fates, now the will of the gods. This Providence, which
rules the universe, is also its mind and its nature, the universal
law and the creative force of all existence. It is not anthropo-
morphic, not a person in any real sense, but a divine power
which can only be presented to the human understanding in
symbols and analogies. Virgil himself believes in it, and
when he comes to stating the core of his belief he abandons
his mythology and speaks of a universal mind : ·

> principio caelum ac terram camposque liquentis
> lucentemque globum lunae Titaniaque astra
> spiritus intus alit, totamque infusa per artus
> mens agitat molem et magno se corpore miscet.[2]
>
> (VI, 734-7)

When such a power decides that Rome shall rule the world,
it is not a personal whim, like the support which Homer's
gods give to Troy, but something deep in the nature of things,
a natural, inevitable process, whose reasons are not to be
discerned, but which is real and therefore right. Any
attempt to oppose it is not so much wrong as foolish ; for it
cannot be frustrated. The mission which Virgil believed to
be Rome's was a natural development whose causes lay in the
divine nature of the universe.

An idea of this kind may appeal to religious convictions
but need not arouse religious emotions. It was held by Stoic
philosophers who hardly believed in a personal god and found
little satisfaction in attempts to enter into relations with him.
Virgil was not like this. He was religious in an old-fashioned
way that consorts strangely with his philosophical theories.
In no great poem do signs and omens play such a part as in

[1]   Each man's acts shall bring
  Him toil or luck. Jove's rule is one for all ;
  The Fates shall find a way.

[2] First, earth and heaven and the watery plains,
  The moon's bright sphere and the Titanian stars
  An inner breath sustains ; in all the limbs
  Mind moves the mass, mixt with the mighty frame.

the *Aeneid*. At every turn of the action and in every crisis Aeneas is helped by some manifestation of divine help. No epic hero lives more closely to the gods than he, or needs their help more. His feelings towards them have a warm humanity; he treats them as his friends and allies. There is an affectionate devotion in his prayer to Apollo :

> Phoebe, gravis Troiae semper miserate labores.[1] (VI, 56)

Aeneas calls on the god's compassion and regards him as a guardian and a helper. When he comes to Italy and invokes the native divinities, it is in a similar spirit :

> nymphae, Laurentes nymphae, genus amnibus unde est,
> tuque, o Thybri tuo genitor cum flumine sancto,
> accipite Aenean et tandem arcete periclis.[2]
> (VIII, 71-3)

Virgil sees the divine powers of the world as potential protectors with whom a man can form something like a human relationship. This belief gives humanity and reality to his general theory of the universe and shows how dependent man is on the gods in all his actions.

Virgil's religion is of so personal a kind that it can hardly be content with abstractions and theories. Especially his sense of the difference between good and evil was so strong that it forced him to accept old beliefs about the reward of the good and the punishment of the wicked after death. Such beliefs, which had their roots in Greece and were held by Orphics and Pythagoreans, were not universal in Rome. The Stoics with their insistence on self-respect as the foundation of morality did not need any scheme of rewards and punishments in the afterworld. Others, like Cicero, believed in rewards for the good but denied the existence of Hell. Virgil presents an almost Christian scheme of Heaven, Purgatory and Hell. In his Elysium he places all the types that he loved and admired, — men who die for their country, good priests and seers, inventors, and benefactors of mankind,

> quique sui memores alios fecere merendo.[3] (VI, 664)

---

[1] Phoebus, who pitied Troy's sore agony.
[2] Laurentine Nymphs, Nymphs of the river race,
And father Tiber, with thy holy wave,
Receive Aeneas, keep him safe at last.
[3] All who by service are remembered still.

VIRGIL AND THE IDEAL OF ROME

In contrast to them are those who are sent to eternal punishment in Tartarus. Here, in addition to the notorious sinners of legend, are some specifically Roman types, and we may discern half-hidden references to Antony who took bribes to make laws and to Clodius who committed incest with his sister. The fault of these wicked souls is that they despised the gods, and are therefore the opposite of Aeneas, who with all his failings never fails in his devotion to them. Between the exalted spirits of Elysium and the lost souls of Tartarus is the mass of common men who pass through a kind of Purgatory and revisit the earth in new shapes, until in the end they are so purified by the divine fire that they too can take their place with the blessed. The scheme of rewards and punishments after death provides a practical reason for good actions in this world.

It is impossible to say how deeply Virgil believed in the details of this scheme. He seems to suggest that it is a dream, and perhaps he means it to be no more than a myth, a symbolical presentation of the vital truth that the Divine Spirit cares about the actions of men. In any case Virgil must have felt that something like this was true and that it was important for men to believe in it. His whole theory of Rome is built on his conception of its divine mission and assumes the validity of religious belief. In his youth he had admired Lucretius, and he must have seen how the Epicurean poet, who denies that the gods care about men, comes equally to deny the worth of such an effort as Rome's and to advocate a philosophic detachment from political activities. Lucretius indeed regards all public life as a futile expense of effort :

> certare ingenio, contendere nobilitate,
> noctes atque dies niti praestante labore
> ad summas emergere opes rerumque potiri.[1]
>
> (II, 11-13)

It might even be thought that the political confusion which preceded the Augustan age was due to a lack of beliefs, especially of religious belief, and that the most obvious result

[1] In rivalry of intelligence or birth,
And struggle with vast effort night and day
Till they emerge upon the heights of power
And lay hands on the empire of the world.
(R. C. Trevelyan)

of this was a feeling that nothing was really worth the trouble. Virgil denies this doubt and its conclusion. He shows his own conviction not merely by presenting a complete picture of the afterworld but by making Aeneas a different man after he has seen it. The vision of his descendants finally removes all doubts and hesitations and strengthens his will to pursue his predestined task. Virgil evidently felt that a belief in divine justice was a necessary basis to a belief in Rome.

The spiritual uneasiness which Virgil saw and tried to heal in his contemporaries was also his own. He knew, more than anyone, the melancholy and the doubts which prey upon the human soul. There is no gaiety and little joy in the *Aeneid*. Its predominating mood is a kind of resigned sadness, a feeling that life is a heavy burden and that most hopes are doomed to disappointment. When Aeneas sees the spirits hurrying to Lethe before being reincarnated and sent back to earth, he asks :

> quae lucis miseris tam dira cupido ? [1] .(VI, 721)

and the words, with their assumption that the desire to live is an infatuate passion, are characteristic of Virgil's outlook. This melancholy rules many important episodes in the poem. It fills the Sack of Troy ; it invades even the quiet life which Helenus and Andromache have found in Sicily ; it emerges at the end of the vision of Roman history with the death of the young Marcellus ; it enters into the fighting in Italy with the death of Pallas ; it closes the poem with the departure of Turnus' lamenting spirit to the shades. Aeneas finds no spiritual exultation in the cause which he upholds and no pride or pleasure in the adventures through which he passes. The first is for him a long series of efforts and dangers :

> per varios casus, per tot discrimina rerum
> tendimus in Latium,[2]   (I, 204-5)

and the second are so painful even in retrospect that he finds it hard to speak of them to Dido :

> infandum, regina, iubes renovare dolorem.[3] (II, 3)

[1] Why this dread, sad longing for the light ?

[2] Through many dangers, many a change and chance
We move to Latium.

[3] Past words, O queen, the grief you bid me wake.

81

The goal, to which he is called, seems to mock his attempts to reach it, as he says when he compares his own destiny with that of Helenus and Andromache:

> vobis parta quies ; nullum maris aequor arandum,
> arva neque Ausoniae semper cedentia retro
> quaerenda.[1] (III, 495-7)

Aeneas feels that his goal appears only to vanish again, and that those who have no such task as his are much to be envied.

This melancholy rises out of Virgil's doubts and misgivings. Behind his belief in the Roman achievement we can see his uncertainty about its reality and its worth. This slips out almost by chance when he seems to question the value of fame to Aeneas' nurse, Caieta, who is buried in a place that is to bear her name for ever:

> et nunc servat honos sedem tuus, ossaque nomen
> Hesperia in magna, si qua est ea gloria, signat.[2]
> (VII, 3-4)

Virgil, who elsewhere sets some store on glory, seems here to doubt if it exists or is worth winning. So too he questions even the worth of those funeral ceremonies which he describes with so affectionate a care. The flowers which Anchises imagines himself to throw on the dead Marcellus are but an "empty rite", and Aeneas wonders if the dead Lausus will find any consolation by joining the spirits of his fathers:

> teque parentum
> manibus et cineri, si qua est ea cura, remitto.[3]
> (x, 827-8)

The immemorial consolation which mankind has found in a reverent treatment of the dead seems here to mean little to Virgil. He is so uncertain of its worth that he intrudes his doubts into the very moment when he might well feel the force of the argument that some kind of survival after death is owed at least to our affections. Even after the vision of

[1] Your rest is won ; no seas have you to plough,
Nor yours to seek Ausonian fields that move
For ever backward.

[2] Thy honour keeps the place ; Hesperia marks
Thy bones, if in that any glory be.

[3] I give thee to thy sires'
Ashes and ghosts, if that be aught to thee.

Elysium which answers so many doubts and means so much to Aeneas, Virgil mysteriously brings his hero from the Underworld by the ivory gate through which false dreams come to men. Some think that this is simply an indication of time ; for after midnight the gate of true dreams is closed. Yet the ordinary reader surely feels a suggestion that what Aeneas has seen is something like a dream, even if not a false dream. Despite his asseverations of religious belief and his trust in the Roman mission, Virgil seems to be not quite free from doubts and uncertainties and to wonder whether the pageant of Roman history has not some of the unsubstantiality of dream.

This haunting uncertainty gives its special character to Virgil's view of human life and even adds nobility to his special conception of what a man ought to be. What matters is that he should do the right things despite his misgivings and doubts. He must trust that all is for the best and that the end will be good. So when Aeneas believes that he has lost most of his ships and is deeply stricken in spirit, he controls his fears and comforts his companions with the words

> o passi graviora, dabit deus his quoque finem.[1] (I, 199)

The reward of such faith and labour is hardly in any personal advantage. Aeneas performs his duty because the gods have laid it upon him ; the glory which will reward him will belong more to Rome than to himself. In depicting him and others like him Virgil gives a new turn to an old heroic idea. Homer believed that a man owed great actions to an ideal of manhood and that in his short span of life he must do all that he can to show that he is really a man. This is the philosophy which he gives to Sarpedon :

> νῦν δ' ἔμπης γὰρ κῆρες ἐφεστᾶσιν θανάτοιο
> μυρίαι, ἃς οὐκ ἔστι φυγεῖν βροτὸν οὐδ' ὑπαλύξαι,
> ἴομεν, ἠέ τῳ εὖχος ὀρέξομεν, ἠέ τις ἡμῖν.[2]
>
> (Il. XII, 326-8)

These words, which are the truest expression of the old heroic outlook, are accepted by Virgil in his own way. When Pallas

---

[1] You have known worse ; this also God will end.

[2] Since, despite what we do, death's dooms now gather above us,
Countless, and no man alive may fly from them nor escape them,
On to the fight, and gain our desire, or yield it to others.

is doomed to die and calls on the divine Hercules to help him, Jupiter forbids any help and gives the reason :

> stat sua cuique dies, breve et inreparabile tempus
> omnibus est vitae ; sed famam extendere factis
> hoc virtutis opus.[1] (x, 467-9)

Man has his allotted span of life, but that is all the more reason why he should display his *virtus* while he lives. The words come from so august an authority that we may see Virgil's own thought in them. The claim of his heroes is that in their short lives they do all that they can to win the right kind of glory by actions which are in themselves painful and difficult and to strive for an end which they themselves do not fully understand.

In the *Aeneid* Virgil presented a new ideal of heroism and showed in what fields it could be exercised. The essence of his conception is that a man's *virtus* is shown less in battle and physical danger than in the defeat of his own weaknesses. The chief obstacles which Aeneas finds are in himself, and his greatest victories are when he triumphs over them. Even in battle his highest moments are when he sees past the fury of the fight to some higher end of unity and harmony. Conversely, Dido and Turnus fail because, despite their innate nobility and strength of will, they give in to their passions and desires. Virgil's idea of heroism is quite different from Homer's because it depends much less on physical gifts than on moral strength and is displayed not merely in battle but in many departments of life. Moreover, Homer's heroes never question the worth of the glory which they seek, but Aeneas, hampered by doubts and misgivings, is unsure not only about his glory but about his whole destiny. This uncertainty is one of his greatest trials, and he shows his worth by pursuing his task despite all his doubts about it. His success is all the greater because it is won largely in spite of his own human feelings. In him Virgil displays what man really is, a creature uncertain of his place in the universe and of the goal to which he moves. To the distrustful and uncertain Augustan age this conception came with the urgency of truth, and Virgil's immediate and lasting success was due

---

[1] To each his day. Irreparable and brief
Is all men's life ; but to spread fame in deeds,
Is manhood's task.

84

to his having found an answer to the spiritual needs of his time. In the vision of Rome he presented an ideal strong enough to win the devotion of his contemporaries, and in his belief in sacrifice and suffering he prepared the way across the centuries to those like Marcus Aurelius and St. Augustine who asked that men should live and die for an ideal city greater and more truly universal than Rome. Once Virgil had opened up a new vision of human worth and recast the heroic ideal in a new mould, he set an example which later poets could not but follow. They might not accept his interpretation of human destiny in all its details, but they felt that he had marked out the main lines for epic poetry and that any new heroic ideal must take account of what he said.

III

CAMÕES AND THE EPIC
OF PORTUGAL

The first epic poem which in its grandeur and its universality speaks for the modern world was written by a Portuguese. And this is right. For the achievement of Portugal in the years between the first expeditions of Prince Henry the Navigator in the fifteenth century and its incorporation in the dominions of Philip II in 1580 is one of the wonders of history, and marks with dramatic significance the transition from the Middle Ages to modern times and from a limited Mediterranean outlook to a vision which embraced half the globe. A small country, poor in population and in natural resources, ruled the seas and commanded an empire round the Cape of Good Hope to the East Indies and the China Sea. What Genoa and Venice had done in the Mediterranean, what Holland and England were later to do in the Indian Ocean, the Portuguese did in all the seas of the Eastern Hemisphere for a crowded century, although the voyage from Lisbon to Calicut lasted a year and was accompanied by all the perils of uncharted waters, shipwreck, scurvy, hostile natives and absence of communications. Of this far-flung dominion remains still survive in forts and churches built on African and Indian coasts, Abyssinian highlands and fever-stricken beaches of southern China, in bronze figures of Portuguese musketeers from Benin and Burma, in words which have passed into Cingalese and pidgin-English, in stories of ancient fights which still echo in Malayan songs, in huge areas still under the Portuguese flag, in the memories of imperial splendour which still hover uneasily in the minds of the Portuguese and stir them at intervals to assert their old pride or to blame themselves for being inferior to their great ancestors. An achievement of this kind, equal in scale and enterprise to the Spanish conquest of the New World and even more costly in life and more dramatic in the brevity of its heyday, deserved the prize of epic song. By a happy chance it found a poet who was not only pre-eminently gifted to sing of it, but was himself singularly a man of his times, a soldier in foreign lands, a scholar of wide and humane learning, a man of charming sensibility and noble heart, a true son of the Renaissance as it developed by the Tagus and of that Portugal which looks out onto the Atlantic and has found in it " the cradle and the grave of its glories ".

Luis de Camões (c. 1524–1580) was disciplined by a life which had more than a just share of the disappointments and defeats upon which genius is supposed to thrive. In his youth, when he studied at the University of Coimbra, then in the height of its glory, he laid up that classical learning which moulded his art and filled his mind with the seductive visions of Pagan antiquity. As a young man he fought in Morocco and paid with the loss of an eye for a knowledge of the Moorish character and methods of war. Imprisoned in Lisbon for taking part in a street fight, he was released on condition that he served the King in India and he, who was already turning from pastoral poetry to the poetry of heroic achievement, was flung into a reckless, dangerous, humiliating life of adventure. In 1553 he sailed from Lisbon and was away for seventeen years. On his travels he learned the lure of the sea, which plays so magically through his poetry. At Goa he found so bitter a disillusionment that he called it " the step-mother of all honest men ", but there he studied the lives of men Christian and Hindu, marked the habits of the Indians, and mastered what he could of their geography, history and religion. He took part in military expeditions up the Malabar Coast and to the Red Sea. In 1556 he sailed east by way of Malacca and the Molucca Islands to Macao, where a grotto still keeps his memory and his name. Two years later he began his long, painful, interrupted voyage home. He was shipwrecked off the mouth of the Mekong River in Siam, and lost all his possessions except the manuscript of his poem to which he clung while he swam to land. At Goa he was again imprisoned, nor, when he was at last released, were his troubles at an end. He was delayed at Mozambique by illness and poverty, and he did not reach his beloved Lisbon till 1570. For years he had been at work on his great epic, Os Lusiadas, and in 1572 it was published. Legends have clustered round Camões' last years, and though it is now doubted whether he died in beggary, he had few comforts or consolations. In 1578 he heard of the appalling disaster of Alcazar Kebir, where King Sebastião and the flower of the Portuguese nobility, blessed by the Pope and fortified with a sacred banner, an arrow of St. Sebastian, and the sword of old Affonso Henriquez, the first king of Portugal, were slaughtered by the Moors in Moroccan sands. In 1580 Camões died. The date has a tragic significance ; for it was the year in which Portugal lost its independence to Spain. Before Philip II came in state to Lisbon to assume his inheritance, Camões had written to the Captain-General of Lamego : " All will see that so dear to me was my country that I was content to die not only in it but with it ". His actual death may have been caused by the plague, but his work was done, and he had no wish to live any longer.

Scholar and soldier, humanist and man of the world, Camões was uniquely fitted to write the epic of Portugal. His knowledge was gained both from books and from life. His aim was to write for his own country a poem which should rival the *Aeneid* in artistic perfection and in national aim. He understood what he was doing ; for he was an accomplished Latinist, who knew the Latin poets with a lover's intimate knowledge, and hardly a page of *Os Lusiadas* fails to awake some echo of them. He seems not to have known Greek, but he probably read Homer in Lorenzo Valla's Latin version, and to a man of his imaginative sensibility the vision of Hellenic splendour was bright enough in its Roman reflections. He was equally well acquainted with Spanish and with Italian and had learned the new style of writing which had come from Italy to Portugal. His decision to write an epic was in accord with his times ; for even in Portugal, which had lacked epics in the Middle Ages, the cultivated Antonio Ferreira was urging poets to celebrate their country's history in epic song. Camões' poem was the product of its age equally in its classical reminiscences and in its national subject. His companion for some twenty years, it was intended to rival the epics of antiquity in art and to surpass them in truth and nobility. Camões begins with a conscious challenge to Virgil, with his own version of *arma virumque cano* :

As armas e os Barões assinalados.[1]   (I, I, I)

----

[1] Arms and the men above the vulgar file.
(Fanshawe)

His theme, he claims, will put Odysseus out of court; his Vasco da Gama will equal Aeneas in renown. He addresses the King of Portugal as Virgil addresses Augustus, and he is confident that his poem will become famous through the world.

Camões' attempt to rival Virgil in epic poetry provides an instructive comment on the literary theories of the time, and especially on Vida's *Ars Poetica* published at Cremona in 1527. Vida lays down rules for a poet's education, and chance willed that Camões should follow them. In his excellent classical education, in his youthful acquaintance with country life in the valleys of the Mondego and the Tagus, in his experience of love and his experience of war, in his distant travels and in the knowledge of the world which he gained from them, he learned in abundant measure the lessons which Vida demanded. Since it is likely that he knew Vida's work and accepted its main postulates, we need not be surprised that he followed up his natural advantages with a close study of Virgil's text and was proud to make his poem Virgilian in more senses than one. Only by such means, he seems to have felt, could he rise to the height of his great theme. Such a belief was of course dangerous. The poet might follow his model too closely and do imperfectly what had already been done perfectly. But Camões did not fail. He gives new meanings to ancient themes, adapts old devices in a fresh and brilliant way, and applies the ideal of Rome with creative originality to his own day. He sets a distance between himself and Virgil both in his metre, which is the *ottava rima* of Ariosto, and in his language, which, despite its classical air, is singularly lucid, direct, natural and swift. When we first read him, we hardly think of Virgil; so well has Camões absorbed the principles of epic construction and used them in his own way. Later we see how great his debt is, but such is his mastery of his material that his personal impress is on almost everything. Indeed at times he uses his model so freely that he seems to criticise it and to think that he can better it. The result is that we compare *Os Lusiadas* with the *Aeneid* not as an imitation with an original, but as one poem with another of the same kind.

The title *Os Lusiadas*, or *The Sons of Lusus*, challenges comparison with *Iliad* and *Aeneid*. It is a conscious classicism. The sons of Lusus are the Portuguese, who were believed to be descended from Lusus, the eponymous hero of Lusitania. The word, which Camões learned from Portuguese poets who wrote in Latin earlier in the sixteenth century, conveys an air of distinction, of association with the ancient world, and shows Camões' wish to set his poem in the Roman tradition. It also shows something else. The poem is not, like the *Aeneid*, called after a man but after a people. Though the *Aeneid* is the poem of Rome, it is so indirectly ; *Os Lusiadas* is much more directly the poem of Portugal and of what Camões calls " the illustrious Lusitanian soul ". What Virgil does implicitly and symbolically, Camões does almost by straightforward narrative. He saw that Virgilian epic could deal with much more than the fortunes of a single man, and he boldly went beyond his master's plan. His poem is a history of his country from its beginnings to his own time. But neither his Virgilian model nor his own artistic instinct allowed him to present this merely as annals ; he was no Ennius or Layamon. *Os Lusiadas* is constructed with practised skill and has a fine bold design. The central, uniting theme is Vasco da Gama's discovery of the sea-route to India in 1498. His voyage and arrival provide the main structure of the poem and occupy about three-quarters of its ten Cantos. Around it Camões has woven the rest of Portuguese history. In Cantos III–IV Gama's narrative covers the salient episodes from the earliest times to his own voyage, and in Canto X Venus prophesies the exploits of the Portuguese in India from Gama's return to the vice-royalty of João de Castro in 1545 ; in Canto VI an incidental story gives a vivid picture of mediaeval chivalry in Portugal, and in Canto VIII great Portuguese leaders receive special attention on the banners of Gama's flag-ship. Just as Virgil conveys the wider prospects of Roman history in prophecy, vision and works of art, so Camões, on a much more generous scale, builds the history of Portugal round his central theme. He lays equal emphasis on his chief hero, Vasco da Gama, and on the people of which Gama is so typical a representative. His voyage is a turning-point in the long heroic story. In it the Portuguese find an outlet for the qualities which they have already shown to be theirs, and their success in it proves that once their power has entered these new fields, nothing should be able to withstand it.

If we compare the construction of *Os Lusiadas* with that of the *Aeneid*, we can see what special advantages Camões gained. First, since the actual story of Portugal receives far more attention than Virgil gave to that of Rome, the poem is more obviously a national epic and has a greater variety since it covers different centuries and spreads to different continents. The episodes may come in a simple, historical order, but this shows much judicious choice and art. They are not only dramatic and exciting, but they illustrate what is most significant in the character and destiny of the Portuguese. In the south-western corner of Europe the Portuguese nation, which Affonso Henriquez founded, had to secure its independence against two main enemies, the Moors and the Spaniards. That is why the three battles which Camões presents at some length are Ourique, where in 1139 the nation was born in battle against the Moors, Salado, where in 1340 Affonso IV helped the King of Castile to rout the Moors, and Aljubarrota, where in 1385 João I defeated a Spanish attempt to conquer Portugal. So too when the future of Portuguese India is prophesied, Camões shows a judgment equally selective and sound. The generals and viceroys to whom he gives most attention are those who most deserve it ; — Duarte Pacheco, who really laid the foundations of the Indian Empire ; Francisco and Lourenço de Almeida, who by the capture of Quiloa and Mombasa secured the communications with the East ; Affonso de Albuquerque, who through the establishment of outposts at Aden, Ormuz and the Malacca Strait tried to make the Indian Ocean a Portuguese Sea, and João de Castro, who organised and consolidated the Malabar Coast from Goa to Ceylon. These great men receive more attention than the other rulers of India, and posterity has endorsed Camões' estimate of their worth. He chooses his subjects with insight, and each choice contributes to his interpretation of Portuguese history.

The great men whom Camões celebrates are typical of their country in their characters and their fortunes. Foremost are the great kings whom he names in his Introduction and whose achievements he tells later. These figures of noble royalty, who challenge comparison with Charlemagne, take first place in the creation, defence and expansion of Portugal. The first is the crusader Affonso Henriquez, who founded the Portuguese kingdom by freeing the country round Lisbon from the Moors. In him Camões indicates the divine protection which watched over the birth of Portugal. For in the battle of Ourique, where Affonso defeats the Moors, he is sustained by a vision of the Cross before the battle, and after it shows his gratitude by composing the royal arms from the five shields of the kings who have been killed and the thirty pieces of silver for which Judas betrayed Christ and which are now in part redeemed. The life of this king is of long struggles against enemies within and without his territories. He is the typical crusader, the champion of Christendom and the scourge of the heathen, and his career shows under what favourable auspices the young country fought its way into existence. Of his successors the two most remarkable are Affonso IV and João I. Affonso IV is the protector of Portugal against Moorish invasion and the gallant ally of Spain against the vast African army which invades Europe and is defeated at Salado. His courage has its hard and even its brutal side, and his reign is marred by the cruelty with which he permits the hideous murder of his son's mistress, Inez de Castro. He is the typical mediaeval king, compounded of different elements, formidable and worthy of his title " o bravo ". João I, the founder of the House of Aviz, starts a new age. After becoming king of a disintegrated country and having to restore order at home, he defeats Spain and carries his victorious armies to Africa, where he begins the expansion of Portugal overseas by the capture of Ceuta. The last king whom Camões presents is João II, who conceives the project of reaching India by the Cape of Good Hope and sends Gama out on his quest. Through these great figures Camões marks the progress of Portugal from a small state on the Tagus to a great empire stretching across half the world.

Below the kings, but hardly less important, are the great counsellors and generals, Egas Moniz, Nuno Alvarez and Fuas Roupinho. The first, the faithful servant of Affonso Henriquez, is a true son of the crusading age, who is ready to offer his own life as a surety for his master and shows the great national quality of loyalty :

Ó grão fidelidade Portuguesa ![1]   (III, 41, 1)

[1] O noble Portuguese fidelity !

The second is the constable of João I and the hero of Aljubar-rota, who in an eloquent appeal summons the wavering lords to war and tells them that if their courage were equal to their king's, they could overthrow the world. Like the young Scipio at Canusium, he puts life into the despairing army and himself takes a prominent part in the subsequent victory. He is the perfect servant of a great king, a man who trusts in his divine guidance and the justice of his cause :

De Deus guiada só e de santa estrêla.[1]   (VIII, 29, 2)

The third is the brave captain who defeats the Moors on land and on sea and later dies fighting against them in a foreign land, a patriot ready to make any sacrifice :

Olha como, em tam justa e santa guerra,
De acabar pelejando está contente.[2]
(VIII, 17, 6-7)

Each of these men presents a different aspect of chivalry and comes from a different age, but all of them act not for their own glory but for their royal masters and their country. In them Camões depicts the Portuguese character in action and shows what qualities have made and kept Portugal.

Camões did not, however, believe that the Portuguese character was compounded only of virtues. History showed that there were national faults, and Camões stresses two, a voluptuousness which breeds irresponsibility and creates disorder, and a sense of justice which verges on cruelty. He may well have been right about both. The first was all too natural in a Latin and Southern people ; the second left ugly scars and memories in the history of India. Camões' account of King Fernando shows that while he understood love, he could judge it fairly. By his attachment to a Spanish woman this king imperilled his kingdom, and only a popular rising saved it from disaster. Camões finds it hard to condemn the king outright, but he sees how dangerous a passion love can be to those in high places, and his judgment is just :

Que um fraco Rei faz fraca a forte gente.[3]   (III, 138, 8)

[1] Guided by God and his good star alone.
(Fanshawe)
[2] See how content in just and holy war
He is to meet his death in battle's din.
[3] For a weak king makes a strong people weak.

93

At the other extreme are those whose sense of duty makes them too hard, and the chief example is the formidable Affonso de Albuquerque, the greatest of the Portuguese Viceroys in India. Camões admires his extraordinary achievements, but turns aside from them to deplore his cruelty in sentencing to death a soldier who had been with a woman intended for the Queen's court. The facts are not fully established, and the historian Ossorio thought that Albuquerque was justified. Camões' tender heart felt otherwise :

> Parece de selváticas brutezas,
> De peitos inumanos e insolentes,
> Dar extrêmo suplício pela culpa
> Que a fraca humanidade e Amor desculpa.[1]
>
> (x, 46, 5-8)

Many would endorse Camões' judgments both on King Fernando and on Albuquerque. The episodes on which he dwells illustrate qualities not merely of these two men but of the nation which produced them. His fairness and candour are characteristic of him. He has a high ideal for his countrymen and is not content to pass over their faults in silence.

A second advantage which Camões found in his subject and in his historical method was that he was not concerned with an imaginary past but with recorded history or with a present of which he was himself in part a witness. Instead of having to describe battles in a lost heroic age and to resort to imaginary archaeology, he can fill his story with convincing and realistic details which are based on fact. Himself a soldier, he saw the past through his own experience. Homer has a like air of actuality, but Homer's scene is narrower than that of Camões. Camões draws on the admirable Portuguese historians, Ruy de Pina, Barros and Castanheda, as Shakespeare drew on Holinshed, and though he keeps to the facts, he sees them with his own imaginative and discerning eyes. There is no sham romance and no anachronism about his mediaeval battles. He knew what war was and that its essentials had hardly changed from the bloody slaughter of Ourique :

[1] It seems to me of savage breasts the style,
Of an inhuman and insulting gall,
To make a man for such a fault to die
As love and human frailty qualify.

(Fanshawe)

94

> Cabeças pelo campo vão saltando,
> Braços, pernas, sem dono e sem sentido,
> E doutros as entranhas palpitando,
> Pálida a côr, o gesto amortecido,[1]
>
> (III, 52, 1-4)

to the blare of the trumpets at Salado :

> A canora trombeta embandeirada
> Os corações, à paz acostumados,
> Vai às fulgentes armas incitando,
> Pelas concavidades retumbando,[2]
>
> (III, 107, 5-8)

and the stricken field of Aljubarrota :

> Aqui a fera batalha se encruece
> Com mortes, gritos, sangue e cutiladas.[3]
>
> (IV, 42, 1-2)

When he came to his own times, he used his personal observation with splendid effect. He had seen strange weapons and methods of war in the East and must have helped to operate the prized military inventions of the age. In short and vivid phrases he calls up the attempt of the Samudri of Calicut to destroy Pacheco's fleet with Greek fire, the bulwarks and palisades of Malacca, the catapults and mines used in the defence of Diu, the arrows which the wind turned back upon the Persian archers at Ormuz, the poisoned darts of the Javanese, the elephants of Hydal-Khan, the flag of Portugal raised high over captured Columbo. This is war as it was fought in the sixteenth century.

This actuality pervades the poem. Since the Portuguese empire lay on and across the seas, it is right that its poet should know them well and be able to write finely about them. From the first words about Gama's fleet at sea :

[1] Heads from the shoulders leap about the field ;
Arms, legs, without or sense or master, fly.
Others, their panting entrails trailing, wheel'd,
Earth in their bloodless cheek, death in their eye.
(Fanshawe)

[2] The banneretted trumpet cries aloud
And wakens hearts that have grown used to peace ;
Makes men take up again resplendent arms,
And rounded hills re-echo fresh alarms.

[3] With deaths, with groans, with blood, with gashes dire,
The battle cruel above measure grows.
(Fanshawe)

> Já no largo Oceano navegavam,
> As inquietas ondas apartando ;
> Os ventos brandamente respiravam,
> Das naus as velas côncavas inchando,[1]
>
> (I, 19, 1-4)

it is clear that the poet is a sailor. This knowledge of the sea
appears at every stage of Gama's voyage, in strange pheno-
mena like the Southern Cross, the Fire of St. Elmo, and the
water-spout, in all the horrors and dangers of voyages in
unknown waters :

> Súbitas trovoadas temerosas,
> Relâmpados que o ar em fogo acendem,
> Negros chuveiros, noites tenebrosas,
> Bramidos de trovões, que o mundo fendem.[2]
>
> (v, 16, 3-6)

It is a sailor who admires the use of the astrolabe, who
describes how the ships' bottoms are scoured of the limpets
and weeds which have collected on them or how the scurvy
makes the sailors' flesh swell and putrefy in the mouth, who
tells how a storm falls suddenly on the fleet and breaks the
main-mast of a ship, while the half-dazed crew lower the
top-sails or climb into the rigging. When Virgil describes
a storm and the emotions which it awakes in Aeneas, he
discovers many incidental beauties, but his words are those of
a landsman who has a deathly horror of shipwreck. Camões
writes as a man of action who knows the dangers all too well
but also knows how they are to be encountered.

The newly discovered lands were as full of marvels as the
new seas. The geographical decoration which Vida recom-
mended from maps and globes if not from travel was for
Camões largely a record of what he himself had seen and
noted with eager, curious eyes. The visual variety of his
poem is much enhanced by his skilful choice of vivid details.

---

[1] They now went sailing in the ocean vast,
Parting the snarling waves with crooked bills ;
The whisp'ring Zephyr breath'd a gentle blast,
Which stealingly the spreading canvas fills.
(Fanshawe)

[2] Sudden and fearful storms the air that sweep ;
Lightnings that with the air the fire do blend ;
Black hurricanes, thick nights, thunders that keep
The world alarm'd, and threaten the last end.
(Fanshawe)

Sometimes they come from common life, like the sails made of palm-leaves at Mozambique, or the striped cotton clothing of the men who work them. At other times they take on a romantic majesty, as when the people of Melinde wear purple caftans and silken clothes, and their king, on whom Camões spends three stanzas, has a golden collar, velvet sandals covered with gold and pearls, and a richly wrought dagger, while a servant holds an umbrella over him as he rides in his royal barge to the music of twisted trumpets. In contrast to him are the simple ways of ordinary natives, the Kaffirs delighted by the crystal beads, scarlet caps and little bells with which the Portuguese try to do barter, the women riding lazily on oxen, the presents which they bring of sheep and poultry, their songs and dances which awake echoes of Virgilian shepherds in the poet. In India above all there was much to capture Camões' fancy. He gives a vivid picture of the Samudri's palace with its spreading pavilions and pleasant groves, of the Samudri himself who sits in state while an old man, kneeling on the ground, gives him a betel-nut to chew, of the monstrous Hindu deities with their violent colours and many limbs. When he turns to the farthest East, he is hardly less circumstantial and notes much of interest that he has heard or seen, the cannibal Gueons who tattoo their flesh, the Indo-Chinese who believe that after death their souls pass into animals, the strange people of Pegu said to be born from a woman's union with a dog. He conjures up the scenes of this remote geography, the nutmeg-pigeons of the Banda Archipelago, the sandal-trees of Timor, the submarine plants of the Maldive Islands, the volcanoes of Tidor and Ternate, and the Great Wall of China. Without seeming to stray from his main theme Camões touches on almost the whole East as his age had discovered it.

Into this vast setting with all its variety and colour Camões introduces real men. His hero, Vasco da Gama, is to be a rival to Virgil's Aeneas :

> Dou-vos também aquele ilustre Gama,
> Que para si de Eneas toma a fama.[1]
> (I, 12, 7-8)

---

[1] Th' illustrious Gama in the rear I name,
Who robs the wandering Trojan of his fame.
(Fanshawe)

97

The claim is well founded. If Aeneas' voyage led to the foundation of Rome, Gama's voyage not only began the Portuguese Empire in the East but altered the history of the world by revealing to a self-contained Europe vast prospects of enterprise in Africa and Asia. Gama's discovery was almost as important as that of Columbus, and his actual voyage was a finer feat of scientific navigation. If Aeneas founded the universal empire of Rome, a similar claim might be made for Gama and Portugal, as Venus says when she reveals the earth to him :

> Eis aqui as novas partes do Oriente
> Que vós outros agora ao mundo dais.[1]
>
> (x, 138, 1-2)

The performance and its results were on a truly Roman scale. Camões chose his subject well, but his choice of a hero created difficulties. Virgil could fashion his Aeneas as he pleased and make him a symbol of the Roman character, but Gama could hardly fulfil the same function in the same way for Portugal. His record was known to everyone. He was no knight-errant ; he was not even so great a soldier as Pacheco or Albuquerque. A man of extraordinary ability, of great determination and foresight, he lacked the more glamorous qualities of heroism. Even the success of his voyage somehow detracts from its romance. Its conclusion, exciting enough at the time, has not in retrospect the wild improbability of what befell Cortés and the Pizarros. Even the India which he discovered was not so strange or so unknown as the realms of Montezuma and the Incas. To make a hero of so real a man as Gama called for considerable dexterity.

The most striking quality of Camões' presentation of Gama is its truth to history. If we leave out the mythological elements, which serve a separate purpose, the voyage follows the route to India which Gama discovered and which Camões knew from his own experience. In the story he selects salient events, as he is bound to do, but he does not add or invent, and even his selection bears some relation to

---

[1] Thus hast thou all the regions of the East,
Which by thee giv'n unto the world is now.
(Fanshawe)

the account given by one of Gama's own crew in his log-book. The main episodes are few, — the fight at Mozambique, the lucky escape from Mombasa, the welcome at Melinde, the storm in the Indian Ocean, the arrival at Calicut, the inconclusive negotiations with the Indian ruler and the departure. Almost any of these might have been disguised and dramatised into something more heroic or romantic, but Camões is content to tell of each very much as it happened. He does not even exaggerate Gama's rôle. The result is different from anything done before in epic. At first sight readers used to Ariosto or even to Homer and Virgil may find *Os Lusiadas* a little flat. The adventures of the Portuguese are so lifelike that we may miss something in them, until we see that this was Camões' intention and that he aims at securing an effect of truth and reality. He believed that his truth was as interesting as fiction and his poem was written on that principle. In his quiet way he has created a noble and serious poetry. His Gama is not a great warrior like Achilles or even like Aeneas. His qualities are more subtle and more practical. His genius is for success, and despite reverses and accidents, despite his own mistakes and miscalculations, he succeeds and reaches India. The qualities demanded of him and displayed so conspicuously by him are not those of the great Portuguese kings and viceroys. Gama is great because he carries out successfully a difficult task as he has been ordered. He is a new kind of hero, with something of the astuteness of Odysseus and the perseverance of Aeneas, but these are not his chief claims. What counts most is that he is a great servant of Portugal and displays its characteristics in a highly effective way. Camões knew that there were other noble types, and in their own place he praised them. Gama is one type among others. He is not like Aeneas the representative of a nation's soul, but a real man who is interesting and admirable for his own sake and for the sake of the country which bred him.

Gama's greatest quality is his unshakable endurance in his long and difficult task. The first mention of him sets the note :

Vasco da Gama, o forte Capitão.[1]   (I, 44, 1)

----

[1] Vasco de Gama, a most valiant guide.
(Fanshawe)

The bravery thus announced is not of the old heroic kind, but an unbroken determination which carries Gama through the dangers and uncertainties of his voyage. At the end of Canto VI, when the fleet has at last reached India, Camões draws his moral. He contrasts the luxurious life at home, full of choice pleasures and happy security, with the continual effort demanded by such a voyage. Those who undertake a task of this kind must always be on their guard :

> Vigiando e vestindo o forjado aço,
> Sofrendo tempestades e ondas cruas.[1]
>
> (VI, 97, 3-4)

They must by sheer force of character keep collected and even gay when cannon-balls tear off their comrades' limbs ; they must live on rotten food in freezing climates ; they must scorn display and wealth and honours in the conviction that these are only worth winning if they are won by hard effort. This is the spirit which takes Gama to India, and Camões shows it at work. His Gama knows next to nothing of the route to India and has to find it as he goes. He suffers a grave check when the pilot whom he takes on at Mozambique proves to be a traitor ; when storm attacks the fleet and the sailors cry out in fear of death, he may well feel that his whole enterprise has failed ; even when he reaches his goal, he meets with serious hindrances and reverses. But he holds to his task and never admits the possibility of defeat. At the close of Canto I Camões dwells on the extreme uncertainties which encompass such an undertaking :

> No mar tanta tormenta e tanto dano,
> Tantas vezes a morte apercebida ;
> Na terra tanta guerra, tanto engano,
> Tanta necessidade aborrecida ![2]
>
> (I, 106, 1-4)

Gama endures all these things and goes on to his goal undismayed and undeterred.

---

[1] By clothing steel, encount'ring hunger, drouth,
Watchings, high winds, and billows overgrown.
(Fanshawe)

[2] By sea how many storms, how many harms,
Death in how many sev'ral fashions drest !
By land how many frauds, how many alarms,
Under how many wants sunk and opprest !
(Fanshawe)

When his more ruthless qualities are not called into action, the great captain maintains the high style and noble manners which befit a king's ambassador. In dealing with natives his first step is to invite them to enjoy his hospitality, and he spreads his wines before the men of Mozambique and Mombasa. In the true tradition of chivalry he makes such gifts as he can. At Mozambique he shows with pride his armoury; when the King of Melinde comes to greet him, Gama dresses himself in crimson Venetian satin with gold buttons, an Italian sword and a plumed cap. His conversation has the dignity and restraint proper to his station. There is a splendid moderation in his answer to the enquiries of the excited Moors at Mozambique:

> Os Portugueses somos do Ocidente,
> Imos buscando as terras do Oriente.[1]
>
> (I, 50, 7-8)

Never was great errand expressed in so simple words. But when Gama feels called to say more, he does so in grand style, as when he explains to the Mozambiquers that he and his company are Christians and need no sacred books, since all that matters is written in their souls, or when he thanks the King of Melinde for his generous hospitality. He has the pride which does not seek to boast or to show its power unnecessarily. That is why he refuses to fire his guns at Mozambique: he knows

> Que é fraqueza entre ovelhas ser leão.[2] (I, 68, 8)

His long defence of his actions to the Samudri of Calicut is a masterpiece of dignified remonstrance. Adroit flattery, virtuous indignation, and persuasive argument are well mingled in it. What he says is quite true, but it is so put that even the Samudri's suspicions are lulled. In all his behaviour Gama is a great nobleman and a worthy ambassador of the Portuguese king in foreign lands.

Camões' choice of subject and of hero brought him many advantages and gave a modern and realistic character to his

---

[1] We are the Portugueses from the West,
We go to seek the countries of the East.
(Fanshawe)

[2] To be a lion among sheep, 'tis poor.
(Fanshawe)

poem. His subject was undeniably up to date, and if he succeeded in making a great poem of it, he might well claim to be a Portuguese Virgil. But the theories and taste of his time demanded more than this. It was not enough to rival Virgil in a new kind of heroic narrative; he must keep many of Virgil's characteristics and decorative effects and especially he must satisfy a scholarly taste for learned allusions. Just as Virgil adapts themes and phrases from Homer, so Camões decked his poem with echoes and hints of classical myth. No doubt he did so with eager enthusiasm; for the world of classical fancy and history was among his first and most enduring loves. Modern taste, however, may find it hard to appreciate his less concealed classicisms, his deliberate imitations of Roman poetry, and his mythological references. His head and heart were so full of ancient verse that at times he seems too eager to reproduce it and looks almost a translator. But this is to misunderstand him. His classical references and reminiscences are more than what his public expected of him, more even than his own indulgence in a devoted loyalty; they are his tribute to Latin civilisation, his confession of faith in what he believed to be most important in the European inheritance, his acknowledgment of a debt to the past and to the language which his own Portuguese so resembled that he made Venus claim that there was hardly any difference between them:

> E na língua, na qual quando imagina,
> Com pouca corrupção crê que é a Latina.[1]
>
> (I, 33, 7-8)

The revival of learning in the fifteenth and sixteenth centuries was much more than an academic or even a literary matter. It gave the world something that it lacked, a strong sense of secular life. To all matters not theological the precedents of Greece and Rome gave a new zest and confidence. The ancient achievements in government, in science and in the arts inspired the men of the Renaissance with a new outlook and new impulses. They felt more at home in the world now that they knew something of their own historical origins. So

---

[1] And in the charming music of their tongue
Which she thinks Latin with small dross among.

(Fanshawe)

Camões stresses the connection of modern times with ancient, the unbroken continuity of the tradition, and the many similarities between Portugal and ancient Rome. In the great plan of his poem the classical tradition has a special place; for the new contact of West and East brought to the fore the special qualities which Europe owed to antiquity. The Roman heritage, quite as much as any differences of religion, differentiates Europe from Asia and Africa. The East, despite its wealth and its immemorial past, is in the last resort uncivilised because it lacks this humanising force. Camões was deeply conscious of this, and it explains the emphasis which he gives to the ancient world.

We may, however, understand and approve of Camões' classicism in principle and yet feel that he indulges it too freely. Its precedents seem to haunt him as Homer's haunted Virgil and to create a similar difficulty by not always appearing quite at home in a new setting. For instance, when Camões describes morning or evening, he does so in a rich mythological manner which tends to look a little too elaborate and artificial. Yet there is a justification for it. In an account of morning:

> Já o raio Apolíneo visitava
> Os Montes Nabateios acendido,[1]
>
> (I, 84, 1-2)

the appearance of Apollo in this remote African setting may seem hybrid, but it hints at the juxtaposition of East and West which takes place when Gama arrives on African shores. More complicated and more allusive are some lines on evening:

> Mas já o claro amador da Larisseia
> Adúltera inclinava os animais
> Lá para o grande lago que rodeia
> Temistitão, nos fins Ocidentais.[2]
>
> (X, I, 1-4)

The allusion passes from Coronis through her lover, Apollo,

---

[1] Now visited th' Apollinean ray
The Nabathean mountains with a smile.
(Fanshawe)

[2] But now the Larissean lass's friend,
Who for a wealthier lover did forgo
The god of verse, his setting steeds did bend
O'er the great lake of silver Mexico.
(Fanshawe)

whom she betrayed, to Mexico, where Apollo, the god of light, is now sinking. Yet even this oblique and Alexandrian reference gains some strength by being brought into connection with the world beyond the Western seas. The light that illumines Europe from the East is seen as spreading to the remotest corners of the world. And even here Camões' poetical instinct shows him that classical allusion is not enough; for he continues in his most charming and most simple manner:

> O grande ardor do Sol, Favónio enfreia
> Co'o sôpro que, nos tanques naturais,
> Encrespa a água serena, e despertava
> Os lírios e jasmins, que a calma agrava.[1]
>
> (X, I, 5-8)

For Camões antique mythology had a peculiar brightness which neither allegory nor the grand style had yet dulled. He felt drawn to use it when some sight touched his fancy, and certainly had no misgivings that it might be thought incongruous.

Camões also uses his classical learning in quite a different way. In his attempt to rival Virgil he has to show that some of his modern themes are worthy of the Virgilian muse and he does this by adapting famous passages of Virgil to suit them. This is of course a characteristic of learned poetry, which by awakening echoes of some other poem seeks to add beauty and dignity to its own subject. Just as the Romans used Greek poetry in this way, so the poets of the Renaissance used Roman. It is wrong to treat passages of such a kind as if they were mere plagiarism. The poet does not wish to pass off the work of others as his own; he aims rather at making us see his theme in the light of some other theme honoured and glorified by classical verse, and find a complex pleasure in the association of the new with the old. So, for instance, when Camões tells the tragic story of Inez de Castro, the beautiful young mistress of the young prince Pedro, he tells how she is led off to be murdered:

---

[1] Sol's burning rays Favonius did suspend
With that cool breath which makes, where it doth blow,
Becalmèd jessamines erect their heads
And naked lilies sit up in their beds.

(Fanshawe)

Para o céu cristalino alevantando,
Com lágrimas, os olhos piedosos,
Os olhos, porque as mãos lhe estava atando
Um dos duros ministros rigorosos.[1]

(III, 125, 1-4)

The scene has a genuine pathos and would touch many who
had never read Virgil, but it is not meant primarily for them.
It is addressed to those who will at once remember Virgil's
account of Cassandra :

ad caelum tendens ardentia lumina frustra,
lumina, nam teneras arcebant vincula palmas.[2]

(*Aen.* II, 405-6)

The effect of such a reminiscence is manifold. It puts Inez
in the same class of victims as Cassandra and gives her a
special claim on our compassion ; it gives a purely learned
pleasure in letting us recognise whence the poet's thought
comes ; it enables us to compare his version with the original
and to see how the Portuguese is softer and less epigrammatic
than the Latin.

When Camões takes an idea from Virgil, he usually
acclimatises it and gives it a new individuality. Virgil for
instance more than once tells how physical nature mourns the
death of some human being. When Affonso Henriquez dies,
Camões imagines a similar lamentation :

Os altos promontórios o choraram,
E do rios as águas saüdosas
Os semeados campos alagaram,
Com lágrimas córrendo piedosas.[3]

(III, 84, 1-4)

The old theme takes a new shape. The land, for which the
dead king has done so much and which is in a political sense

[1] Lifting unto the azure firmament
Her eyes, which in a sea of tears were drown'd,
Her eyes, for one of those malevolent
And bloody instruments her hands had bound.
(Fanshawe)

[2] Vainly to heaven uplifts her burning eyes,
Her eyes, for bonds restrain her tender hands.

[3] Him did the lofty promontories moan :
With all their streams the widow'd rivers wept,
And overflowing the fields newly sown
With rueful tears the next year's harvest swept.
(Fanshawe)

his creation, mourns him as a lost friend. The "pathetic fallacy" of mourning nature ceases to be a trope and hints at some deep companionship between landscape and man. The main theme had been sanctified by Virgil, but Camões works it in so well that there is hardly a hint of erudition about it. Again, Virgil in a famous passage [1] describes the sound of a trumpet through a wide countryside and tells how different places hear it and mothers clasp their children to their breasts. The beauty of his lines gains much from the affection with which he names the actual places, the lake of Trivia, the sulphurous streams of Nar, the wells of Velinus. His trumpet sounds among places familiar to his readers and has a special, local appeal for them. In his account of Aljubarrota Camões also sounds a trumpet:

> Deu sinal a trombeta Castelhana,
> Horrendo, fero, ingente, e temeroso;
> Ouviu-o o monte Artabro, e Guadiana
> Atrás tornou as ondas de medroso.
> Ouviu o Douro e a terra Transtagana;
> Correu ao mar o Tejo duvidoso;
> E as mães que o som terríbil escutaram,
> Aos peitos os filhinhos apertaram.[2]

> (IV, 28, 1-8)

This trumpet sounds down all the rivers of Spain and Portugal and threatens war to all who dwell by them. Camões has widened the scene and given it a national, rather than a local, importance, to suit his setting of a Portugal invaded by Spaniards.

In transforming his Virgilian model to suit his times and his country Camões, naturally enough, made free use of similes. Of all the devices of Greek poetry the simile has had the most remarkable career. Unlike many oral poets, Homer uses similes on a large scale and puts into them those experi-

---

[1] *Aen.* VII, 514-18.
[2] Castilian trumpets did the onset sound,
Loud, furious, dismal, terrible and hoarse;
Heard it Artabor's Mount, and underground
Her way did frighted Guardiana force:
Heard it the Dwere, and Alentecho round:
Tagus looks back, then hastens on his course:
And mothers who that baleful noise did hear,
Clasp to their breasts their tender babes for fear.

(Fanshawe)

ences and scenes which he could not put into his heroic narrative. Virgil followed him closely and seldom went beyond his range of subjects. Camões takes up the tradition and shows how well he understands the real function of the simile. Its chief use is to provide a break in the narrative by suggesting something outside its events which illustrates them. The point of comparison varies, but usually it is a mood or tone and makes us think that there is something more in what happens than appears in the mere account of it. Some of Camões' similes come from books, others from life, but they are always fresh and apposite and give the relief and illumination which a simile should. Even when he follows a well-worn path, his instinct keeps him from being conventional. For instance, Virgil, copying Homer by way of Catullus, compares the dying Euryalus to a flower weighed down by rain or cut down in a cornfield. Camões follows this example and produces for the death of Inez de Castro something that is nobly and delightfully his own :

> Assim como a bonina que cortada
> Antes de tempo foi, cândida e bela,
> Sendo das mãos lascivas maltratada
> Da menina que a trouxe na capela,
> O cheiro traz perdido e o côr murchada :
> Tal está, morta, a pálida donzela,
> Sêcas do rosto as roas e perdida
> A branca e viva côr, co'a doce vida.[1]
>
> (III, 134, 1-8)

The main intention of the simile is the same as in Virgil ; it illustrates the withering of a beautiful creature in death. But the details are changed and new associations are started. The poppy or field-flower is replaced by the daisy ; for the daisy is the symbol of girlhood in mediaeval poetry and calls up a world of chivalry and romantic devotion. The theme is elaborated, and the cheeks of Inez are " red and white "

[1] Like to a daisy-flow'r with colours fair,
By virgin's hand beheaded in the bud
To play withal, or prick into her hair,
When sever'd from the stalk on which it stood,
Both scent and beauty vanish into air,
So lies the damsel without breath or blood,
Her cheeks' fresh roses ravisht from the root
Both red and white, and the sweet life to boot.
(After Fanshawe)

because this was the mediaeval way of praising a girl's beauty. Coming perhaps from *The Song of Solomon*, — " My beloved is white and ruddy ", — it passed into Provençal verse in such lines as those of Arnaut de Marueil :

> La fassa fresca de colors
> Blanca, vermelha pus que flors,[1].

and thence into the early songs of France and Portugal. Inez is beautiful, young and innocent, and is celebrated in the graceful imagery of courtly love. Camões takes the classical form and recreates it into something more suited to his subject and more significant for his own world.

Camões equally finds similes for which there is no classical precedent. When he had to describe an unfamiliar phenomenon, he found that a novel simile helped him to be more exact. He had, for instance, seen a waterspout and been much impressed by it ; so he makes Gama describe one, carefully and accurately, to the King of Melinde. A thin vapour rises in the air and begins to revolve, then throws out a tube to the sky, grows larger and draws up water from the sea while a dark cloud hangs over its top. The strange phenomenon demands precise description, but to relate it more closely to common experience Camões adds a simile :

> Qual roxa sanguessuga se veria
> Nos beiços da alimária (que, imprudente,
> Bebendo a recolheu na fronte fria)
> Fartar co'o sangue alheio a sêde ardente ;
> Chupando, mais e mais se engrossa e cria,
> Ali se enche e se alarga grandemente :
> Tal a grande coluna, enchendo, aumenta
> A si e a nuvem negra que sustenta.[2]
>
> (v, 21, 1-8)

[1] Her colouring, so fresh and bright,
More than a flower's, red and white.

[2] As a black horse-leech — mark it in some pool !—
Got to the lip of an unwary beast,
Which, drinking, suck'd it from the water cool,
Upon another's blood itself to feast ;
It swells and swells, and feeds beyond all rule,
And stuffs the paunch, a rude unsober guest :
So swell'd the pillar, with a hideous crop,
Itself, and the black cloud which it did prop.
(Fanshawe)

The leech, swelling with blood, is an excellent parallel to the swelling waterspout. There is even a point in the beast which has sucked it up unexpectedly ; for the waterspout itself is highly unexpected. To convey the significance of this strange new sight Camões draws his simile from common rustic life. His method is Homer's ; for Homer often compares great events to small without detracting from their grandeur. But the subject and its details are Camões' own. From this piece of simple observation he makes a parallel which is not only visually but emotionally relevant ; the waterspout is sinister and frightening, and so too in its own small world is the leech. The simile is in the true epic tradition, fresh, apposite and effective.

By such means Camões adapts the Virgilian technique and gives a Virgilian character to his poem. But this would not be enough for the theorists of epic in his age. He must also follow his model in relating his human events to some scheme of things and provide a metaphysical or theological background. In other words, he must have divine personages in his poem, as Virgil and Homer had before him. Lucan indeed omitted the gods from his *Pharsalia*, but he was censured for it by Petronius, and his example was not followed. The epic was expected to give a comprehensive picture of life and would fail in this if the gods were left out. It might also fail to reach the right heroic tone ; for to this the gods of Virgil indubitably contribute. When Camões wrote an epic on the Virgilian model, he must decide what to do about the gods. They must be present in some form, but it was not easy to decide in what. Since Camões lived in a Christian age, he might perhaps be expected to use some kind of mythological machinery based on Christianity. No doubt this would have been acceptable in the sixteenth century, when few would have felt, as Boileau did in the seventeenth, that any such attempt led to a falsification of divine truths and that to set the figures of Christian belief in such a poem was

> Du Dieu de vérité faire un dieu de mensonges.

Even so there was a serious artistic objection to such a procedure. The God and the Saints of Christianity are not easily placed in a heroic poem ; for, as Dryden says, " the machines of our Christian religion, in heroic poetry, are much

more feeble to support that weight than those of heathenism ".
The alternative was to keep the Pagan gods and to give them
a new significance. It is true that they had long ago ceased
to be worshipped and that some might regard them as devils
or creations of the Devil. But the revival of learning had
given them a new life. For the moment many accepted them
at least as creatures of noble fancy. So Camões, true to his
love of antiquity, chose to introduce them, to make them
appeal aesthetically to the imagination and at the same time
to give them a serious place in his main scheme.

It is sometimes assumed that Camões treated the Olympian
gods as literary conventions, as figures who represent abstract
qualities or natural forces. Such was the method of the
seventeenth century when Boileau identified Minerva with
prudence, Venus with beauty, Jupiter with thunder and
Neptune with the sea. The method is more than familiar,
but it is not that of Camões. It is true that his Neptune is a
god of the sea and his Mars of war, but even these allegorical
figures take on some kind of personality when the first holds
court in his submarine palace or the second strikes his spear-
shaft on the floor of Olympus in angry defence of the Portu-
guese. Camões' Venus is much more than beauty, his
Jupiter than thunder, his Bacchus than wine. His mythology
is far less abstract and arid than that of the seventeenth
century ; it reveals a deeper and more sympathetic under-
standing of the antique gods than Corneille felt when he
demanded their presence in poetry :

> Qu'on fait d'injure à l'art de lui voler la fable !
> C'est interdire aux vers ce qu'ils ont d'agréable.

Between Camões and this kind of decoration there lies a great
dispute about the whole relation of heathen beliefs to a
Christian society, a dispute which left a place for the gods of
heathendom only by making them sacrifice much of their
reality. Camões still breathes the air of the Renaissance and
believes that the ancient gods are worthy of honour. He does
not indeed follow Pico della Mirandola who worked out a
system to equate the doctrines of Plato with those of the
Church. For Camões' concern is not intellectual but
aesthetic ; his gods and goddesses come not from philosophy
but from poetry. He is more like Raphael, who in his

Parnassus displayed the divine figures of antiquity as a counterpart to those of Christianity. They were for him as supreme in the arts and sciences as the Church was in religion and morals ; they were even real, in the sense that they embodied forces powerful in the human heart and in the conduct of life. In the Renaissance the two worlds could exist side by side. Camões accepted the paradox and made the most of it.

To simplify his theological machinery Camões uses only a small number of divinities, and all who really matter are Jupiter, Venus and Bacchus. The first two owe something to Virgil ; the third is Camões' own choice and almost his own creation. Jupiter prophesies the great future that awaits the Portuguese ; he is in some sense connected with the Fates ; his decrees may be disputed but in the end they are accomplished. He is magnificent and majestic :

> Num assento de estrêlas cristalino,
> Com gesto alto, severo e soberano.[1]
> (I, 22, 3-4)

All this is in the Virgilian tradition. The Father of the gods, who once favoured Rome and foretold its greatness, now does the like for Portugal. Camões again shows his belief that his country is the natural and destined successor of Rome. Venus too owes much to Virgil. As the ancestress of Rome and champion of Aeneas she now transfers her protection to Portugal. No doubt Camões was delighted that she was also the goddess of love, but his choice is justified by other reasons. The goddess of Rome loves Portugal :

> Por quantas qualidades via nela
> Da antiga tam amada sua Romana.[2]
> (I, 33, 3-4)

She personifies the Western and European spirit which has grown on Roman foundations and finds a new mission in the East. In all her actions Venus displays this spirit or supports it in others. She embodies a civilising harmony, a spirit more

---

[1] Upon a crystal throne with stars emboss'd
Sublime the Father sat, worthy that place.
(Fanshawe)

[2] For the much likeness she observ'd in them
To her old Rome, for which she had such passion.
(Fanshawe)

creative and more orderly than she has in Virgil. Her special
task is to favour the Roman outlook in the modern world.
In opposition to her is not Juno but Bacchus. Bacchus is no
doubt chosen partly because he was connected with India
and was believed once to have conquered it. He is not the
god of wine or of Dionysiac ecstasy, but the spirit of the East
in its vanity, cunning and disorder. Camões found some such
view of him in Statius' *Thebaid* where Bacchus is followed
by a curiously mixed company :

> sunt illic Ira Furorque
> et Metus et Virtus et numquam sobrius Ardor.[1]
> (IV, 661-2)

So in *Os Lusiadas* Bacchus aptly typifies these qualities of the
East which are opposed to the order and reason of the West.

As in the *Aeneid* the main conflict in heaven is between
Venus and Juno, so in *Os Lusiadas* it is between Venus and
Bacchus. Jupiter holds the final decision but stands aside
from the struggle. It is fated that the Portuguese shall come
to India, but Bacchus is determined to postpone the evil day
for as long as possible and to put every hindrance in their way,
while Venus is no less determined to give help. The issue,
which pervades the poem, is made clear in the first scene on
Olympus, which shows Venus and Bacchus at loggerheads.
The first crisis comes on the African coast, when Bacchus sets
out to create mistrust and hatred in the Moors for the Portu-
guese and to lure his enemies to destruction. At Mozambique
he disseminates dark rumours, but is foiled by Gama's
watchfulness. So he makes the fleet come to Mombasa,
where he disguises himself as a Christian and raises a Christian
altar which naturally deceives the men whom Gama sends to
report on the situation. Camões indulges a quaint fancy
when he makes Bacchus worship at this altar :

> e assim por derradeiro
> O falso Deus adora o verdadeiro.[2]
> (II, 12, 7-8)

[1]   With him are Rage and Wrath,
Valour and Fear and never sober Zeal.

[2]   from whence it doth ensue
That the false god came to adore the true.
(Fanshawe)

The Portuguese believe that the inhabitants are Christian and try to enter the harbour, but, to their great surprise, their ships will not move, — because Venus and her Nymphs prevent them. The whole scene is of a radiant beauty. The goddess and her Nymphs are as lifelike as if they came from Virgil or Ovid. But the episode has its symbolical significance. It shows the conflict between dark powers of suspicion, hatred and deceit, which fight against Gama, and other powers, which save him from destruction and may justly be regarded as providential. Superhuman forces are engaged on both sides ; the spirits of West and East, of civilisation and barbarism, are at work. Nor is all this mere fancy ; it has a basis in history. The Portuguese really believed that there were many Christians in Africa who would welcome them. Even the intervention of Venus is not too removed from fact ; for as Gama was entering the harbour at Mombasa, a false manœuvre by one of his ships made the Moors think that their plot was discovered, and their agitation put the Portuguese on their guard and made them leave for Melinde.

The second crisis between Venus and Bacchus takes place in the Indian Ocean. Determined to prevent the fleet from reaching India, Bacchus invokes the powers of the sea to send a storm. The fleet is in great peril, but Venus intervenes in time and calms the waters. The storm is real, even historical, if we assume that Camões has transposed to this time and place the fearful storm which fell on Gama in the Atlantic when he was on his way home, and into it Camões has put details gained from his own experience. The storm is the last obstacle which the explorers have to pass before reaching their goal. Having suffered from the malignity of men, they now suffer from the malignity of the elements. Once again Venus and Bacchus stand for supernatural powers that help or obstruct the Portuguese. The spirits of East and West include powers of nature as well as of man. Bacchus creates violence and disorder in the elements ; Venus restores calm and order. The divinities stand for something not easily labelled but revealed in their actions. Venus, with Mars to help her, is a protecting power of Western order, Bacchus is the opposite. The beneficent forces of the world, which arise from civilisation, are no less displayed in nature ; the evil forces, which fill men's hearts with hatred and distrust, are akin to the violent natural powers which discoverers have to face. In Venus and Bacchus Camões gives a fundamental conflict in the world, a strife between opposites in which one or the other must yield. In the result Venus wins. Bacchus wastes himself in intrigues and fails; Venus rewards those whom she supports and gives them peculiar delights in her Island. In his Pagan mythology Camões has found new symbols to display the real issues that he sees in Gama's voyage. The discovery of India is important not only for its historical results but because it is a great victory for harmony and order in physical nature and in the human heart.

In creating again for his own times the gods and goddesses of Olympus Camões found a task that suited him perfectly. From the opening of the Council in Heaven in Canto I to the last words of Venus in Canto X he never fails to make the most of his opportunities. He makes his divinities majestic and attractive, and he sets the right note by emphasising their sublimity. The first gathering of the gods takes place in an ample, Olympian air. They come

> Pisando o cristalino Céu formoso,
> Vem pela Via Láctea juntamente.[1]
>
> (I, 20, 5-6)

There Jupiter is seated on his throne, and when the gods have taken their seats in due order, he addresses them in language which befits their lofty station:

> Eternos moradores do luzente,
> Estelífero Polo e claro Assento.[2]
>
> (I, 24, 1-2)

When the Council is finished, they depart with royal courtesies and deep obeisance. In the celestial sublimity of this first scene Camões sheds on Olympus a light worthy of Correggio

---

[1] Treading in clusters the diaphane skies
Thorough the Milky Way their course they bent.
(Fanshawe)

[2] Eternal dwellers of the tow'r divine
And empyrean hall with starrèd vault.
(Fanshawe)

ainting; his effect is not
poetic imagination which
mpian gods from Roman
vision of them. The powers
iverse have the glory and the
sm brings to the objects of its
yond time and the other limita-
und the antithesis of his troubled
gings. With his high sense of style
ew into them much that he most
l intention gives depth and interest
he gods, but their first claim on him
re the gods of his great love, the antique

ove for them Camões found in his divinities
of power. Even the grave Virgil pauses to
enchants Aeneas with her ambrosial beauty,
ributes to these powerful beings qualities that
l eye. So Camões, true to the ancient tradition,
conscious of their beauty. His Venus is a
nbol, but she is still a goddess. When she comes
cue of the Portuguese fleet at Mombasa, Camões
e spirit of the Italian Renaissance in his glowing
of her:

Nos ombros de um Tritão, cum gesto aceso,
Vai a linda Dione furiosa;
Não sente quem a leve o doce pêso,
De soberbo com carga tam formosa.[1]

(II, 21, 1-4)

The Nereids are fit company for her as they sweep the white foam with their silver tails. The protectress of Portugal is still the goddess of love and beauty, and the poet is proud that his country should be favoured by her. So when she visits Jupiter to entreat his help for the Portuguese, Camões is more daring even than the Roman poets in making her display her naked beauty without any false shame:

[1] Upon a Triton's back, with kindled face,
The beauteous Erycina furious rode.
He, to whose fortune fell so great a grace,
Feels not the rider, proud of his fair load.
(Fanshawe)

115

Os crespos fios de ouro se esparziam
Pelo colo que a neve escurecia ;
Andando, as lácteas têtas lhe tremiam,
Com quem Amor brincava e não se via.[1]
(II, 36, 1-4)

In this splendid appearance she exerts all her charm
divine father, who is entirely overcome by them and p
to do all that she asks. In this scene Camões, like
presents a divine contrast to his earthly events. Hi
have their own glory, but the glory of the gods is differer
beyond human range.

Such scenes show what the antique gods were for Can
In them he found figures of delight and beauty, bril
contrasts to the world which he saw about him. They
powers of the spirit which give light and glory to hum
achievements and grant an unreckonable reward to those w
honour them ; they are the forces which have created t
best elements in European life as Camões knows it. Thei
memory must have comforted him through many dark hours
among the hateful intrigues of Goa or on the stricken shores
of Africa. In their own way and in their own place they are
real. Camões believes in them and honours them. Free from
the theological inhibitions of the Middle Ages and hardly
touched by the Counter-Reformation, he works out his own
way of bringing the Olympian gods into his poem. What
even Ariosto does not do, Camões does gaily and confidently.
His divinities play an indispensable part in his poem, and it
would be vastly poorer without them. Through their inter-
actions with men it moves, like most great epics, at two levels.
The human action has its own grandeur, but it acquires
greater dignity because the gods have a part in it. The grim
struggles of the Portuguese discoverers are one side of the
picture ; the other side contains all that the gods represent,
the glory and the delight that they bring, the order which
they create. In adhering to this convention of epic poetry
Camões wins a triumphant success. Like Correggio and

---

[1] The golden tresses on her shoulders fell,
Whose whiteness smuts the fleece of onfall'n snow :
Her breasts, and those ev'n their own milk excel,
Play'd with by unseen Cupid, trembling go.

(Fanshawe)

Raphael, he understands the ancient gods and sees their meaning for his own time.

Camões, however, was no Pagan but a Catholic, proud to be a subject of a Christian king, and his Portuguese owe much of their dignity to their championship of the Christian cause against Moors and idolatrous Indians. He had therefore to show what place his Olympian gods have in his scheme of the universe and what is their relation to his Christian beliefs. Since his gods are symbolical, there should be no great difficulty about accommodating them to some comprehensive Christian system, especially at a time when such harmonies had been attempted by more than one Italian thinker. Camões is, however, inconsistent on this point. He gives at least two explanations, and they are irreconcilable. The most emphatic and explicit is that which probably meant least to him. In Canto IX, after his account of the Island of Loves, he devotes three stanzas to explaining that the whole scheme is allegorical, that the Island is only an emblem of glory and that the gods and heroes of the ancient world are nothing but human beings whom fame has immortalised :

> Não eram senão prémios que reparte,
> Por feitos imortais e soberanos,
> O mundo co'os varões que esfôrço e arte
> Divinos os fizeram, sendo humanos.
> Que Júpiter, Mercúrio, Febo e Marte,
> Eneas e Quirino e os dois Tebanos,
> Ceres, Palas, e Juno com Diana,
> Todos foram de fraca carne humana.[1]
>
> (IX, 91, 1-8)

The explanation is worse than an anticlimax ; if we treat it seriously, it spoils much of the poem. For Jupiter, who has decided the future destinies of Portugal, and Venus, who has so nobly helped their fulfilment, are of no importance if they

---

[1] What meant they but an immortality
Giv'n by the world for actions soveraign,
To such as arts or arms advanc'd to high
And heav'nly pitch, being born of human strain ?
For Jove, Apollo, Mars and Mercury,
Aeneas, Romulus, the Thebans twain,
Juno, Diana, Ceres, Pallas, all
Dwell, as you do, in brittle earthen wall.
(Fanshawe)

117

are human beings of whom only the glorious names survive. It has been thought, with good reason, that these stanzas are a late addition required by the censor or inserted to placate him. Rather than sacrifice his divinities altogether Camões explains them away. He may well have thought that those who really understood him would not be deceived by such a device, while possible enemies might be deluded into thinking that after all he was orthodox. In any case the explanation is inconsistent with what Camões says elsewhere in his poem and should not be treated as his last word.

Camões' real explanation is more profound and more satisfying. It is that his divinities are symbols for different activities of the one supreme God, subordinate powers to whom various special functions are allotted. Camões hints at this in Canto I at the beginning of the assembly on Olympus :

> Deixam dos Sete Céus o regimento,
> Que do Poder mais alto lhe foi dado,
> Alto Poder, que só co'o pensamento
> Governa o Céu, a Terra e o Mar irado.[1]
>
> (I, 21, 1-4)

Here the Highest Power cannot be Jupiter, for Jupiter controls one of the seven spheres ; it can only be a Supreme Deity above him. In Canto X the idea is elaborated. Venus explains the structure of the universe and begins by denying that the ancient gods are anything but fables ; but from this discouraging start she goes on to show their real place :

> E também, porque a Santa Providência,
> Que em Júpiter aqui se representa,
> Por espíritos mil que tem prudência
> Governa o mundo todo que sustenta.[2]
>
> (X, 83, 1-4)

---

[1] They leave the patronage of the seven spheres
Which by the Highest Pow'r to them was giv'n,
The Highest Pow'r, who with an eye-brow steers
The earth, the raging ocean, and the heav'n.
(Fanshawe)

[2] As likewise because Holy Providence,
Which shadow'd is by Jupiter in verse,
Doth by a thousand ministers dispense
His gifts to the supported universe.
(Fanshawe)

Jupiter is Divine Providence, not God Himself, but an attribute of Him, and, as Venus goes on to say, this power is called God because it belongs to Him, just as the angels are sometimes called gods. A little later she adds :

> Emfim que o Sumo Deus, que por segundas
> Causas obra no Mundo, tudo manda,[1]
> > (x, 85, 1-2)

and makes all clear. If Jupiter is Divine Providence and God works through second causes, Camões' gods and goddesses are neither fictions nor allegories nor famous men and women of the past but celestial powers who in their several spheres carry out the commands and will of the Supreme Being. They are even aspects of Him, and their powers are His.

That such was really Camões' belief is proved by the way in which he works his divinities into the action of his poem. When Venus or Mercury intervenes to help Gama, it is not to them that he offers prayer or thanks but to the God of his fathers. When, for instance, Mercury appears in a dream to him at Mombasa, the Captain takes the warning, but speaks of a heavenly guide :

> Que o Céu nos favorece e Deus o manda.[2]   (II, 65, 2)

When Venus saves the fleet, Gama ascribes the deliverance to Providence and ends with a solemn prayer to his own God :

> Ó tu, Guarda Divina, tem cuidado
> De quem sem ti não pode ser guardado ![3]
> > (II, 31, 7-8)

Even more striking is the great prayer which Gama offers up during the storm in Canto VI. He prays to the God who delivered Israel from the Red Sea and Paul from shipwreck and addresses him in words of noble piety :

[1] In fine, Almighty God, who rules the round
World, by his second causes, He commands.
> (Fanshawe)

[2] Heav'n is our Guide, and God our course directs.
> (Fanshawe)

[3] O thou Guardian divine, to guard him deign,
Who without Thee doth guard himself in vain.
> (Fanshawe)

Divina Guarda, angélica, celeste,
Que os Céus, o Mar e Terra senhoreias.[1]
(VI, 81, 1-2)

His prayer is answered, — but by Venus. The paradox is
abundantly clear, and Camões stresses it. When dawn
comes, it is her star that shines, as it were, with a message of
hope:

Mas já a amorosa Estrêla scintilava
Diante do Sol claro, no Horizonte.[2]
(VI, 85, 1-2)

Then follows her intervention, and the seas are calmed. Just
as Camões' Jupiter is Divine Providence, so his Venus has
some qualities of Divine Love. He paints her in all the
bright colours of Latin poetry, but she is none the less a
beneficent power in a Christian universe, the love which
looks after the good and rewards them in the end. Camões
must have given great thought to his gods and goddesses.
He treats them with subtlety and insight and relates them
closely to his main scheme.

Gama's voyage to India, and the history of Portugal, in
which it is a turning-point, provides Camões with his main
theme. They give him the heroes which he needs for his
national epic. But he seems to have felt that to confine him-
self to such themes was to make his poem too grave and too
austere, that it needed some diversion of a different kind.
Much of *Os Lusiadas* comes from a world which owes little
to Virgil and bears no resemblance to the starker kinds of
heroic poetry. Yet even in this Camões might have claimed
that Virgil provided him with a precedent. For Virgil had
introduced into his heroic frame something of the romantic
poetry of Alexandria and made use of fancies which were out-
side the heroic scope. So Camões felt himself justified in
giving part of his epic to a kind of poetry which might seem
to be far removed from it. The most popular poem of his
time was the *Orlando Furioso* of Ariosto, published in 1516.
This great work belonged to a great tradition. It followed

[1] Protector of the quires angelical,
Whom heav'n and earth and angry seas obey.
(Fanshawe)

[2] But see, the amorous star, with twinkling ray,
Conspicuous in the Eastern Hemisphere.
(Fanshawe)

naturally where Boiardo had led the way. For lovers of poetry in the sixteenth century the Italian chivalrous epic, brilliant, gay, romantic, debonair, pictorial, was what mattered most. It was admired and loved by Camões, who felt that his own poem must find some relation to it and show its superiority. If his readers expected from him something like the *Orlando Furioso*, they must learn that he offered something truer and nobler. In his Introduction he stresses this three times, when he claims that his subject is truer than the stories of Rodomonte, Ruggiero and Orlando, that his Portuguese kings match Charlemagne, and that the Twelve of England are as good as the Twelve Peers. He challenges a great and popular poetry, and he suggests that, although what he tells is true, it is in every way as interesting and delightful as the imaginations of Ariosto.

In attempting to combine this kind of poetry with his heroic story Camões set himself a difficult task. Despite its historical connections with heroic epic, chivalrous epic moves in another sphere of the spirit and makes few calls to serious ambition or high resolve. Camões adds much colour and life to his poem by using some themes of chivalrous epic, but he introduces them circumspectly with a proper regard to their relevance in their new place. Some themes indeed he omits. The miraculous, which Boiardo carried to such superb lengths, is missing from any action of Camões' human characters. Even love is confined almost to the single story of Inez de Castro, which is based on history and told in a tragic spirit with a high classical style. But there were other themes which could be adapted to a new setting without spoiling the balance of the poem. For instance, the chivalrous epic was much attached to jousts and tournaments with their proper accompaniment of injured damsels championed by gallant knights. Such a subject appealed to Camões' tender, dreaming, amorous soul, and he makes his own use of it. In his Introduction he forecasts what is to come :

> Pois pelos Doze Pares dar-vos quero
> Os Doze de Inglaterra e o seu Magriço,[1]
> (I, 12, 5-6)

[1] For the Twelve Peers, I other Twelve bestow
That passed to England, and Magrizzo one.
(Fanshawe)

and in Canto VII the story of the Twelve of England is told during a storm by Fernão Velloso. At first sight it has little connection with the tournaments of Ariosto. The poet claims that it is historical. It took place in the reign of João I of Portugal and Richard II of England, and John of Gaunt played a leading part in it. Camões found the story in the chivalresque novel of Ferreira de Vasconcelos and accepted it as true. So indeed it may in part have been. An event tactfully suppressed by English chroniclers did not suffer the same fate from Portuguese writers, who saw that it brought nothing but honour to their country. Camões tells it with a serious, instructive purpose. The crew discuss what kind of tale they wish to hear, and the love-stricken Lionardo asks for a tale of love, but Velloso overrules him on the ground that such a subject is out of place in their situation and that a tale of chivalry is better. Camões prepares the way for the Twelve of England with care and makes it clear that he does not treat it as a mere invention of romance.

The tale, however, has obviously something in common with such tales as that of Rinaldo and Ginevra in the *Orlando Furioso*. Both have much the same outline. The womanhood of one nation is grossly libelled by its men and seems defenceless against their calumnies ; fortunately the men of another nation come to the defence and prove their case by triumphing in a tournament ; in the actual fight one injured woman seems to be without a champion until an unknown knight arrives and carries all before him ; once the victory is won, the victors go off to adventures in foreign lands. Such are the main elements that Ariosto took over from the legends of the Swan-Knight and Camões found in his novel. Of course Camões' sources are not entirely to be trusted as history, but Camões believed in their veracity and told his story in a realistic, historical spirit. This is his version of the Age of Chivalry as it really existed, and in essentials he is surely right. His narration reflects a real state of society and follows a correct geography. John of Gaunt furthers the claims of the Portuguese because they have helped him to fight against Spain ; the Twelve travel to England with the consent of the English king ; Magriço goes his own way that he may visit Spain, France and Flanders. All this is circumstantial and even probable. Yet the episode has the thrills and the graces of chivalry, not merely in the beginning when women's honour assumes so great an importance, but in the final tournament with the king on his throne, the horses champing their golden bits, the lady, who has no champion, sitting forlornly in black, the sudden arrival of Magriço at the crucial moment, the shock of the encounter :

> Picam de esporas, largam rédeas logo,
> Abaixam lanças, fere a terra fogo.[1]
>
> (VI, 63, 7-8)

In the end all is well. The honour of English womanhood has been vindicated by the Portuguese knights, who go on their various ways to new adventures. Such is Camões' art that he takes this episode and gives it the glamour of chivalrous romance without detracting from its reality.

Another, less tractable theme of chivalrous epic is the brutal giant who frightens men by his revolting appearance and inflicts hideous tortures on them, — like Ariosto's Galigorante, who from his hidden haunt in the sands traps unwary wayfarers of both sexes and eats them. He is almost the ogre of fairy-tale, and his kind might seem to have no place in the discovery of India. Yet on it Camões has built one of his most renowned and most original episodes, the appearance of Adamastor. When the fleet reaches the southernmost point of Africa, on a calm night a cloud rises and grows until it is seen to be the figure of a giant. Camões spares no details of his repellent aspect, from his scowling face, squalid beard, and hollow eyes to his filthy hair, black mouth and yellow teeth. He is as large as the Colossus of Rhodes, and his deep, ugly voice makes the hair stand up on those who hear it. Like any other giant, he abuses the Portuguese for breaking into regions which he regards as his private domain and forbidden to all strangers, and proceeds to foretell horrors and destruction to them. Then he tells his own story, which is of course one of injured innocence. He sought marriage with Thetis, but was foiled by a trick. When he believed that she was his, he found that his embraces were wasted on a rock. There is a gross, ogreish bestiality about

---

[1] Spurs are clapp'd to, reins slacken'd in a trice,
Spears coucht in rest ; fire from the struck ground flies.
(Fanshawe)

his ardour when he thinks that he has won the object of his desires :

> Como doido corri de longe, abrindo
> Os braços para aquela que era vida
> Dêste corpo, e começo os olhos belos
> A lhe beijar, as faces e os cabelos.[1]
>
> (v, 55, 5-8)

Like other monsters, Adamastor is extremely sorry for himself and hates everyone. When he disappears with loud weeping and a howl over the sea, he shows that, despite his ugly threats, he is defeated. His character and appearance come largely from chivalrous epic and through it from fairytale, but Camões has transmuted him into something more remarkable and more significant.

Adamastor is convincing because he is related to fact and because his forecasts of evil belong to history. He foretells disasters, all of which occurred in the regions round South Africa in the years after Gama's voyage. The first, ironically appropriate in its victim and specially pleasing to Adamastor, is the storm that brought death to the first European to round the Cape, Bartolemeu Dias. The second is the death of the great Viceroy, Francisco de Almeida, who paid for the destruction of Quiloa and Mombasa by falling on African soil in a chance fight with natives when he was on his way home to Lisbon. The third is the fearful catastrophe which befell Sepúlveda, who had been governor of Diu and was returning with his beautiful and loved wife, Leonor. They were shipwrecked, and after hideous treatment by the natives, saw their children die before they themselves died of starvation and thirst. Adamastor dwells on the horrors which await them :

> Verão morrer com fome os filhos caros,
> Em tanto amor gerados e nascidos ;
> Verão os Cafres, ásperos e avaros,
> Tirar à linda dama seus vestidos ;

---

[1] With open arms, far off, like mad I run
To clip therein my joy, my life, my sweet :
And, clipt, begin those orient eyes to kiss,
That face, that hair, that neck, that all that is.
(Fanshawe)

Os cristalinos membros e preclaros
À calma, ao frio, ao ar, verão despidos,
Depois de ter pisada, longamente,
Co'os delicados pés a areia ardente.[1]

(v, 47, 1-8)

The Cape of Storms, which Adamastor personifies, was indeed to bring many agonies and disasters to the Portuguese in their early voyages round it. It is not without reason that he prophesies woe to Gama and his successors :

Sabe que quantas naus esta viagem
Que tu fazes, fizerem, de atrevidas,
Inimiga terão esta paragem,
Com ventos e tormentas desmedidas ![2]

(v, 43, 1-4)

When Camões wrote, these perils were familiar, and Adamastor might well seem to represent a hideous and hostile force of nature. The ogre has become something more formidable than a figure of fairy-tale.

Just as Bacchus symbolises the difficulties which the Portuguese meet on their journey to the East, so Adamastor symbolises a natural obstacle, the passage round the Cape of Storms, the point where East meets West and disasters are common. As the ancients believed that no man could safely sail beyond the Pillars of Hercules, so in the sixteenth century some may have believed that even after Dias had rounded it, the Cape set a natural limit to sailing. The Portuguese pass this limit and have to pay for it. Their triumph over it is part of the whole process by which they bring order and civilisation to remote places. Camões shows this is in his own way. When he makes Adamastor one of the Giants, the companion

[1] Starv'd shall they see to death their children dear,
Begot and rear'd in so great love. The black
Rude Caffirs, out of avarice, shall tear
The clothes from the angelic lady's back.
Her dainty limbs of alabaster clear
To heat, to cold, to storm, to eyes worse wrack
Shall be laid naked, after she hath trod
Long time with her soft feet the burning clod.
(Fanshawe)

[2] This know : as many ships as shall persever
Boldly to make the voyage you make now,
Shall find this point their enemy for ever
With winds and tempests that no bound shall know.
(Fanshawe)

of Enceladus, Aegeus and Centimanus, and the enemy of Jupiter, he indicates that he belongs to an old chaotic state of things which Divine Providence has now decided to control. The myth is carried further in Adamastor's amorous pursuit of Thetis. She is a sea-goddess, and she refuses his advances. The sea is to belong not to primaeval powers like him but to the Portuguese. Adamastor's real inheritance is the rock which he finds in her place, thick with scrub and thorn, a fit emblem of his Antarctic world. Even he himself is turned to earth and has become the Cape; it is only his phantom that appears to Gama. The sea, which he once sought for bride, flows round him and increases his anguish. Camões' myth presents the triumph of the Portuguese over untamed forces of nature and their reward in becoming masters of the sea. The horror which the vision of Adamastor arouses is based on a natural fear of going too far and has a real relation to experience. The grisly and revolting phantom is an apt symbol of the horrors which may well appal those who break into waters where no men have sailed before.

In the Twelve of England and in Adamastor Camões turns themes of chivalrous epic to his own serious purpose, but he was a lover of beauty in so many forms that when the magic of Ariosto was on him he could hardly fail sometimes to release his spirit in flights of pure fancy and imaginative delight. When he does this, he confines himself to his divinities; his men are not allowed to transcend the bounds of mortality. A signal case is in Canto VI where Bacchus travels to the marvellous realms of the sea-gods whose help he wishes to win. Ariosto delighted in marvellous journeys, and this is in his tradition. It is true that even here the symbolical element is not altogether lacking and makes a brief appearance in the sculptures of the submarine palace which depict the triumph of the gods over the giants and the gifts which earth owes to the sea, and show the conquest of disorder by order in a way that harmonises with the Portuguese conquest of the seas. But these details are incidental. The main features of the episode are pure delight. On sands of fine silver Bacchus finds towers of crystal and diamond, gates of gold inlaid with pearl, a new earth with its own grass and trees and flowers. The company matches the setting. Here are the Nymphs dear to the poet's heart, Tethys in her finely woven veil, Amphitrite with her dolphin, Ino with her child who plays with golden shells. Here too are stranger beings, Glaucus in the shape of a fish, and the incomparable Triton, whose uncombed hair is of sea-weed, on whose beard grow mussels, and whose cap is a large lobster-shell. As he swims naked through the water, hundreds of shell-fish hang about him :

> Camarões e cangrejos e outros mais,
> Que recebem de Febe crescimento,
> Ostras e briguigões, do musco sujos,
> As costas co'a casca os caramujos.[1]
>
> (VI, 18, 5-8)

With his conch he summons the assembly, who, like the gods of Olympus, sit in due order on their thrones and hear Bacchus' complaint. We feel that this corrupt and ingenious god takes advantage of their innocence and that they have no real desire to help him in his fell designs, so charmingly are they presented.

The adaptation of themes from Boiardo and Ariosto was not without perils for Camões. They appealed so powerfully to him and called out so fine a response that they do not always consort easily with his grave and heroic subject. The difficulty can be seen in one of his most brilliant and most famous episodes, the Island of Loves in Canto IX. On their homeward voyage from India the weary explorers are guided by Venus to an earthly paradise under her protection, and into it Camões flings all his love of natural beauty. Ariosto had written of marvellous landscapes and magical gardens, and made them equally attractive whether they belong to the vicious Alcina or the virtuous Logistilla, while the finest is that which St. John shows to Astolfo in Paradise. Camões may owe something to any or all of these, but his ideal Island is on a greater scale and contains a greater variety of delights. Whereas Ariosto uses four stanzas for the landscape of Paradise, Camões uses ten for his Island, and a whole sylvan scene is conjured into existence. But even here Camões shows his independence. The beauties of his Island are all natural. In Ariosto's Paradise the flowers are jewels :

[1] As crayfish, shrimps, and other fish that crawls,
Receiving theirs from the pale moon's increase,
Oysters and periwinkles with their slime,
Snails, with their houses on their backs, that climb.
(Fanshawe)

Zaffir, rubini, oro, topazi, e perle
E diamante e crisoliti e iacinti
Potrìano i fiori assimigliar, che per le
Liete piaggie v' avea l' aura dipinti,[1]
(*O.F.* XXXIV, 49, 1-4)

but Camões' flowers are those which he knew and loved in his own Portugal, — violets, roses, lilies and hyacinths. In Ariosto the birds are as unearthly as the flowers :

Azurri e bianchi e verdi e rossi e gialli,[2] (*Ib.* 50, 2)

but in Camões they are more familiar :

A longo a água o níveo cisne canta
Responde-lhe do ramo Filomela.[3]
(IX, 63, 1-2)

Camões paints the landscape of his own country as he saw it with the homesick eyes of exile. He lingers lovingly on the heavily fruited trees, the fresh waters, the lush grass, the wild animals that seem tame. His mariners are rewarded with such a sight as he himself must often have imagined when he was in the blistering and dusty East.

In this respect the Island of Loves, unknown to geography, suits Camões' main design. An ideal landscape like this may well sustain adventurers in distant places and seem a fitting reward to them after long absence from home. But the landscape is not all. Such scenes are often associated with the pleasures of love, as Ariosto makes Alcina's garden a setting for bodily delights. Camões evidently felt this magic, and when he dreamed of an ideal garden, he was not altogether able or willing to deprive it of attractive inmates. So when Venus wishes to refresh the wanderers, she includes amorous pleasures among her benefits. Her Nymphs lure the sailors with song and dance, bathe in the streams or hide in the woods. The sailors catch glimpses of them and give pursuit. The Nymphs enter into the spirit of the sport, and, after suitable

---

[1] Here sapphire, ruby, gold and topaz glow,
Pearl, jacinth, chrysolite, and diamond lie,
Which well might pass for natural flowers which blow,
Catching their colour from the kindly sky.
(W. S. Rose)

[2] Azure, and red, and yellow, green and white.
(W. S. Rose)

[3] Along the lake the snowy swan did sing,
Him Philomela answers from a bough.
(Fanshawe)

resistance, allow themselves to be captured :

> Pouco e pouco, sorrindo e gritos dando,
> Se deixam ir dos galgos alcançando.[1]
>
> (IX, 70, 7-8)

Then follows a scene of universal love-making. The Nymphs give themselves up to their captors, and the woods are loud with caresses, kisses, laughter and promises of eternal affection. The essentially human character of all this gaiety is typified in the episode of Lionardo. He has hitherto been unsuccessful in love and feels that his desires are doomed to defeat, but even he is now successful. He sees the nymph Ephyre, pursues her, and appeals to her with such passion and sincerity that she yields to him :

> Cair se deixa aos pés do vencedor,
> Que todo se desfaz em puro amor.[2]
>
> (IX, 82, 7-8)

Camões had known the miseries of unrequited love and may have put something of himself into Lionardo. In any case Lionardo's adventure confirms the impression that the amorous delights of the Island are as real as the poet can make them. They are the poetry of desire, of a longing for love returned and unqualified.

Yet once he had allowed his fancy to develop this splendid theme Camões seems to have had misgivings about its appropriateness and even about its propriety. Such excesses of physical joy were somewhat unsuitable to his heroic subject and might shock bigots at home. So, to our surprise and disappointment, he explains that it is all allegorical :

> Que as Ninfas do Oceano, tam formosas,
> Tethys e a Ilha angélica pintada,
> Outra cousa não é que as deleitosas
> Honras que a vida fazam sublimada.[3]
>
> (IX, 89, 1-4)

---

[1] Shrieking and laughing softly in the close,
They let the greyhounds gain upon the does.   (Fanshawe)

[2] All melted in pure love, languidly sweet,
She lets herself fall at the victor's feet.   (Fanshawe)

[3] For these fair daughters of the Ocean,
Tethys and the angelic pencill'd isle,
Are nothing but sweet honour, which these won,
With whatsoever makes a life not vile.   (Fanshawe)

The charming Nymphs and the beautiful Island are, it seems, nothing but the satisfaction which honour and glory bring to those who have done great things. After all the excitement and passion the explanation is a little chilling. Of course it is possible that this is no more intended for the intelligent and humane reader than is Camões' explanation that his gods are merely human beings, and that he said this simply to disarm the censor or to save trouble from the Inquisition. On the other hand, Camões may well be sincere. He has at least good precedent for what he says. Ariosto's gardens are allegorical; Alcina's symbolises vice and Logistilla's virtue. It is true that when we read of them the distinction is not of much importance; for the poem moves in a world of pure imagination where ethical distinctions count for little. Yet Ariosto does so colour his details as to produce an effect. The lusts awoken by Alcina are as ugly as the mental pleasures of Logistilla are pure. The pleasures which Camões gives to his sailors are, if literal, unsuitable for heroes and improper for men. Therefore he follows Ariosto and makes them allegorical. His allegory is not entirely convincing. He virtually asks us to believe that the satisfaction which men find in physical love is like what they find in glory and the world's appreciation of a work well done, and this is not easy to accept. Camões makes his romantic episode fit into his plan, but at a cost. It is the price that he has to pay for allowing his heroic poem to contain a theme which belonged to the different world of chivalrous epic.

In his management of his poem Camões shows a remarkable independence. If he means to rival Virgil, he knows that it must be in his own way. In particular, he assumes that a poet can state his own opinions, which Virgil hardly ever does explicitly or directly. The sixteenth century accorded a position of honour to a poet and listened with respect to what he had to say; it even expected him to have views on matters of serious and general interest. These might be given implicitly, as Virgil gives his. But the poets of chivalrous epic had evolved a simpler method of speaking in their own persons. By such means Boiardo and Ariosto were able to produce many interesting effects in fanciful arguments on such topics as the faithfulness of wives or the proper uses of dishonesty. They were also able to touch on graver matters,

as when Ariosto rises to noble eloquence in his apostrophe to
the Furies who devastate Italy, or his contrast of the barbarity
of contemporary war with the courtesies of old times. Ariosto
usually sets such passages at the beginning of a canto as a
prelude to what follows. Camões followed this tradition, but
altered its details to suit his different aim. He does not
confine such passages to the beginning of a canto, nor himself
to general reflections. Sometimes he philosophises on general
matters, sometimes he speaks about himself. In particular, he
begins and ends his poem with long addresses to King
Sebastião. In his Introduction of eighteen stanzas he com-
mends his poem to the King. It is a statement of literary
aims as well as an appeal to the King to be proud of his
people's achievements. Its length and elaboration show that
Camões treats his subject with a seriousness unfamiliar in
Ariosto. He underlines the main subjects and the national
qualities of his poem; he shows what kind of an epic he
claims his to be. The Introduction creates expectations of
what is coming and gives the poet's conception of his poem.

In Canto X, Camões closes his poem with lessons to be
learned from it. His advice to the King is tactful and respect-
ful but courageous and clear. He urges him to reduce the
rigour of the laws, to promote experienced men to his Council,
to see that the religious orders keep fasting and discipline and
avoid worldly ambitions, and to look after his army. The
advice, given in this liberal spirit, was needed. The young
King lacked experience and judgment, and he had recently
come under Jesuit advisers who inflamed his natural fanati-
cism. Camões felt so strongly that a poet was the voice of his
nation that he was prepared to risk any displeasure that his
frankness might win for him. He felt that something was
wrong with the Portugal of his day:

> E não sei por que influxo de Destino
> Não tem um ledo orgulho e geral gôsto,
> Que os ânimos levanta de contino
> A ter para trabalhos ledo o rosto.[1]
>
> (x, 146, 1-4)

[1] Nor know I by what fate, or duller chance,
Men have not now that life and general gust
Which made them with a cheerful countenance
Themselves into perpetual action thrust.
(Fanshawe)

He could not but contrast the heroic Portugal of his poem with the actual Portugal that he found on his return from India. Something seemed to be lost, and history justifies him in thinking so. The expense of energy and life in the conquest of India had been too great for a small country, and the high spirit of Gama's generation had vanished. Camões calls on the King to restore it. In his poem he has presented the vast scope of Portuguese heroism and the great parts played by her Kings; it is for King Sebastião to be worthy of his ancestors and to revive the ancient spirit.

For Camões the King of Portugal is more than a national monarch. He rules an empire from the rising to the setting sun, and he, much more than the Emperor or the Most Christian King of France, is the champion of European Christendom:

> Vos, tenro e novo ramo florescente
> De uma árvore, de Cristo mais amada
> Que nenhuma nascida no Ocidente,
> Cesárea ou Cristianíssima chamada.[1]
>
> (I, 7, 1-4)

He is a terror to the heathen who are half ready to submit to him:

> Em vós os olhos tem or Mouro frio,
> Em quem vê seu exício afigurado;
> Só com vos ver, o bárbaro Gentio
> Mostra o pescoço ao jugo já inclinado.[2]
>
> (I, 16, 1-4)

A poem which begins in this spirit and then describes the heroic doings of Portugal in the past must inevitably end on a heroic note. Such was indeed expected by the King. Sebastião believed that he was called to conduct a crusade against the heathen and, after abandoning a project for such

---

[1] You fair and tender blossom of that tree
Belov'd by Him, who died on one for man,
More than whatever Western Majesty
Is styled Most Christian or Caesarean.

(Fanshawe)

[2] On you with fixèd eyes looks the cold Moor,
In whom he reads his ruin prophesied:
The barb'rous Gentile, viewing you, is sure
You'll yoke his neck, and bows it to be tied.

(Fanshawe)

a war in the East, turned his mind to Africa and made his first military reconnaissance on the Moroccan coast. The idea of a crusade was more than welcome to his spiritual advisers, and the King himself dreamed of reviving chivalrous ideals. The Turks were advancing into the heart of a Europe rent by religious wars. No wonder that Sebastião, blessed by the Pope, felt that he had to play his part. So too did Camões. His poem ends with an appeal to the King to take the field in Africa:

> Ou fazendo que, mais que a de Medusa,
> A vista vossa tema o monte Atlante,
> Ou rompendo nos campos de Ampelusa
> Os muros de Marroccos e Trudante.[1]
>
> (x, 156, 1-4)

All influences converged to the same tragic end, and the old imperial Portugal perished in the butchery of Alcazar Kebir. It is the irony of Camões' life that the ideal which he proclaimed and which seemed to be justified by history had outlived its strength. His country had become weaker than even he knew.

Camões' conception of kingship is related to the central idea of his poem. In the Portuguese he sees champions of civilisation and Christianity against the corrupt forces of Islam and barbarism. What this meant to him can be seen in the emphasis which he gives to it in Canto VII when Gama's fleet has just reached Calicut. Once again he develops a theme from Ariosto, who had hoped to find champions of Christendom in Francis I, Maximilian, Charles V and Henry VIII. The unity which he imagined proved a mirage, and when Camões wrote, European Christianity was even more divided. In words of savage irony he rebukes the Germans, among whom Luther's work was beginning to show results, for inventing a new creed and fighting against the Pope instead of against the Turks; the English, whose King claims to be King of Jerusalem but who forgets the celestial Jerusalem and turns his sword against the servants of Christ; the

---

[1] Making Mount Atlas tremble at your sight
More than at that of dire Medusa's head,
Or putting in Amplusian fields to flight
The Moors in Fez and black Morocco bred.
(Fanshawe)

133

French, whose King calls himself " Most Christian " but
who allies himself with the heathen, as Francis I did with
Suleiman the Magnificent against Charles V ; the Italians,
who waste their lives in wealth, pleasure and indolence, and
whose vices make them easy victims of tyranny. Camões'
denunciation of Europe is a criticism of Ariosto's hopes. He
shows how little trust could be placed in these rulers and
their countries. When he wrote, the position was worse than
in Ariosto's time. The Council of Trent in 1563 and the
Massacre of St. Bartholomew in 1572, the year in which
Os Lusiadas was published, were signs of the European
discord. So though not all Camões' complaints are quite
contemporary, they are none the less relevant. In this
discredited European company Portugal alone keeps up the
fight :

> Mas, emtanto que cegos e sedentos
> Andais de vosso sangue, ó gente insana,
> Não faltaram Cristãos atrevimentos
> Nesta pequena casa Lusitana.[1]
>
> (VII, 14, 1-4)

The conviction that his country is the real champion of
Christendom is a driving force in Camões' poem.

Camões desires nothing less than a European crusade
against Islam. Its first object must be to drive the " dogs "
out of the Holy Sepulchre. But he is moved by other aims
than this. He feels compassion for the peoples of the Balkans
and Asia Minor who are under Turkish rule :

> Gregos, Traces, Arménios, Georgianos,
> Bradando vos estão que o povo bruto
> Lhe obriga os caros filhos ao profanos
> Preceptos do Alcorão — duro tributo ![2]
>
> (VII, 13, 1-4)

[1] But whilst, mad people, you refuse to see,
Whilst thirst of your own blood diverts you all,
Christian endeavours shall not wanting be
In this same little house of Portugal.
(Fanshawe)

[2] The Thracian, Georgian, Greek, Armenian
Cry out upon you, that ye let them pay
— Sad tribute ! — to the brutish Alcoran
Their Christian children, to be bred that way.
(Fanshawe)

His real sense of European culture and his love for Greece as its cradle filled him with indignation that these other, hardly less holy, lands should be in the enemy's corrupting grip. He even holds out a worldly bait to the divided peoples of Europe that their efforts will be rewarded by splendid plunder, for the East is full of gold. To this project Camões sees one great obstacle : while Islam is united, Europe is divided. Let it close its ranks, and it will conquer ; for not only is its cause just, but modern inventions are on its side :

> Aqueles invenções, feras e novas,
> De instrumentos mortais da artilharia
> Já devem de fazer as duras provas
> Nos muros de Bizâncio e de Turquia.[1]
>
> (VII, 12, 1-4)

Though it is hard to imagine a return to the spirit of Cœur de Lion or St. Louis in the sixteenth century, and though the discoveries of the explorers had turned men's eyes to worlds remoter than the Levant, Camões was not alone in preaching such a crusade. The Popes approved of it, and the battle of Lepanto in 1571, when Don John of Austria destroyed the Turkish fleet, showed that victory was by no means impossible. If a united crusade had been undertaken in a serious spirit, Eastern Europe might have been saved from three centuries of servitude. The Portuguese might well feel that they at least bore their full share of a European duty when they fought against Islam in Africa. It was their ruin, but there is a tragic magnificence in the intensity of their effort to take on the enemy alone. Camões had reason to be proud of his people, and he was moved by more than merely national pride.

Camões felt and believed that Islam was brutal and bestial. He had for this enemy none of the old chivalrous feelings which had tempered the fanaticism of the mediaeval crusaders. Indeed nothing in his poem is more striking than the low characters and mean motives which he ascribes to the enemies of Portugal. Just as Virgil attributes every trick and treachery

---

[1] That Hellish project of the Iron Age,
Those thunderbolts of war, the cannon-ball,
At Turkish galleys let them spit their rage,
And batter proud Constantinople's wall.
(Fanshawe)

to the Greeks in their war against Troy, so does Camões to
the Moors. From the " base Ishmaelite " of his Introduction
to the Moorish efforts to prevent the Portuguese from leaving
India, he never fails to stress the malign and perfidious
machinations of the enemy. In all this company he makes
only two exceptions, the King of Melinde, and the Moor,
Monçaide, who helps Gama at Calicut. He tactfully passes
over the King's religion, but on Monçaide he is more explicit.
He becomes a Christian and his soul is saved :

> Oh ! Ditoso Africano, que a clemência
> Divina assim tirou de escura treva.[1]
>
> (IX, 15, 5-6)

In Camões' view the only way for a Mahomedan to show
virtue is to help Christians. This is a sign of grace and
deserves praise and gratitude. The qualities which the Moors
display in their several ways and places are united in Bacchus.
Just as the celestial struggle is between him and Venus, so the
struggle on earth is between the cunning followers of the
Prophet and the honest protagonists of Christ. For Camões
the struggle exists, or should exist, in the whole world ; it is
the battle of light and darkness, of truth and falsehood. The
whole history of Portugal from the battle of Ourique to the
victories of João de Castro is meant to illustrate it, and Gama's
voyage should show that the old crusading spirit is still alive
and that it still has heavy tasks before it.

This conception of a European mission and of the need
for a modern heroism is no mere dream. Camões knew what
he was saying and was fully aware not only of what such
ventures cost but of the real objections that can be made to
them. He had himself seen that such successes are won only
at a great price and may often seem not to be worth it. He
had himself suffered from the corrupt agents of Portuguese
imperialism, and his natural love of ease and pleasure often
made him protest against the sufferings and humiliations
which life in the East exacted. At times he pauses to lament
his own misfortunes, and at the end of Canto I he suggests
that they are almost too heavy for him to bear :

[1] O happy African, whom Providence
Divine out of infernal darkness drew.
(Fanshawe)

Onde poder acolher-se um fraco humano,
Onde terá segura a curta vída,
Que não se arme e se indigne o Céu sereno
Contra um bicho da terra tam pequeno ? [1]

(I, 106, 5-8)

His passionate attack at the end of Canto VIII on the corrupt-
ing effects of the desire for money is surely based on his own
experience in the Indies. Camões was not a man to hide his
sorrows, and at times he forces them on our notice in a
sudden outburst of melancholy or complaint. He was
certainly without illusions about what the ideal of empire
meant in practice.

Camões even shows how strong a case can be made against
an endeavour like that of the Portuguese in India. Just as
Adamastor prophesies horrors and disasters, so, when the
fleet is about to sail from the Tagus, an Old Man of venerable
mien cries out upon the whole undertaking and denounces
the vanity of fame and the horrors and cruelties which the
desire for empire breeds. In ten great stanzas he thunders
against the imperial ambition, its cost and its demoralising
influence. Almost every one of his arguments has some force
in it, — that glory is a mirage, that the pretence of spreading
religion brings only more horrors, that the prospect of making
money is largely illusory, that the Ishmaelite will always
prove superior in cunning, that it is madness to seek foes afar
when there are other foes near enough at home, that moral
corruption follows the lust for glory :

Dura inquietação d'alma e da vída,
Fontes de desamparos e adultérios,
Sagaz consumidora conhecida
De fazendas, de reinos e de impérios.[2]

(IV, 96, 1-4)

[1] Where may a frail man hide him ? in what arms
May a short life enjoy a little rest,
Where sea and land, where guile, the sword and dearth
Will not all arm 'gainst the least worm of earth ?

(Fanshawe)

[2] Fell tyrant of the soul ! life's swallowing wave !
Mother of plunder and black rapes unchaste !
The secret miner and the open grave
Of patrimonies, kingdoms, empires vast.

(Fanshawe)

This is no mere rhetorical display. Into it Camões has poured much of his own experience, of the bitterness and disillusion which his lyrical poetry expresses so poignantly. It is the other side of the imperial venture, and its inclusion in the poem adds greatly to its depth and truth. Just as Virgil sets his heroic actions against a background of doubt and uncertainty, so Camões sets his against the misgivings and disillusions which must have assailed both him and many of his contemporaries. These things are true, and he does not deny them. Indeed he throws much of his own feeling into them and gives them the appeal of painful, personal knowledge. But he feels that they are not the whole truth nor the most important part of it. The Portuguese mission justifies its ruinous cost by the qualities which it calls into action and the good that it promises to the world.

Os Lusiadas is in many ways the epic of Humanism. The new vision and the new values which came with the revival of learning found in Camões a poet singularly fitted to sing of them. He is a Humanist even in his contradictions, in his association of a Pagan mythology with a Christian outlook, in his conflicting feelings about war and empire, in his love of home and his desire for adventure, in his appreciation of pleasure and the demands of his heroic outlook. But he is above all a Humanist in his devotion to the classical ideal and in his conviction that this was the living force in the imaginative life of Europe in his time. He equates Portugal both with Christianity and with the classical tradition. The Counter-Reformation and the Inquisition hardly touched him, and such small concessions as he made to them do not affect the character of his work. His poem covers a wide range of experience because it was written by a man who was open to many kinds of impression and had a generous appreciation of human nature. Though he has much of the magnificence of the Renaissance, he tempers it with a taste which always knows when to stop. His conception of manhood is fuller and more various than Virgil's. He has indeed something of Homer's pleasure in the variegated human scene and, like Homer, he knows that there can be more than one kind of noble manhood. Os Lusiadas is a true product of that Europe, Christian and classical, of which Camões was so faithful and so distinguished a son.

IV

TASSO AND THE ROMANCE
OF CHRISTIAN CHIVALRY

In 1575, three years after the publication of *Os Lusiadas*, the Italian poet Torquato Tasso completed his *Gerusalemme Liberata* (*Jerusalem Delivered*) at Ferrara. Though he came to know the work of Camões and to pay a handsome tribute to it, he was not influenced by it, and a comparison of his own poem with it shows how differently two poets in the same age can attempt a similar task with similar aims. Both Tasso and Camões set out to write epic because it was the most honourable and most serious poetry that they knew; both used the same metre, the *ottava rima*, which had been a recognised medium of narrative poetry since the thirteenth century and had won sanction and popularity through Boiardo and Ariosto; both had received an excellent classical education and show many traces of it in their poetry, even to the adaptation of phrases and episodes from ancient poets; both were determined to harmonise the popular art of romantic epic with something closer to the Virgilian model; both wrote a remarkably mellifluous and clear language, though Tasso's Italian, polished and refined by his brilliant predecessors, is more subtle and more sophisticated than Camões' more native Portuguese; both believed that an epic poem should expound an inspiring and noble message and make men conscious of their heroic obligations. The two poems and the two poets inevitably call for comparison, but the more we examine them, the less like they are seen to be. Even when they show undoubted resemblances, these are found on analysis to conceal considerable differences of aim and of temper.

Like Camões, Tasso held that an epic must have a serious purpose, and even a definite lesson, and he agreed that the best purpose for it in his time was to exhort the Christian peoples of Europe to unite in a crusade against the heathen. In dedicating his poem to Alfonso II, Duke of Ferrara, Tasso expresses his hope that such a crusade will soon be begun

and his confidence that Alfonso will take a distinguished part
in it. Later in the poem, when a prophecy foretells the great
deeds of Rinaldo's descendants, of whom Alfonso is one,
Tasso returns to this hope and announces his heartfelt desire
that some day Alfonso will carry the cross and the banner of
Ferrara, with its white bird and golden lilies, beyond the
Nile and the Euphrates and exact a full vengeance from the
heathen :

> Qual ei giusta faria grave vendetta
> Su 'l gran tiranno e su l' iniqua setta ![1]
>
> (XVII, 93, 7-8)

This invocation recalls Camões' summons to King Sebastião
to take up arms against the Moors and his lamentations that
the Holy Land is still in the grip of the infidel. And just as
Camões' history provides a background and an inspiration to
his summons, so Tasso finds his subject in the First Crusade,
when the united princes of Christendom successfully delivered
the Holy Land, and connects the past with the present by
making Alfonso's ancestor, Rinaldo, one of his chief heroes.
So far the aims of the two poets are close, but at this point the
differences emerge. Camões really sees the triumph of
Portugal as the culmination of a long historical process, and
his advocacy of a crusade is based on historical arguments;
Tasso has no such foundation for the crusade which he
advocates. It is dictated by abstract considerations of religion
and morality. In him the literary element predominates over
the historical, the imaginative over the realistic. Even his
conception of West and East, of Christian and infidel, lacks
Camões' clear-cut distinction between them. Tasso wrote
about one crusade because he wished to promote another,
but his whole conception is quite different from Camões'
informed and experienced knowledge.

A second point of comparison between Camões and Tasso
is in their combination of romantic or chivalrous themes with
a Virgilian pattern. Whereas Camões keeps such themes in
control and subordinates them to his main purpose, almost
excluding his human actors from them and using them as a
kind of commentary or relief, Tasso allows them a far greater

---

[1] Oh what revenge, what vengeance, shall he bring
On that false seed and their accursèd king !

(Fairfax)

prominence and mingles them with his main heroic story. In fact, while Camões merely embroiders a Virgilian epic with chivalrous ornaments, Tasso imposes a Virgilian manner and majesty on a mass of chivalrous and romantic material. The result is that the *Gerusalemme* is much more fanciful than *Os Lusiadas*. The greater part played in it by romantic themes gives it quite a different character. Whereas Camões is firmly grounded in history, Tasso moves in a world of his own making which intermingles elements of sober fact with many others of pure invention. For this Tasso's circumstances are largely responsible. It was not for nothing that he wrote at Ferrara, which had for a century been the home of chivalrous epic and whose ducal house had taken pride in giving its patronage to Boiardo, to Ariosto, and to Tasso's own father, Bernardo Tasso, the poet of *Amadigi*. Chivalrous epic had become almost a prerogative of Ferrara, and Tasso was both expected and prepared to provide it. It was on this kind of poetry that he had been nourished; it was these masterpieces that he was expected to follow in the new conditions of his own time. In 1562 Tasso, at the age of eighteen, published at Venice his first attempt at narrative poetry in his *Rinaldo*, an epic in his father's manner on one of Ariosto's heroes. In the *Gerusalemme* he had passed from this imitative stage, but he kept much of the old form, though he treated it with a greater seriousness and with a devout sense of a mission.

These differences between Camões and Tasso are accentuated by others no less important. Tasso lacked Camões' knowledge of the world, and, when he finished the *Gerusalemme*, he was only thirty years old. It is a young man's poem, written out of his dreams and desires rather than out of his experience. For this reason it lacks Camões' firm grip on reality, his realism and his common sense. But what Tasso lacks in experience, he makes up in lyrical intensity. Camões, who was a great lyric poet, curbed his lyrical impulses in his epic, no doubt in order to give to it the objectivity which he thought proper to the form. But Tasso approaches and interprets his subject in a lyrical spirit. He feels for his characters as if they were projections of himself; he sets on their lips words of purely lyrical emotion which seem to rise from his own heart; he describes scenes and situations with

all the affectionate delight of imaginative youth; he gives
far more space to speeches than Virgil or Camões does,
perhaps because through them he can find an outlet for his
emotional and exuberant temperament. The result is that
the *Gerusalemme* has an extraordinary intensity and brilliance.
It is much more personal than *Os Lusiadas* or even than the
Aeneid. Though Tasso hardly ever refers to himself or
attempts to interpose his own comments or reflections, as
Camões often does, his effect is remarkably intimate. He has
so imposed his tastes on his story and created such a world of
his own that the *Gerusalemme* gives a pleasure akin to that of
lyric poetry. Tasso poured his dreams and fancies into it
when he was in the full flush of early manhood and at the
zenith of his creative powers. His ardent and passionate
character needed full scope to express itself, and it is fortunate
that he could find this in the epic.

This dissimilarity between the two poets is matched by a
difference in their circumstances. Camões spent much of his
creative life in distant countries and in exacting conditions;
he was a man of the world who knew the brutal facts of life.
Tasso wrote the greater part of the *Gerusalemme* at the court
of Ferrara. His state was not affluent, but he lived in courtly
circles, and his poem was intended for them. They affected
its character as they affected Tasso's own. When he wrote,
Ferrara typified the peculiar state of northern Italian culture
in the triumph of the Counter-Reformation. On the one hand
the free spirit of the Renaissance, with its ideal of the fully
realised individual, was curbed both by the revival of religion
and by unanswerable facts of politics. It was no longer
permissible to combine Christianity with such speculations as
the preceding century had enjoyed, and it was humiliatingly
clear that no Italian state could resist either French invasion
or Spanish domination. On the other hand Ferrara still
maintained the high style of an earlier day and kept up the
external magnificence of the Renaissance. It might lack both
political power and freedom of thought, but it pretended to
be its own master and to have a proud place in the world. In
its imaginative life this pretence was of vital importance. A
poet at Ferrara must pay his tribute to it and keep up the
illusion of grandeur. Indeed the stern facts only made the
imaginative compensation the greater and created an atmo-

sphere of make-believe which found a satisfying outlet in masques and pageants and poetry. Whatever the rulers might really think about the religious or the political situation, they did not expect their poets to discuss it. They preferred them to write as if nothing had happened and as if Italy were still what she was before the French and Spanish invasions or the rise of the Inquisition.

To this situation Tasso responded in a special way. He was a product both of the Counter-Reformation and of court life at Ferrara. In his boyhood he was educated by the Jesuits and received from them not only the classical training which later he turned to such profit but the religious instruction which made him a devout Catholic, anxious not to offend the rules of the Church and far more conscious of what his faith demanded than ever Camões was. If, for instance, his life had been spent in Rome or in any of the Papal territories, he might never have turned his thoughts to chivalry but have written more poetry like his own *Mondo Creato* which described the creation of the world and owed nothing to romantic precedents. But he lived in Ferrara, and chivalry was forced on his attention and found a ready advocate in him. The paradox of his situation and of his character is that while in his religion he was a man of his own times, in his imagination he was a survival from an earlier age, the last member of a poetical dynasty which wrote chivalrous poetry; and like other such survivals, his feeling for the tradition which he inherited was one of romantic devotion. The composition of an epic in the succession of Boiardo and Ariosto made great demands on him and intensified an inner contradiction in him. For while the *Orlando Furioso* belongs to a world of pure art and has no direct relations with actuality, Tasso could not divorce his poem from religion and morality. If one half of him sought a refuge and a solace in pure fancy, the other half insisted that this fancy must be related to something true and edifying. In the *Gerusalemme* each half has its say, and the result is a poem which is consciously and conscientiously Catholic in the spirit of Tasso's own time but is also romantic and chivalrous in the spirit of 1500.

The *Gerusalemme* is a Christian epic not merely in its subject and its exhortation to a crusade but in many of its episodes and in much of its sentiment. The opening lines proclaim its subject :

> Canto l' armi pietose e il Capitano
> . Che il gran sepolcro liberò di Cristo.[1]
>
> (I, I, I-2)

This is not the spirit in which Ariosto proclaims all the delights of chivalrous epic :

> Le donne, i cavallier, l' arme, gli amori,
> Le cortesie, l' audaci imprese io canto.[2]
>
> (O.F. I, I, I-2)

Nor is it the spirit of *Os Lusiadas*, which opens on a patriotic note about the great men and the great doings of Portugal. Both Tasso's hero and his story are emphatically Christian. He writes not about a country but a cause, and his chief figure is memorable by what he did for that cause. Nor does Tasso ever quite forget his Christian purpose. Sometimes he seems to wander away from it, but he always returns to it, especially in moments of crisis and decision. His Crusaders fight for the Cross, and when they die for it, they are honoured as heroic martyrs, as Goffredo honours Dudone :

> Vivesti qual guerrier cristiano e santo,
> E come tal sei morto ; or godi e pasci
> In Dio gli occhi bramosi, o felice alma,
> Ed hai del ben oprar corona e palma.[3]
>
> (III, 68, 5-8)

Camões sometimes strikes such a note, but only rarely, and with him the conception of the Christian warrior is identified with that of the patriotic Portuguese. Tasso clears the issue and makes it plain that his soldiers fight for a single cause,

---

[1] The sacred armies, and the godly knight
That the great sepulchre of Christ did free.
(Fairfax)

[2] Of loves and ladies, knights and arms, I sing,
Of courtesies and many a daring feat.
(W. S. Rose)

[3] For like a Christian knight and champion blest
Thou didst both live and die ; now feed thine eyes
With thy Redeemer's sight, where crowned with bliss
Thy faith, zeal, merit, well-deserving is.
(Fairfax)

which is their religion, and gain from this a special glory. It is therefore right and appropriate that his poem should end with Goffredo offering prayers in the captured Temple of Jerusalem.

This Christian and Catholic character of the *Gerusalemme* comes out clearly in Tasso's handling of Pietro, — Peter the Hermit, — who inspired and started the First Crusade. He does not play a large part, but whatever he does, is decisive. It is he who furthers the divine decision that Goffredo shall command the army and calls for obedience in words which not only echo the need for a united Christendom against the heathen but show the hierarchical view of society as the Church has always advocated it :

> Deh ! fate un corpo sol de' membri amici ;
> Fate un capo, che gli altri indrizzi e frene ;
> Date ad un sol lo scettro e la possanza,
> E sostenga di re vece e sembianza.[1]
>
> (I, 31, 5-8)

Before the assault on Jerusalem he shows the real meaning of the undertaking when he chides Goffredo for considering only the military aspects of the situation :

> Tu movi, o Capitan, l' armi terrene ;
> Ma di là non cominci onde conviene,[2]
>
> (XI, 1, 7-8)

and urges him to make the whole army first attend Mass. When Rinaldo returns from his amorous adventure with Armida, Goffredo, who represents the temporal power, is content to accept his apologies, but Pietro urges Rinaldo to make confession and gives him absolution. Pietro always speaks with authority and can be stern as when he reproves Rinaldo for his faults and tells him that only divine Grace can purify him :

---

[1] Of friendly parts one body then uphold,
Create one head, the rest to rule and guide ;
To one the regal power and sceptre give,
That henceforth may your king and sovereign live.
(Fairfax)

[2] Right well, my lord, these earthly strengths you move,
But let us first begin from Heaven above. (Fairfax)

Chè sei de la caligine del mondo
E de la carne tu di modo asperso,
Che il Nilo o il Gange o l' Ocean profondo
Non ti potrebbe far candido e terso.[1]

(XVIII, 8, 1-4)

Pietro is the spiritual director and the father-confessor of the Crusaders and shows what part Tasso thought a priest should take in the military life. In the last resort Pietro's word is final.

The sentiment which gives this importance to Pietro inspires Tasso to a truly devout poetry, and two passages show how he brings this unfamiliar element into the epic. The first is in Canto XI when Goffredo, on Pietro's advice, orders High Mass to be held for the army. It begins with a procession in which all the priests are arrayed in full vestments ; Pietro carries the cross, and behind him comes the army in procession, the choir singing hymns and Goffredo walking alone while the others follow in pairs. Tasso gives the matter of the chants, which includes the Trinity, the Church, the Apostles and the Martyrs. While the heathen look on amazed from the walls of Jerusalem or cry out blasphemously, the sacrament is taken on the Mount of Olives, where an altar has been erected with candles in golden candlesticks. After the benediction the army returns to camp, refreshed and ready for the battle. The whole ceremony, so happily and so devoutly described, is characteristic of the Counter-Reformation which by making its ritual more varied and more attractive tried to win some of the crowds and the interest which belonged to secular masques and pageants. A second example of this spirit is when Rinaldo makes confession of his sins. Before dawn he goes out alone to the same Mount of Olives and sees the stars above him. He kneels and asks God for forgiveness, and as he prays, the dawn comes. Nature responds to the situation in Rinaldo's soul. When he goes out, the darkness has not yet gone, but there are the first signs of light :

[1] The world, the flesh, with their infection vile
Pollute thy thoughts impure, thy spirit stain ;
Not Ganges, not the seven-mouthèd Nile,
Nor the wide seas, can wash thee clean again.
(After Fairfax)

Quinci notturne e quindi mattutine
Bellezze incorruttibili e divine.[1]
(XVIII, 12, 7-8)

Then when he confesses and light comes, the change marks
the change in him. As the rising day sheds its light on his
helmet and armour, he feels its refreshing breath :

E ventilar nel petto e ne la fronte
Sentia gli spirti di piacevol ôra.[2]
(XVIII, 15, 5-6)

There is nothing factitious in this ; it is simply and sincerely
devout. Tasso creates a special poetry for the brave man who
does penance and frees himself from his burden of guilt.

Tasso weaves this religious spirit into his plot with some
skill. It is not enough for the story that Pietro should merely
assert eternal truths or shrive sinners ; so Tasso fits him into
the ancient mould of the prophet who plays a part in most
epics. Prophecy is needed both because it links up the heroic
past with the present and because it gives an air of pre-
destined inevitability to important actions. When the knights
who have followed Armida return and tell how Rinaldo
rescued them, his own fate is still a mystery. The chief
warrior of the Christian army is lost, and no one knows if he
is alive or dead. But Pietro turns his eyes to heaven, and
a holy light shines in his face :

Pieno di Dio, ratto dal zelo, accanto
A le angeliche menti ei si conduce :
Gli si svela il futuro, e ne l' eterna
Serie de gli anni e de l' età s' interna.[3]
(X, 73, 5-8)

Divinely inspired, he knows not only that Rinaldo is alive and
a woman's thrall, but that heaven is saving him for a noble

[1] On this side night, on that the morning's shine
With beauty incorruptible, divine.

[2] Upon his breast, upon his forehead then
He felt the breath of that delightful hour.

[3] Ravished with zeal his soul approachèd near
The seat of angels pure, and saints divine,
And there he learned of things and haps to come,
To give foreknowledge true, and certain doom.
(Fairfax)

147

destiny and that his descendants will be champions of the
Church. Later, when Goffredo is deeply perplexed by the
enchanted wood, Pietro again prophesies words of comfort.
He knows that the task of breaking the evil magic awaits
Rinaldo, who will return and take Jerusalem. And again the
Hermit's voice and appearance show that he is inspired :

> Parla ei così, fatto di fiamma in volto,
> E risuona più ch' uomo in sue parole.[1]
>
> (XIII, 52, 1-2)

Pietro has the part of a prophet and shows the outward signs
in his face and speech ; in the action he does what Virgil's
oracles and seers do for Aeneas. But the whole part has been
so recast that the prophet is really a man of God.

His religious beliefs created a special problem for Tasso
when he came, according to precedent, to provide the divine
machinery of his poem. Camões' use of pagan divinities was
out of the question. Neither the Holy Office nor Tasso's own
conscience would have allowed it. He adopted the only
alternative, which was to present the God and angels of his
own faith in such a way as to help the story without bringing
them into discredit. His God starts the action by sending
Gabriel to Goffredo with orders to march against Jerusalem ;
when Raimondo prays for help in his battle with Argante, his
prayer is answered, and a guardian angel comes to help him ;
when the battle turns against the Crusaders, God sends
Michael to turn back the infernal hosts who are fighting for
the infidels ; when Goffredo sees his army perishing for lack
of water, and prays for rain, God answers his prayer ; God
even sends him a dream telling him to recall Rinaldo ; in the
last battle Michael appears to Goffredo and shows to him the
celestial hosts fighting on his side. Tasso's God and angels
do very much what the gods of epic usually do. Sometimes
they follow Homeric or Virgilian precedents, as when God
nods in the manner of Homer's Zeus :

> Così dicendo, il capo mosse ; e gli ampi
> Cieli tremaro, e i lumi erranti, e i fissi ;

---

[1] This said, his visage shone with beams divine,
And more than mortal was his voice's sound.
(Fairfax)

148

> E tremò l' aria riverente, e i campi
> De l' oceàno, e i monti, e i ciechi abissi.[1]
>
> (XIII, 74, 1-4)

But usually the literary precedent is accommodated to Christian belief. God answers prayers, even for rain ; his angels are real ministers of help ; Goffredo's dream enforces its practical instructions with noble words on the nature of true glory. Tasso clothes his heavenly figures with all the colour and brightness that he can give them and uses especially the old religious symbols of height and light. His God dwells. in the highest heaven :

> E quanto è da le stelle al basso inferno,
> Tanto è più in su de la stellata spera,[2]
>
> (I, 7, 5-6)

and Michael comes through the night like the sun piercing the clouds :

> Tale il Sol ne le nubi ha per costume
> Spiegar dopo la pioggia i bei colori.[3]
>
> (IX, 62, 5-6)

Tasso's angels reflect the imaginative vision of many Italian painters and are, no doubt, much what he thought angels to be when they appear to men. But behind them he sees something more radiant, a heaven of light and song and harmony :

> D' intorno ha innumerabili immortali,
> Disegualmente in lor letizia eguali.[4]
>
> (IX, 57, 7-8)

It is this that Goffredo is permitted for a moment to see in a dream ; he learns of the living flame which fills it :

[1] At these high words great heaven began to shake,
The fixèd stars, the planets wandering still,
Trembled the air, the earth and ocean quake,
Spring, fountain, river, forest, dale and hill.
(Fairfax)

[2] As far above the clear stars every one
As it is hence up to the highest star.
(Fairfax)

[3] After a storm so spreadeth forth the sun
His rays and binds the clouds in golden strings.
(Fairfax)

[4] On every side the blessèd spirits be,
Equal in joys, though differing in degree.
(Fairfax)

> Questi lucidi alberghi e queste vive
> Fiamme che mente eterna informa e gira.[1]
>
> (XIV, 9, 3-4)

Though Tasso lacks Dante's enthralling and exact vision of a celestial world, he has at least a substitute for it in his place of light and flame. He has a real conviction that angelic powers move in the world and that a heavenly host;

> Milizia innumerabile ed alata[2], (XVIII, 96, 4)

fights for the good.

Against these bright figures, who support the Crusaders, Tasso sets the hosts of Hell, who support the infidels. The literary ancestry of his devils may be found in Vida, Dante, and Claudian, but they would be real enough to men of his time who would have formed their notions of such beings from paintings of the Last Judgment and other subjects in which Italian artists had for centuries indulged their grotesque and macabre fancies. Tasso's method has its advantages. His devils were once angels, but they are so corrupted and ruined that they have lost all their original brightness and become

> Gorgons and Hydra's and Chimera's dire.

Such monsters have none of the ambiguity which has caused so much trouble with Milton's Satan. Perhaps to us they are a little unreal and unconvincing, but no monster is very real to a scientific age, and devils have lost much of their old status. Tasso at least spent care and imagination on them. They are summoned by a trumpet that sounds through Hell:

> Chiama gli abitator de l' ombre eterne
> Il rauco suon de la tartarea tromba:
> Treman le spazïose atre caverne,
> E l' aer cieco a quel romor rimbomba.[3]
>
> (IV, 3, 1-4)

They take their seats on red-hot thrones of brass. The chief

[1] Those shining dwellings, and those living flames
Which everlasting mind informs and turns.

[2] Innumerable armies on the wing.

[3] The dreary trumpet blew a dreadful blast
And rumbled through the lands and kingdoms under;
Through wasteness wide it roared, and hollows vast,
And filled the deep with horror, fear and wonder.

(Fairfax)

of them is indeed formidable, with his eyes like an evil comet and his mouth dripping with blood, and his hideous exterior is matched by a nature no less hideous. The chief characteristic of Tasso's devils is their desire to regain their lost honours. They cannot forget that they have been driven out of heaven, and for this reason they hate God, His Son and mankind. Now they are afraid that their altars will be destroyed by the Crusaders, and therefore they take the side of the infidels and are ready to do any damage or destruction that will prevent the capture of Jerusalem. They are personifications of malice, envy and hatred. Perhaps Tasso himself believed that devils were like this. When in the years after the completion of the *Gerusalemme* his mind became disordered, he was a prey to dark fancies and believed that he was condemned to Hell and heard God saying " Depart, ye accursed into everlasting fire ". The roots of this hallucination may have lain in his early training, and it is possible that he was always haunted by a terror of devils and of Hell. If so, the monsters of the *Gerusalemme* are far from being symbols or inventions; they are reflections of something that lay deep in Tasso's being.

These devils play their part in the poem. After their first council they break loose over the earth and start the chain of events which ends in Armida's attempt to corrupt and divide the Crusaders; the fiend, Aletto, who comes in name and in character from the *Aeneid* but is well acclimatised to her new circumstances, starts troubles in the Christian camp when it is thought that Rinaldo has been treacherously killed, and later excites the Soldan Solimano to take up arms against the Crusaders. The devils take part in the action when they obey the summons of the magician, Ismeno, to haunt the wood where Goffredo intends to cut trees for his siege-engines, and prevent his warriors from passing through it by frightening displays of magic. They help the infidels in battle until God sends Michael to rout them and they retreat to Hell. Their work may be seen in the sulphurous fumes with which Ismeno defends the walls of Jerusalem and which hold up the attack until the wind changes and blows them back on their users. But though the actions of these devils have a supernatural character, which few men in the sixteenth century would have thought strange, Tasso on the whole

makes them work by natural means and through human
agents. Armida's kinsman, Idraote, welcomes their plan to
divide the Christians and acts upon it, but they do no more
than appeal to thoughts and desires which are already active
in him :

> In questo suo pensier il sovraggiunge
> L' angelo iniquo, e più l' istiga e punge.[1]
>
> (IV, 22, 7-8)

The appearance of Aletto as a grave greybeard to Solimano is
effective, because Solimano is already eager to win glory by
defeating the Christians. The devils who fight for the infidels
help them chiefly by strengthening their fury and desperation.
These devils are powers of evil, but they usually work in a
familiar and accepted way by appealing to the base desires
of their victims. They provide such obstacles as Camões'
Bacchus provides to Gama, but, since they belong to religious
belief, they are not allegorical or symbolical. In their motives
and their actions they have the reality which belongs to old-
established creatures of fancy and of conscience.

The war in which God and His angels take one side and
the devils take the other is a crusade, and Tasso was fully
persuaded that such a task was among the highest that men
could undertake. It calls for great qualities of devotion,
perseverance, obedience and courage ; it is a mission that can
be carried out only by unflinching resolve. What Italy is to
Aeneas, Jerusalem is to the Crusaders, and it is no accident
that when they greet their first sight of the city,

> Ecco apparir Gerusalem si vede,
> Ecco additar Gerusalem si scorge ;
> Ecco da mille voci unitamente
> Gerusalemme salutar si sente,[2]
>
> (III, 3, 5-8)

Tasso's words recall Virgil's when Aeneas' company first
sees Italy :

---

[1] At hand was Satan, ready ere men need,
If once they think, to make them do, the deed.
(Fairfax)

[2] Jerusalem, behold, appeared in sight,
Jerusalem they view, they see, they spy,
Jerusalem with merry shout they greet,
With joyful shouts and acclamations sweet.
(Fairfax)

Italiam primus conclamat Achates,
Italiam laeto socii clamore salutant.[1]
(III, 523-4)

Tasso catches the authentic spirit of Virgil when he makes
his epic turn on a quest for what seems almost an ideal goal.
It is true that Jerusalem, like Italy, is a real place and that after
many hazards it is reached, but both the quest and the goal
have a special significance. The effort to take Jerusalem is a
test of Christian manhood as Aeneas' efforts are of Roman
virtus, and the final success is a sign that, after all, the right
qualities have been shown and the right steps taken. The
mixed fortunes of the Crusaders are the ordeal through which
they pass and in which their worth is tested and strengthened.
They are by no means faultless, and much of the delay is due
to their own errors. The desires which Armida inflames in
them not only rob the army of some of its best soldiers but
lead to the killing of Gernando by Rinaldo and to Rinaldo's
choice of exile for himself rather than punishment. When
later the Crusaders think that Rinaldo is murdered, they turn
on Goffredo and threaten him, and only his courage saves a
desperate situation. In a time of drought the spirit of sus-
picion and disobedience again turns on the general, and he
is saved only by his trust in God. The dangers and trials of
the Crusaders are comparable to those of Aeneas, and like
his, they rise in men's own hearts. But these trials are an
essential part of the whole process. By overcoming them the
Crusaders become fit to take Jerusalem. The moral is pointed
out by the Sage to Rinaldo and his companions when they
return from Armida and prepare to join the battle. To him
Tasso gives a version of some famous words of Simonides,
who said that Virtue dwells on rocks hard to climb, and the
new version of the old theme contrasts the life of effort with
the life of pleasure in a way which sums up the spirit of the
Crusade as Tasso understands it :

Signor, non sotto l' ombra in piaggia molle
Tra fonti e fior, tra Ninfe e tra Sirene,
Ma in cima a l' erto e faticoso colle
De la virtù riposto è il nostro bene.

[1] First " Italy ! " Achates cries,
    All with glad clamour cry out " Italy ! "

L

Chi non gela, e non suda, e non s' estolle
De le vie del piacer, là non perviene.
Or vorrai tu lungi da l' alte cime
Giacer, quasi tra valli augel sublime.[1]

(XVII, 61, 1-8)

Tasso gives a new character to the old ideal. His Sage tells Rinaldo that he can win the prize only if he turns his thoughts to Heaven ; he will then be strong in battle against the enemy and not waste his strength in disputes with his own companions. From his classical source Tasso draws a moral which needs little adaptation to fit his Christian soldier.

The war, which should be fought in this spirit, is as real as Tasso can make it. He lived in an age when soldierly prowess was much prized, and he himself, though no soldier, was an accomplished swordsman and horseman and admired the qualities which make a man formidable in battle. Unlike Virgil, he knew too little of war to feel all its horror, and, unlike Boiardo and Ariosto, he did not treat it as unreal and entertaining. He had indeed too little experience of it to write about it with Camões' first-hand knowledge, but he knew something of the use of arms and had learned about battles from books and from the society of soldiers. Considering his handicap, his accounts of fighting are remarkably lively, and even convincing. They may not be history but they are good story-telling. Tasso's warfare follows neither historical records nor the practice of his own time ; it is his own invention, based on the *Aeneid*, on Livy and on chivalrous epic. But this imagined world has its own coherence and verisimilitude. The first assault on Jerusalem, the night attack on the Christian camp, the building and the destruction of siege-engines, the part played by the spy Vafrino who knows Syriac and Egyptian and disguises himself beyond recognition even by his friends, the use of carrier pigeons between the relieving Egyptian army and the beleaguered

---

[1] Not underneath sweet shades and fountains shrill,
Among the nymphs, the fairies, leaves and flowers ;
But on the steep, the rough and craggy hill
Of Virtue stands this bliss, this good of ours ;
By toil and travail, not by sitting still
In pleasure's lap we come to honour's bowers ;
Why will you thus in sloth's deep valley lie ?
The royal eagles on high mountains fly.

(Fairfax)

Saracens, the elephants and dromedaries of the Egyptian army, the final and successful breach of the city walls, and the hand-to-hand fighting in the city, are all circumstantial, exciting and vigorous. Tasso knows how to describe a single combat, whether on horse or on foot, and gives a truly dramatic thrill in the last encounter between Tancredi and Argante; he can describe the chaos, the horrors and the excitements of a general encounter; he takes care to make the plan of campaign convincing, maps the terrain, points out the weak spots in the defence, appreciates the need of supplies and of good communications, and tells with great effect the appalling horrors of drought in eastern lands. His account of the war may bear little relation to what really happened, but it has its own reality and shows what care and thought Tasso gave to it.

In such a war the chief characters on the Christian side have a complex part to play. The epic form demands that they should be convincing as human beings and impressive as warriors, but the Christian purpose demands something more: they must illustrate, either in success or failure, various aspects of the Christian life. Tasso does not follow Virgil's example in concentrating his whole ideal of manhood on almost a single character. His leading crusaders are well differentiated and in their several ways equally lively. His method is that of Homer, who sets a mixed company on both sides in his Trojan War and portrays different types of heroic manhood in Achilles, Hector, Ajax and Odysseus. But just as Agamemnon is Homer's central figure, so Tasso's Goffredo is the axis round which the other characters revolve, and is himself the clearest portrait of a Christian soldier. His dominating characteristic is that he lives entirely for his task:

> E pien di fè, di zelo, ogni mortale
> Gloria, impero, tesor mette in non cale.[1]
>
> (1, 8, 7-8)

For this reason God chooses him to lead the army, and the army welcomes him as its leader. Goffredo receives divine help, not only through the hermit Pietro and a dream sent by God but from the archangel Michael in battle. Sustained by

---

[1] And full of zeal and faith esteemèd light
All wordly honour, empire, treasure, might.
(Fairfax)

such help, he carries out his task in a noble, uncomplaining spirit. His direction of the war shows his capacity for leadership, foresight and control of unruly subordinates. His position often demands that he should act in a way that he himself dislikes, as when he imposes his authority on Rinaldo for killing Gernando or sends Argillano to prison for fomenting sedition. In the dark hours of crisis he behaves with great courage and dignity, as when he faces the malcontents alone and unarmed or endures all the suspicions and hatred which rise against him when the army suffers from lack of water. In battle he is among the bravest and takes an important part in the final assault. Though he resembles Aeneas in the weight of his responsibilities and in his submission to divine guidance, he has little of Aeneas' melancholy or indecision. He is a full man at the start, and such he remains.

Since Goffredo is the commander of a Christian army, his task has a special character. He is not a knight of the old kind who can pursue prowess to his heart's content. His duty is to command his army and to conduct the campaign. His heroism is limited by his position, and from Tasso's point of view this is right. It is made clear by the dream which God sends to Goffredo to tell him that the actual capture of Jerusalem must be left to Rinaldo:

> A te le prime parti, a lui concesse
> Son le seconde ; tu sei capo, ei mano
> Di questo campo ; e sostener sua vece
> Altri non puote, e farlo a te non lece.[1]
>
> (XIV, 13, 5-8)

Since Goffredo's sphere is thus defined, he is wrong when, even with the best of reasons, he yields to any consideration but his command of the army and what is required for victory. For instance, when Armida comes to him and inflames his warriors with a false tale of injured innocence, Goffredo is less touched than the others by her and his first decision is that his conditions do not allow him to help her. In this he is right, but he allows his decision to be overruled,

---

[1] The first is thine, the second place is his,
Thou art this army's head, and he the hand ;
No other champion can his place supply,
And that thou do it doth thy state deny.

(Fairfax)

and disasters follow. His natural courtesy and respect for
the feelings of his officers impair his judgment and make him
forget that his first and only task is to lead the army against
Jerusalem. Again, when the attack on the city is being
prepared, Goffredo means to conduct it in person and clothes
himself suitably for the assault, until he is stopped by
Raimondo, who points out that the risk is too great for a
commander-in-chief to take :

> L' anima tua, mente del campo e vita,
> Cautamente, per Dio, sia custodita.[1]
> (XI, 22, 7-8)

Goffredo has such responsibilities that he must subordinate
everything to them, even his own feelings of courtesy and his
natural desire to be in the forefront of the battle.

Of the other crusaders Tancredi and Rinaldo are the most
important. They derive their chief interest from their loves
and romantic adventures, but in battle they play their parts
and throw some light on Tasso's conception of Christian
chivalry. Tancredi embodies the courtly virtues and might
have been modelled on Baldassare Castiglione's famous book,
Il Cortegiano (*The Courtier*). No one has a better style or a
nobler heart than he :

> O più bel di maniere e di sembianti,
> O più eccelso ed intrepido di core.[2]
> (I, 45, 3-4)

When his comrade Rinaldo is in danger of punishment for
killing Gernando, Tancredi stands up for him and pleads
that such a noble cannot be treated like a common soldier.
He is singularly free from envy or resentment and bears
patiently with the harsh treatment that he has received from
Baldovino. He is a fine swordsman, and his greatest feats
are in single combat, whether against Argante or Rambaldo
or Clorinda. Reflective in the face of danger, as when he
comes to Armida's castle, his reflection never impedes his
will or hampers his forcefulness in action. He shows courtesy

[1] Your happy life is spirit, soul and breath
Of all this camp ; preserve it then from death.
(Fairfax)

[2] With majesty his noble countenance shone.
High were his thoughts, his heart was bowed in vigour.
(Fairfax)

and generosity even to his victim and his enemies. When Erminia is his prisoner at Antioch, he respects her womanhood and her rank and leaves her in the enjoyment of her position ; he twice offers mercy to Argante in his last fight with him and, unlike Achilles, demands that his enemy's corpse be properly buried. Though he is badly wounded, he insists on being carried into Jerusalem, since he has taken a vow that he will die there, and once there he takes command of troops abandoned by their own leader. Behind the courtier and the crusader is the soldier who shrinks from no danger and who, when his martial temper is aroused, is indeed formidable. After offering Argante his life and hearing his offers refused, he kills him with relentless fury :

> Poi la spada gli fisse e gli rifisse
> Ne la visiera, ove accertò la via.[1]
>
> (XIX, 26, 3-4)

In Tancredi Tasso presents the ideal of the courtier and soldier as it was cultivated at Ferrara.

Rinaldo differs from Tancredi in being not a courtier but a romantic adventurer. When he is fifteen years old, he hears

> La tromba che s' udia da l' Orïente,[2]   (I, 59, 8)

and he travels alone in remote lands until he joins the Crusade at the age of eighteen. In his independence, his sense of personal honour, and his youthful ardour, he is an uneasy subordinate. He cannot endure insults, and in his high temper he kills Gernando. His pride prevents him from accepting punishment, and it is characteristic of him that he goes off alone to seek adventure in foreign lands :

> Gir fra' nemici ; ivi o cipresso o palma
> Acquistar per la fede ond' è campione ;
> Scorrer l' Egitto, e penetrar sin dove
> Fuor d' incognito fonte il Nilo muove.[3]
>
> (V, 52, 5-8)

But this difficult temper has in it the makings of great heroism.

---

[1] Therewith he thrust and thrust again his blade,
And through his ventil pierced his dazzled eyes.   (Fairfax)

[2] The trumpet sounding from the Orient.

[3] To go among his foes, and win or palm
Or cypress for the faith he champions,
To pass through Egypt and beyond and go
Where undiscovered the Nile's waters flow.

Even before his departure Rinaldo has shown that he is the best of the Crusaders in battle, and when he returns, spiritually strengthened and reformed, he performs prodigies of valour. He leaps on the wall of Jerusalem, attacks the door of the temple, and in his assault on the Egyptian army does things

> Incredibili, orrende, e mostruose.[1] (xx, 54, 8)

So swift is his handling of his sword that he seems to have three swords in his hand, and where he goes, there is not so much battle as slaughter. It is he who kills the formidable Adrasto and the Soldan Solimano. Rinaldo is the crusader who comes nearest to being a hero in the old sense. He has the heroic pride and sense of honour, but in him these are eventually curbed and disciplined until they are turned to the use of his Christian cause, although they lose none of their fierceness in the actual fighting.

Against these figures Tasso sets his infidels. Their real leader is the Soldan Solimano, for whom Tasso shows much of the respect in which the historical Crusaders held such opponents as Saladin. Indeed Tasso may have had Saladin in his mind when he created Solimano; for he makes him an ancestor of Saladin and hear from the magician Ismeno of his descendant's power and gallantry. Solimano is an incarnation of warlike pride and determination. He shows his spirit when, deserted and discomfited in battle, he refuses to give in:

> Veggia il nemico le mie spalle e scherna
> Di novo ancora il nostro esilio indegno ;
> Purchè di novo armato indi mi scerna
> Turbar sua pace e il non mai stabil regno.
> Non cedo io, no : fia con memoria eterna
> De le mie offese eterno anco il mio sdegno.
> Risorgerò nemico ognor più crudo,
> Cenere anco sepolto e spirto ignudo.[2]
>
> (IX, 99, 1-8)

---

[1] Things wondrous, strange, incredible he wrought.   (Fairfax)

[2] Let Godfrey view my flight, and smile to see
This mine unworthy second banishment,
For armed again soon shall he hear of me,
From his proud head the unsettled crown to rent ;
For as my wrongs, my wrath etern shall be,
At every hour the bow of war new bent ;
I will arise again, a foe, fierce, bold,
Though dead, though slain, though burnt to ashes cold. (Fairfax)

Solimano is singularly lacking in guile or treachery; he prefers an open fight to anything else and is as fine a soldier as any on the Christian side. His pride refuses to admit that he can be defeated and his own actions almost justify his claims. In the attack on the Christian camp he does prodigies of valour, as when he kills Argillano with a single stroke through shield, helmet and head down to the throat. He takes command of a dispirited populace when he enters Jerusalem secretly by night, and hears disparaging talk about himself without resentment. He is ready to do all that is asked of him and to be relentless in his treatment of cowards and traitors. When the Christians attack the city, he is foremost in the defence, and even when they break in, he maintains a desperate resistance. He even shows a tender, human side when he weeps for the death of Lesbino and is for a moment unable to continue the fight:

> Tu piangi, Soliman? tu che distrutto
> Mirasti il regno tuo col ciglio asciutto?[1]
>
> (IX, 86, 7-8)

It might almost be said that Solimano's only fault is that he is a pagan. Tasso has not Camões' deep distrust of all heathen as such, and his Solimano has many virtues which would do honour to a Crusader. But because he is a pagan and lacks any supernatural help except from devils, he collapses at the last. When he is confronted by Rinaldo, we expect him to put up a defiant and desperate resistance, but Tasso gives him a different end. He, who has been so active and courageous, fails. Like Turnus, he resembles a frustrated figure in a dream. Something has gone out of him:

> Ma non conosce in sè le solite ire,
> Nè sè conosce a la scemata forza.
> Quante scintille in lui sorgon d' ardire,
> Tante un secreto suo terror n' ammorza.[2]
>
> (XX, 106, 3-6)

[1] Thou weepest, Soliman, thou that beheld
Thy kingdoms lost, and not one tear could yield.
(Fairfax)

[2] Yet felt not in himself his courage old,
His wonted force, his rage, and hot desire;
His eyes that sparkled wrath and fury bold
Grew dim and feeble; fear had quenched their fire.
(Fairfax)

He collapses almost without resistance and dies. It is as if in the last resort the formidable pagan who lacks divine help must inevitably be defeated by his Christian opponent.

If Solimano represents infidel power and magnificence, Argante represents infidel courage and pride. Into him Tasso has put something of Virgil's Mezentius; he is

> Impaziente, inesorabil, fero,
> Ne l' arme infaticabile ed invitto,
> D' ogni Dio sprezzator, e che ripone
> Ne la spada sua legge e sua ragione.[1]
> (II, 59, 5-8)

He shows his lack of chivalry when he accepts a sword from Goffredo and says that the Christians will soon learn to what uses he can put it. He is rudely critical of his own leaders, as when he chides Aladino for his inactive conduct of the war. He is devoured by a desire for glory and is confident that the war can be settled by a single combat between himself and some leading Christian champion. He will not tolerate that anyone else should take his place in action or danger; he will not even allow Clorinda to go out alone to destroy the enemy's siege-tower. He exults over his defeated foes, as over Ottone, whose life he contemptuously spares:

> Renditi vinto, e per tua gloria basti
> Che dir potrai che contro me pugnasti.[2]
> (VI, 32, 7-8)

This pride is based on great physical courage, both in attack and in defence, and more than once Argante's unshakable resistance is compared to that of a mountain. He never submits or yields, and in his last fight with Tancredi refuses the offers of mercy made to him. Even in death his body presents a formidable aspect:

---

[1] Bold was his heart, and restless was his sprite,
Fierce, stern, outrageous, keen as sharpened brand,
Scorner of God, scant to himself a friend,
And pricked his reason on his weapon's end.
(Fairfax)

[2] Yield thee my slave, and this thine honour be,
Thou may'st report thou hast encountered me.
(Fairfax)

E poi vider nel sangue un guerrier morto
Che le vie tutte ingombra, e la gran faccia
Tien volto al cielo, e morto anco minaccia.[1]
(XIX, 102, 6-8)

He lives entirely for war, and for the honour that he finds in
it. He is not a leader like Solimano but a warrior who is
moved only by the desire for his own glory. He is not even a
victim of love, and the revenge which he swears to take for
Clorinda is prompted entirely by loyalty to a dead comrade
in arms. He is primitive, pagan man, untouched by divine
grace, but in his own way formidable and even noble.

In these different respects Tasso makes his epic both heroic
and Christian, both Virgilian and contemporary. The old
standards of prowess have a new meaning in his Crusaders;
the old devices of epic pass ingeniously into the new setting.
Yet if Tasso had composed all his poem in this spirit, it would
lack much that has been most admired in it and would repre-
sent only a part of Tasso's imaginative experience. Indeed
when Tasso diversified his epic with themes far removed from
Virgil and much closer to Ariosto, he answered a deep need
in his own nature. The martial story appealed only to a part
of him, and he well might feel unable to maintain it through-
out his twenty-four books. The story of the First Crusade
was as serious and as instructive as anyone could desire, but
Tasso was young and passionate, full of lyric frenzy and fiery
dreams, and his great poem could not but reflect these as
much as his more solemn aspirations towards a Christian
heroism. The result is that large parts of the *Gerusalemme*
are a poetry of romantic fancy. In them Tasso disregards
ordinary life much as Ariosto disregarded it, and they can
rightly be called romantic because they are an escape from a
world of rules and obligations to a world of fancy and dream.
To combine such themes with a historical Crusade imposed a
difficult task on the poet. It was not enough for Tasso that
these episodes should be delightful; they must also be in
some sense serious and suited to his general purpose. They
must have something more than charm or excitement and

[1] And saw where lay a warrior murdered new,
That all bebled the ground, his face to skies
He turns, and seems to threat, though dead he lies.
(Fairfax)

.must touch on important problems in human life. Tasso, who complained in his letters that he could not enjoy such freedom as Ariosto, evolved his own way of introducing fanciful subjects into his poem and fitting them into his scheme of things.

The precedent of chivalrous epic provided Tasso with a subject that appealed deeply to him, — the miraculous. If he had any qualms about introducing it into his poem, he overcame them. It was proper to chivalrous epic, and it provided Tasso with an opportunity to enjoy himself in wild fancies. In his liking for it Tasso ran counter both to the literary pundits, who held that magic had no place in a heroic poem, and to the priests, who took the view that it was impious. Tasso preferred to follow Ariosto and to agree with the mass of his contemporaries, who believed that magic existed but had no very clear ideas about it. From it he extracted his own kind of poetry. In Boiardo the magic is usually entertaining, in Ariosto it is sometimes entertaining, sometimes frightening, but in neither poet does it provide a criticism of life or bear a close relation to real experience. With Tasso it is different. It is as if he put into his magic some of his own frustrations and unfulfilled desires, some of his irrational fears and fancies. He related it to human experience and gave it a new force and relevance. He accepted in part the sacerdotal view that magic is the work of devils, and made his infidel magicians like Ismeno use it,

> Ismen, che trar di sotto ai chiusi marmi
> Può corpo estinto e far che spiri e senta ;
> Ismen, che al suon de' mormorati carmi
> Sin ne la reggia sua Pluto spaventa.[1]
>> (ii, i, 3-6)

But he felt its claims too strongly to confine it to devils and infidels and boldly tried to give it a new interpretation.

The claim of the uncanny and supernatural in art is that it appeals to our own fears and gives a shape and coherence

---

[1] Ismen dead bones laid in cold graves that warms
And makes them speak, smell, taste, touch, see and hear ;
Ismen with terror of his mighty charms
That makes great Dis in deepest Hell to fear.
                                        (Fairfax)

to them. Tasso, himself a prey to many strange dreads and hallucinations, was able to make poetry out of them and to show on what feelings they are founded. This special kind of poetry may be seen in his enchanted wood. The Crusaders need timber for their siege-engines, and decide to get it from a wood. The magician, Ismeno, tries to stop them by summoning devils to haunt the wood, and many strange results follow. Into this striking episode Tasso weaves some of the less intelligible fears of the human soul. The wood is from the start unlike other woods ; it is thought to be sacred to the heathen gods, and there is something sinister and frightening in it :

> Qui s' adunan le streghe, ed il suo vago
> Con ciascuna di lor notturno viene.[1]
>
> (XIII, 4, 1-2)

The old idea of a haunted wood is developed and made more effective when Ismeno, with one foot unshod and charms thrice repeated, strikes the earth with his rod and summons the evil spirits to take charge against the Christians. They come slowly and unwillingly, but they come :

> Veniano innumerabili, infiniti
> Spirti, parte che in aria alberga ed erra,
> Parte di quei che son dal fondo usciti
> Caliginoso e tetro de la terra.[2]
>
> (XIII, 11, 1-4)

Ignorant of all this, the Christians send parties to cut the trees, but the wood-cutters are filled with a nameless dread and come back with dismayed and confused stories. Even the soldiers sent to guard them are overcome by fear and horror when they hear hideous noises like the cries of beasts or the sounds of trumpets and thunder. This fear, like all fear, does not know of what it is afraid, and Tasso conveys its reality in

---

[1] United there the ghosts and goblins meet
To frolic with their mates in silent night.
(Fairfax)

[2] Legions of devils, by thousands, thither come,
Such as in sparsèd air their biding make,
And thousands also which by Heavenly doom
Condemnèd lie by deep Avernus' lake.
(Fairfax)

a simile which is surely based on his own hallucinations :

> Qual semplice bambin mirar non osa
> Dove insolite larve abbia presenti,
> O come pave ne la notte ombrosa,
> Immaginando pur mostri e portenti.[1]
>
> (XIII, 18, 1-4)

The emotional experience which informs Tasso's enchanted wood is this nameless, irrational dread.

This vague horror soon takes a more concrete form. Different warriors offer to see what they can do and refuse to admit that the wood can frighten them. The first to go is Alcasto, who is a type of purely animal courage, a man who fears nothing because he is too stupid to know what fear is :

> L' uom di temerità stupida e fera.[2]   (XIII, 24, 3)

He goes out confidently, and finds a flaming castle in his way, fortified with instruments of war and held by strange monsters. His courage gives way, and he soon runs away. In him Tasso shows how a naturally bold man can feel afraid when he meets something entirely unfamiliar. The devils know his weakness, which is that his stupidity hampers him when he comes across something outside his experience. Alcasto is succeeded by Tancredi, whose life has just been blasted by the death of Clorinda. He has unwittingly killed her, though deeply in love with her. Tancredi's experience in the wood is quite different from Alcasto's. He leaps boldly through the flames and finds that they do not burn him ; when clouds and storms follow, he takes no notice, and they vanish. But the devils play on him in a more sinister way. He comes to a green space, and in the middle of it is a tall cypress, with an inscription which tells him that the wood is full of ghosts who should not be disturbed. He strikes the tree with his sword, and

---

[1] As silly children dare not bend their eye
Where they are told strange bugbears haunt the place,
Or as new monsters, while in bed they lie,
Their fearful thoughts present before their face.
(Fairfax)

[2] A man both void of wit and void of dread.
(Fairfax)

drops of blood ooze out of it, and a voice speaks claiming to be that of Clorinda and telling him that in striking her he is a murderer. The effect on Tancredi is appalling, and he too runs away. The devils know his weakness and take advantage of it. In his grief for Clorinda, he feels that he is a murderer. Tasso marks his state with a remarkable simile:

> Qual infermo talor, che in sogno scorge
> Drago o cinta di fiamme alta Chimera,
> Se ben sospetta o in parte anco s' accorge
> Che simulacro sia, non forma vera,
> Pur desia di fuggir ; tanto gli porge
> Spavento la sembianza orrida e fera ;
> Tale il timido amante appien non crede
> Ai falsi inganni, e pur ne teme e cede.[1]
>
> (XIII, 44, 1-8)

Tancredi's fear is quite different from Alcasto's. He knows that this is a hallucination, but none the less in his weakened state of will and his haunted conscience he is frightened. Since he is not master of himself, he cannot defy the terrors which the wood holds for him.

The enchantment is finally broken by Rinaldo. He too is a great hero. He has returned from his sojourn with Armida, and has made solemn confession of his faults. He is therefore a full man and at peace with himself, as the grief-stricken Tancredi is not. In the recent past Rinaldo has been the slave of a woman and has wasted himself in voluptuous ease. So it is on the possibility of these weaknesses that the devils play when he goes into the wood. He is greeted not by monsters or flaming castles but by a scene of idyllic bliss. The trees are loud with the song of birds and the music of waters ; a great bridge of gold rises over a river and disappears when Rinaldo crosses it ; he hears the sound of voices and of instruments :

[1] As the sick man that in his sleep doth see
Some ugly dream, or some chimera new,
Though he suspect, or half persuaded be,
It is an idle dream, no monster true,
Yet still he fears, he quakes and strives to flee,
So fearful is that wondrous form to view ;
So feared the knight, yet he both knew and thought
All were illusions false by witchcraft wrought.

(Fairfax)

Ma il coro uman, ch' ai cigni, a l' aura, a l' onda
Facea tenor, non sa dove si cele ;
Non sa veder chi formi umani accenti,
Nè dove siano i musici stromenti.[1]

(XVIII, 24, 5-8)

All this magic is meant to revive Rinaldo's old love of beauty
and of pleasure and lull his present purpose. But he pays no
attention to it and goes on his way boldly until he is faced by
a stronger temptation. He is greeted by figures like Dryads
who sing and dance about him and bid him welcome to the
grove. They are, it seems, the companions of Armida, and
then from a myrtle the shape of Armida herself appears. She
appeals to his love and his compassion, but Rinaldo is un-
moved and his old love does not stir in him. She then tries
to frighten him with threats and by taking strange forms, but,
still unmoved, he strikes the myrtle with his sword, and the
magic spell is broken once and for all. The skies thunder and
the earth roars, but Rinaldo does not care, and the devils
leave the wood. Rinaldo's triumph over the devilish enchant-
ment is that of a man who is completely master of himself
and no longer a prey to his former weaknesses. So the
episode of the wood closes, with its implicit lesson that evil
magic of this kind can be encountered successfully only by
those who know what evil is and are not moved by its allure-
ments.

Tasso presents an even more penetrating account of
magic in Armida. Taught by Idraote, who communes with
devils, she is a great enchantress. Her first devastating effects
on the Crusaders are due to her beauty and her consummate
histrionic powers, but once she has caused discord among
them and made ten of them follow her, she shows other gifts.
When the ten knights come with her to a castle by the Dead
Sea and find a feast spread for them, Armida produces a rod
and a book and turns her victims into fish. As one of them
says :

Non so come ogni gamba entro s' accoglia,
Come l' un braccio e l' altro entri nel tergo

[1] The human voices sung a triple high,
To which respond the birds, the streams, the wind,
But yet unseen those nymphs, those singers were,
Unseen the lutes, harps, viols which they bear.
(Fairfax)

M' accorcio e stringo ; e su la pelle cresce
Squamoso il cuoio ; e d' uom son fatto un pesce.[1]

(x, 66, 5-8)

Though she resembles Homer's Circe and Ariosto's Alcina, Armida acts from different motives. The transformation of her victims is intended to impress them so with her power that they will forsake their own faith and embrace hers, and she warns them that, if they refuse, she can turn them into birds or plants or rocks, though for some unexplained reason she is actually content to throw them into a dungeon. Armida is an infidel witch, and her magic comes from evil sources. That is no doubt why Tasso, unlike Ariosto, attaches no moral significance to the transformation of the Crusaders into fish. Ariosto suggests that such victims deserve what they get, and that their new shapes reflect their brutish characters. But in such a case the witch has some justice on her side, and Tasso prefers to keep Armida in the full power of her wicked intentions. Like his other powers of evil, she has her place in his general plan.

Just as the enchanted wood tests the characters of those who go into it, so Armida tests those who come into her orbit, and especially Rinaldo. Rinaldo is Tasso's most romantic hero. As the ancestor of Tasso's patron, Alfonso II, he receives special prominence, and into him Tasso has put many of his own desires. Rinaldo's character is sketched for us when God looks down on the Christian leaders and sees him :

Scorge in Rinaldo ed animo guerriero
E spirti di riposo impazïenti ;
Non cupidigia in lui d' oro o d' impero,
Ma d' onor brame immoderate ardenti.[2]

(1, 10, 3-6)

---

[1] My legs and feet both into one were brought,
My arms and hands into my shoulders sliding,
My skin was full of scales, like shields of brass,
Now made a fish, where late a knight I was.

(Fairfax)

[2] In young Rinaldo fierce desires he spied,
And noble heart of rest impatient ;
To wealth or sovereign power he naught applied
His wits, but all to virtue excellent.

(Fairfax)

He is a young man, aflame for honour, and honour includes success not only in arms but in love. As yet love has not touched him, but he is ripe for it, and Tasso suggests that it will soon assail him :

> Se il miri fulminar ne l' arme avvolto,
> Marte lo stimi ; Amor, se scopre il volto.[1]
>
> (I, 58, 7-8)

When Armida comes to the camp, he does not yield to her charms as the others do, but, in the troubles which follow, in a fit of angry pride he kills Gernando and exiles himself from the crusading army rather than submit to punishment. At first Armida hates him and wishes to revenge herself on him because he has freed the ten knights whom she has imprisoned. She uses her arts to catch him, and on an island in the Orontes her magic begins to work. He sees in the water a beautiful figure which looks like a nymph or a goddess or a siren, and he hears a song of entrancing beauty which tells him that youth is too short to be spent in anything but pleasure and that virtue and fame are but idle words :

> O giovinetti, mentre aprile e maggio
> V' ammantan di fiorite e verdi spoglie,
> Di gloria e di virtù fallace raggio
> La tenerella mente ah non v' invoglie ![2]
>
> (XIV, 62, 1-4)

The song lulls Rinaldo to sleep, and appeals to hidden desires in him. The young man who lives for honour is pierced by this call to pleasure. While he sleeps, Armida comes up, falls in love with him, and carries him off in her magic chariot to her palace in the Fortunate Islands beyond the ocean. The magic has worked perfectly. It has woken the one force in Rinaldo which can subdue his desire for glory, and has given him into her power.

She has indeed much to offer him beside her beauty and love. In Canto XVI Tasso presents the palace and garden of

[1] Armèd, a Mars, might coyest Venus move,
And if disarmed, then god himself of Love.
(Fairfax)

[2] Ye happy youths, who April fresh and May
Attire in flowering green of lusty age,
For glory vain, or virtue's idle ray,
Do not your tender limbs in toil engage.
(Fairfax)

M

Armida in a way that makes almost all other such creations seem dull. On the top of a mountain, above the snow-line, she has built a place of everlasting spring. It has all that a man can desire, all the natural beauties of hills and valleys, caves and grottoes; the fruit, like that in the garden of Alcinous, grows all the year round; there is " a sweet disorder " in the mixture of natural and artificial:

> Stimi (sì misto il culto è col negletto)
> Sol naturali e gli ornamenti e i siti.
> Di natura arte par, che per diletto
> L' imitatrice sua scherzando imiti.[1]
>
> (XVI, 10, 1-4)

In this enchanted place everything seems to make music, and the birds sing in harmony with the breezes and the waters:

> Vezzozi augelli infra le verdi fronde
> Temprano a prova lascivette note.
> Mormora l' aura, e fa le foglie e l' onde
> Garrir, che variamente ella percote.
> Quando taccion gli augelli, alto risponde;
> Quando vantan gli augei, più lieve scote;
> Sia caso od arte, or accompagna, ed ora
> Alterna i versi lor la music' ôra.[2]
>
> (XVI, 12, 1-8)

The whole setting is a triumph of enchantment, and those who are under its spell feel no need for anything outside. It is Tasso's myth of a complete sensuous joy. It alone could keep Rinaldo from his normal activities, and it does so with entire success. It is, of course, wrong, and must come to an end, but, in the interval, it overwhelms the senses and creates an unbroken illusion of happiness. It is Tasso's strongest

---

[1] So with the rude the polished mingled was
That natural seemèd all and every part;
Nature would craft in counterfeiting pass,
And imitate her imitator art.
(Fairfax)

[2] The joyous birds, hid under greenwood shade,
Sung merry notes on every branch and bough;
The wind that in the leaves and water played
With murmur sweet, now sung, and whistled now:
Ceasèd the birds, the wind loud answer made,
And while they sung, it rumbled soft and low;
Thus were it hap or cunning, chance or art,
The wind in this strange music bore his part.
(Fairfax)

and most alluring magic. He created it out of his own long-
ings and dreams, and into it he put much of himself. He
knew what appeal Armida's charms would have for a young
voluptuous man like Rinaldo, and he set it out in all its power.

There is another side to this magic. Seen from the inside
it is complete and satisfying, but from the outside it looks
different. It is wrong that Rinaldo should enjoy himself here
instead of doing his duty with the Crusade, and steps are
taken to recall him. The two knights who go to fetch him
have to deal with an almost supernatural situation and must
use magic against magic, their own good methods against the
evil methods of Armida. In describing their actions Tasso
resorts almost to allegory. They must of course know what
they are doing, and therefore they have a map of the laby-
rinthine entrances to Armida's resort. They encounter
various beasts, which seem to represent the bestial appetites
of man, and defeat them with a wand which represents their
own purity. They pass the dangerous stream of laughter; for
laughter undermines the serious purpose of their undertaking.
They take no notice of an apparently beautiful woman, who
offers them happiness ; for like Ariosto's Alcina, she is really
Lust, and means nothing to them. They bring the love-sick
Rinaldo to his senses by showing him his reflection in a magic
mirror, a symbol for the truth which reveals how ugly a thing
may be which seems beautiful from the inside. The imagery
is simple and old-fashioned, but it is important because it
gives Tasso's interpretation of the episode. Armida's garden
is not intended to be only delightful. It is delightful, but it is
based on wrong desires and illusions. Brought into contact
with virtue and truth it ceases to exert its charm, and Rinaldo
leaves it as soon as he sees himself as he really is and hears
the call to manhood :

> Qual sonno o qual letargo ha sì sopita
> La tua virtude ? o qual viltà l' alletta ?
> Su su ; te il campo e te Goffredo invita ;
> Te la fortuna e la vittoria aspetta.[1]
>
> (XVI, 33, 1-4)

---

[1] What letharge hath in drowsiness up-penned
Thy courage thus ? what sloth doth thee infect ?
Up, up, our camp and Godfrey for thee send,
Thee fortune, praise and victory expect.
(Fairfax)

Armida's magic, which appeals so deeply to certain instincts in him, can be countered only by awaking other powers which see it in its true character and are not deluded by it.

In these cases Tasso is on orthodox ground in giving magical powers to infidels who consort with devils. In one case, however, he treats magic differently and makes it an instrument for good in the hands of a Christian. The Sage, to whom Pietro directs the knights in search of Rinaldo, has a knowledge and powers which in their own way rival Armida's. He takes the knights under the water to his dwelling in a cave which shines with jewels and where he keeps state with gold plate and a hundred servants. He is at pains to explain that all this comes from a knowledge acquired by natural and correct means :

> Ma spiando men vo da' lor vestigi
> Quale in sè virtù celi o l'erba o il fonte ;
> E gli altri arcani di natura ignoti
> Contemplo, e de le stelle i vari moti.[1]
> (XIV, 42, 6-9)

This Sage in fact gets his knowledge from the stars, which he watches from Lebanon or Carmel, and the learning, which he acquired in his pagan days before he was baptised by Pietro, has now taken on a new character. The suggestion is that, whereas of old his arts were turned to evil ends, now they are turned to good. He is a Christian sage who studies profane knowledge in a pious spirit. Such a conception met with some hostility from Tasso's critics, who thought that any claim to such knowledge was wrong. But Tasso argued in reply that the knowledge which the Sage imparts inspires and strengthens other men to virtue, while the fact that he learned it in his pagan days is merely a reflection of the fact that most profane knowledge comes from the Greeks. Just as Tasso himself sought to be a scholar and a philosopher, so his Sage is one, and has a clear view of what relation his knowledge should bear to God :

---

[1] But of all herbs, of every spring and well,
The hidden power I know and virtue great,
And all that kind hath hid from mortal sight,
And all the stars, their motions, and their might.
(Fairfax)

E in Lui m' acqueto. Egli comanda e insegna
Mastro insieme e signor sommo e sovrano ;
Nè già per nostro mezzo oprar disdegna
Cose degne talor de la sua mano.[1]

(XIV, 47, 1-4)

The Sage's powers are as great as Armida's but they are
inspired by God and directed to good ends. Tasso believed
that knowledge could, if properly followed, be more powerful
than witchcraft, and felt that it was really a means to a good
life. It may seem to work marvels, but they are not marvels
to those who are properly instructed in the ways of nature.

Tasso illustrates the Sage's powers in a special way. He
sends the knights to Armida's island by putting them in a
miraculous boat which covers the distance in a short time.
It is directed by a woman who is not like other women :

Crinita fronte ella dimostra, e ciglia
Cortesi e favorevoli e tranquille :
E nel sembiante a gli angioli somiglia ;
Tanta luce ivi par ch' arda e sfaville.[2]

(XV, 4, 1-4)

Her dress is always changing colours like the feathers on a
dove's neck and seems now red, now blue, now green. She
assures the knights that, with her to guide them, the seas will
be calm, and she keeps her promise to bring them safely and
swiftly to Armida's island. Though Tasso does not say so,
the changing colours of her dress show that she is Fortune,
and she favours the knights in their enterprise. But she is
a special kind of Fortune, not variable and fickle, but sub-
ordinate to the Sage's wisdom ; he has sent her with them
to be their servant and their guide. In other words, the Sage's
knowledge enables him to command Fortune for his good
designs ; she is not incalculable but a power in a divinely

[1] In him I rest, on him my thoughts depend,
My lord, my teacher, and my guide is he ;
This noble work he strives to bring to end ;
He is the architect, the workmen we.
(Fairfax)

[2] Upon her front her locks were curlèd new,
Her eyes were courteous, full of peace and love ;
In look a saint, an angel bright in show,
So in her visage grace and virtue strove.
(Fairfax)

ordered universe who helps the good. The speed and ease with which her boat travels is an indication of the help she can give to men when they do what is right. Moreover, it is significant that Tasso makes her foretell to the knights the discoveries of Christopher Columbus. Though the subject of his poem and his own limited experience prevented Tasso from giving such a picture of the world as we find in Camões, here at least he suggests wider horizons when the lady tells how in the future unknown seas will be opened to sailing :

> Un uom de la Ligurìa avrà ardimento
> A l' incognito corso esporsi in prima :
> Nè il minaccevol fremito del vento,
> Nè l' inospito mar, nè il dubbio clima,
> Nè s' altro di periglio o di spavento
> Più grave e formidabile or si stima,
> Faran che il generoso entro ai divieti
> D' Abila angusti l' alta mente acqueti.[1]
>
> (xv, 31, 1-8)

Columbus is an example of a man who trusts himself to Fortune because he possesses true knowledge, and his case underlines Tasso's moral that if men set out in this spirit, nothing can withstand them.

Tasso, then, works his marvels into his poem with some dexterity and adapts them to his new outlook. Their significance is deepened by his illustrative or symbolical use of them. On the one side are the dark powers which take advantage of human weakness, on the other the powers of light and knowledge which help activities directed to good ends. What was before an ornament or a delightful episode in the epic is thus remodelled and changed. Tasso's use of marvels throws some light on his treatment of another subject even more favoured by chivalrous epic, — love. He follows Ariosto in giving it an important place in his poem, but he does so in his own way.

---

[1] A knight of Genes shall have the hardiment
Upon this wondrous voyage first to wend,
Nor winds nor waves, that ships in sunder rent,
Nor seas unused, strange clime, nor pool unkenned,
Nor other peril or astonishment
That makes frail hearts of men to bow and bend,
Within Abila's strait shall keep and hold
The noble spirit of this sailor bold.

(Fairfax)

His view of women was different from Ariosto's. He was still a young man, and his passionate temperament felt all the lure of womanhood; he lacked Ariosto's saving humour which gave a ridiculous side even to so charming a creature as Angelica; he lived in a time when the notion of honour demanded that a man should suffer for love and devote his life to it. But though Tasso portrays several men and women in love, he builds them on a similar plan by making their loves frustrated, anxious and unhappy. No doubt there is a psychological explanation for this in Tasso's own character, but it fits well into the plan of his poem. Just as his knights have to overcome obstacles, so do his lovers; just as his magic may have its wrong side, so too may his love. He saw all life as a struggle, and his lovers pass through as many obstacles and ordeals as his soldiers.

The importance which love has for Tasso is shown early in the poem in the episode of Sofronia and Olindo. They are young Christians living in Jerusalem. Olindo is deeply in love with Sofronia, but he is too shy to speak of it, and she has no notion of what he feels:

> Ei che modesto è sì, com' essa è bella,
> Brama assai, poco spera, e nulla chiede;
> Nè sa scroprirsi, o non ardisce, ed ella
> O lo sprezza, o nol vede, o non s' avvede.[1]
> (II, 16, 3-6)

The pair are naturally well matched; for both have heroic instincts and are of the stuff from which martyrs are made. So when the infidel tyrant Aladino orders a general massacre of Christians because an image of the Virgin, stolen at his orders from a church, has been mysteriously removed from his clutches, Sofronia gives herself up and untruthfully claims to have taken it. The tyrant accepts her story and condemns her to be burned. Her veil and mantle are torn from her, her hands are bound, and she is set on a pyre, a virgin-martyr in the true taste of the Counter-Reformation. When Olindo hears what has happened, he is so distressed

[1] She fair, he full of bashfulness and truth
Loved much, hoped little, and desirèd naught;
He durst not speak by suit to purchase ruth;
She saw not, marked not, wist not what he sought.
(Fairfax)

and so eager to save Sofronia that he goes to the tyrant and says that not she but he removed the image. Aladino orders him to be bound and set on the same pyre, and the two seem likely to die together. The effect on Olindo is that he, who has for so long been shy and tongue-tied, now bursts into protestations of passionate love and in words which are hardly saintly reveals his amorous dreams :

> Ed oh mia morte avventurosa appieno !
> O fortunati miei dolci martiri ! ,
> S' impetrerò che giunto seno a seno
> L' anima mia ne la tua bocca io spiri,
> E, venendo tu meco a un tempo meno,
> In me fuor mandi gli ultimi sospiri.[1]

(II, 35, 1-6)

For this Sofronia reproves him, and tells him that he should be weeping for his sins. Fortunately at this point Clorinda intervenes ; the couple are released and get married. Frustrated and unhappy love is forced to a crisis in suffering and even then seems unlikely to find a happy ending, until good luck puts everything right. We see the conflict between passion and piety, and the sudden twist by which passion is sanctified.

This episode prepares the way for other more complex situations. In one case Tasso presents a triangle of lovers. Erminia loves Tancredi who loves Clorinda who loves no one. The situation is even more complicated because Erminia and Clorinda are pagans, and Clorinda is a woman warrior who fights on the opposite side to Tancredi. In him Tasso presents the young warrior whose life is devoured by a single, agonising passion. So God sees him :

> Vede Tancredi aver la vita a sdegno,
> Tanto un suo vano amor l' ange e martira.[2]

(I, 9, 3-4)

[1] Yet happy were my death, my ending blest,
My torments easy, full of sweet delight,
If only with my breast upon thy breast,
My soul onto thy lips could take its flight ;
And thou, with me upon my bosom pressed,
Thy latest sighs with mine couldst then unite.
(After Fairfax)

[2] Tancred he saw his life's joy set at naught,
So woe-begone was he with pains of love.
(Fairfax)

176

Tancredi first saw Clorinda by a stream with her helmet off, and he has been in love with her ever since :

> E sempre ha nel pensiero e l' atto e il loco
> In che la vide, esca continua al foco.[1]
>
> (I, 48, 7-8)

This love dominates and disorganises his life. It interferes with his martial prowess and makes him utterly miserable. In the middle of a fight he makes a declaration of his love to Clorinda, but she is not moved by it, and the battle continues. When he has undertaken to fight Argante, he thinks that he sees Clorinda riding away and pursues her, thus not only deserting his duty but letting himself fall into many troubles and perils. When he returns, tragedy comes. Clorinda goes out at night to destroy a siege-engine, succeeds in doing so, but is shut out from the city afterwards. Tancredi, not seeing in the darkness who she is, fights her and at last deals her a fatal blow. Only too late, when she uncovers herself, does he know her, and the effect on him is heart-breaking :

> Tremar sentì la man, mentre la fronte
> Non conosciuta ancor sciolse e scoprio.
> La vide ; la conobbe ; e restò senza
> E voce e moto. Ahi vista ! ahi conoscenza ![2]
>
> (XII, 67, 5-8)

His disaster overwhelms and unmans Tancredi. He can think of nothing but her death and of his responsibility for it.

Into this tragic story Tasso has woven his own special kind of consolation. The first problem he has to solve is the difference of faith between Tancredi and Clorinda, and he does this with great dramatic skill. On her last night, before she goes out to burn the siege-engine, Clorinda hears from the faithful old eunuch Arsete the story of her birth and early childhood. It seems that her parents were Christians, but, owing to troubles at her birth, she has never been baptised.

[1] Her shape, her gesture, and her place in mind
He kept, and blew love's fire with that wind.
(Fairfax)

[2] With trembling hands her beaver he untied,
Which done he saw, and seeing knew her face,
And lost therewith his speech and moving quite ;
Oh woeful knowledge, ah unhappy sight !
(Fairfax)

A divine figure in a dream told Arsete to baptise her when she was young, but he did not do so; the vision has re-appeared, and Arsete is full of anxiety. For the moment Clorinda decides to continue in her pagan beliefs, and in this spirit she goes to her last fight. Then, as she lies fatally wounded, her spirit feels a change, and she asks Tancredi to baptise her :

> Parole ch' a lei novo un spirto ditta,
> Spirto di fè, di carità, di speme ;
> Virtù ch' or Dio le infonde ; e, se rubella
> In vita fu, la vuole in morte ancella.[1]
>
> (XII, 65, 5-8)

In this new temper she forgives Tancredi :

> Amico, hai vinto : io ti perdon . . . perdona
> Tu ancora.[2]   (XII, 66, 1-2)

Tancredi baptises her with water fetched from a spring in his helmet, and she dies a Christian.

The trouble which Tancredi suffers from his love for Clorinda does not end with her death. He is so overcome with grief and shame at killing her that he loses all control of himself. He longs to die, laments over the dead body, and lies on his bed weeping. His comrades try to comfort him, but without success, and the situation is so serious that Pietro, who looks after his Christian flock as a good shepherd looks after his sheep, reproves him for his persistence in grief and his refusal to accept the will of heaven :

> Rifiuti dunque, ahi sconoscente !, il dono
> Del Ciel salubre, e 'ncontra lui t' adiri ?
> Misero, dove corri in abbandono
> A' tuoi sfrenati e rapidi martiri ? [3]
>
> (XII, 88, 1-4)

---

[1] A spirit new did her those prayers teach,
Spirit of hope, of charity, of faith ;
And though her life to Christ rebellious were,
Yet died she his child and handmaid dear.
(Fairfax)

[2] Friend, thou hast won. I pardon thee . . . and thou
Pardon me.

[3] Thou dost refuse of heaven the proffered grace,
And gainst it still rebel with sinful ire,
Oh wretch ! Oh whither doth thy rage thee chase ?
Refrain thy grief, bridle thy fond desire.
(Fairfax)

Pietro at least prevents Tancredi from killing himself and lightens some of his sorrow, but he is still a broken man. His cure comes when a vision of Clorinda appears to him in sleep and thanks him for saving her soul by baptism. She tells him that their love, which had no happiness in this world, will be rewarded in the next :

> Quivi io beata te amando godo, e quivi
> Spero che per te loco anco s' appresti,
> Ove al gran Sole e ne l' eterno die
> Vagheggerai le sue bellezze e mie.[1]
>
> (xii, 92, 5-8)

Comforted by this hope, Tancredi buries Clorinda, and recovers himself for the battle. By this means Tasso solves his complex situation with the difficult problems that it raised. The love, which has been so agonising and so disturbing on earth, will be fulfilled in heaven ; the difficulty of a Christian's love for a pagan woman is solved by her becoming a Christian ; the obstacles which this love creates in Tancredi and which are such a hindrance to his life have in the end made a better and more complete man of him. This is his special ordeal, and with divine help he surmounts it.

Erminia's love for Tancredi is a kind of counterpart to Tancredi's love for Clorinda. Equally frustrated and hopeless, it is more tender, more helpless, more feminine. She fell in love with him when he sacked Antioch and treated her with chivalrous courtesy. When she watches the Christian warriors from the walls of Jerusalem, she sees him again and is overwhelmed by an emotion which she has great difficulty in hiding :

> Pur gli spirti e le lagrime ritiene,
> Ma non così, che lor non mostri alquanto ;
> Chè gli occhi pregni un bel purpureo giro
> Tinse, e roco spuntò mezzo il sospiro.[2]
>
> (iii, 18, 5-8)

[1] There still I love thee, there for Tancred fit
A seat preparèd is among the blest ;
There in eternal joy, eternal light ;
Thou shalt thy love enjoy, and she her knight. (Fairfax)

[2] But sighs and tears she wisely could suppress,
Her love and passion she dissembled well,
And strove her love and hot desire to cover,
Till heart with sighs, and eyes with tears ran over. (Fairfax)

Her crisis comes when Tancredi is wounded. She broods over his wounded state and imagines that he is dying; she is skilled in herbs and feels that she can cure him. But she is the victim of a violent inner conflict. While love calls her to help him, honour tells her not to go:

> E fan dubbia contesa entro al suo cuore
> Duo potenti nemici, Onore e Amore.[1]
> (VI, 70, 7-8)

Love triumphs over honour, and Erminia decides to risk her good name by going to Tancredi. She disguises herself in Clorinda's armour and goes out attended only by a squire and a serving-woman. The squire goes ahead with her message to Tancredi, who receives it kindly, thinking that it comes from Clorinda. But Erminia herself fails to reach the Christian camp. Two men on guard are deceived by her armour and give chase to her. She, who is no warrior, is completely terrified and rides off alone into the country, not knowing where she is and foiled in her attempt to find Tancredi.

Erminia's desire to heal Tancredi is prompted by love, and Tasso suggests that this love is not quite honourable. Erminia dreams of marriage with Tancredi, but seems to be quite happy at the thought of his love without it. So when she flies defeated from her quest, she has for the moment lost both her love and her self-respect. The two powers, who were at war in her, have been equally defeated. Her sick and stricken soul needs healing and finds it in a sunlit, pastoral world to which by accident her horse brings her. She lies down wearily and sleeps, and when she wakes, she is greeted by a delicious scene of water, flowers and trees. This is a setting for some simple shepherds who welcome Erminia and give her a home. After her troubles and sorrows she finds peace and happiness with this warm-hearted family which lives away from the world. No doubt Tasso himself often dreamed of such a release from the complications of court life, and it is significant that the shepherd once lived in the court at Memphis but left it because he could endure it no

---

[1] For in the secret of her troubled thought,
A doubtful combat, love and honour fought.
(Fairfax)

longer. So Erminia finds a respite from her troubles and a time to regain her lost self-respect. She is still obsessed by her love for Tancredi, sings songs about him and carves his name on trees. Her life with the shepherds gives her a chance to recover from her shattered state and to be ready for her destiny when it comes.

It comes in due course. Erminia, after leaving the shepherds and joining the Egyptian army, still loves and seeks Tancredi. So she gladly joins the spy Vafrino and comes with him to the Christian Army. She arrives just after Tancredi's fight with Argante, when Argante is dead and Tancredi lies wounded, exhausted and unconscious on the ground. She seems to find all her hopes ruined :

> Dopo gran tempo i' ti ritrovo appena,
> Tancredi, e ti riveggio, e non son vista,
> Vista non son da te, benchè presente ;
> E trovando ti perdo eternamente.[1]
>
> (XIX, 105, 5-8)

But Tancredi is still alive, and Erminia nurses him back to life. When he regains consciousness, he asks tenderly who is nursing him and is content that it is Erminia. So at last she is rewarded by being able to save the life of the man she loves and to know that he is grateful to her. But this is her only reward. Tancredi is pledged to Clorinda, and cannot and would not marry Erminia. Indeed we hear no more of her being with him. Wounded though he is, Tancredi is carried into Jerusalem and asks no more about Erminia. Her love is as unfulfilled in this life as Tancredi's own love for Clorinda, but, unlike him, she has no consolation that she will be joined to her beloved in Heaven. Yet though Erminia's love is thus unsatisfied, she has been ennobled and transformed by it. The tenderness and devotion which she shows in her care for Tancredi are finer than her old reckless desires. For her, love is in the end its own reward.

The love of Rinaldo and Armida is fraught with greater issues than that of Tancredi for Clorinda or of Erminia for

---

[1] Tancred, I have thee, see thee, yet thine eyes
Looked not upon thy love and handmaid kind ;
Undo their doors, their lids fast closèd sever,
Alas, I find thee for to lose thee ever.
(Fairfax)

Tancredi. In it Tasso assails a complex problem both in art
and in morals. Armida might have been nothing but a witch ;
she is in fact a formidable witch and a devoted infidel. Her
great assets are her beauty and her intelligence, both of which
Tasso displays at work. He dwells lovingly on her beauty ;
she resembles the Cnidian Venus, with her golden hair, her
cheeks like roses and ivory, her shapely breasts like snow.
He does not shrink from showing her sexual appeal :

> Come per acqua o per cristallo intero
> Trapassa il raggio, e nol divide o parte ;
> Per entro il chiuso manto osa il pensiero
> Sì penetrar ne la vietata parte.[1]
>
> (IV, 32, 1-4)

This beauty is combined with an uncommon skill in playing
on male emotions. Armida is an accomplished actress.
With becoming modesty she tells her tale of imaginary woe
and accepts Goffredo's first refusal of help with an equally
becoming resignation. She manages the large company of
men who fall in love with her and keeps them on tiptoe with
expectation and desire as she varies her moods and methods :

> Usa ogni arte la donna, onde sia côlto
> Ne la sua rete alcun novello amante ;
> Nè con tutti, nè sempre un stesso volto
> Serba, ma cangia a tempo atti e sembiante.[2]
>
> (IV, 87, 1-4)

Even when the ten knights follow her, Armida keeps up her
enticing ways until the fatal moment when she appears with
her rod and book and changes her victims into fishes. Tasso's
first presentation of Armida is of an extremely clever and
beautiful woman who uses her gifts for wrong ends. She is
indeed a dangerous temptress, conceived by a man who knew
the full power of such temptations as hers.

---

[1] As sunbeams dive through crystal or through wave
To spy the store-house of his springing gold,
Love-piercing thought so through her mantle drave
And in forbidden regions wandered bold.
(Fairfax)

[2] All wily sleights that subtle women know
Hourly she used, to catch some lover new.
None kenned the bent of her unsteadfast bow,
For with the time her thoughts her looks renew.
(Fairfax)

Armida's chief victim is Rinaldo, the greatest knight among the Christians. Their love is Tasso's most exciting flight of fancy. He conveys the hold which Armida has on Rinaldo and his utter subservience to her. But this life of pleasure, so delightful to hear of, has its other side. It is wrong, because Rinaldo forgets his duty and is the slave of a woman. The proper relations between man and woman which Milton summed up in his Adam and Eve,

Hee for God only, shee for God in him, (*P.L.* IV, 299)

are reversed :

L' una di servitù, l' altra d' impero
Si gloria ; ella in sè stessa, ed egli in lei.[1]
(XVI, 21, 1-2)

In her pride and vanity Armida is like a peacock or a rainbow. Her love is sensual and selfish. She is the incarnation of the Eternal Feminine in its most dangerous and most corrupting shape. All womanly tricks are at her command, and Tasso shows her power by an adaptation from Homer. Homer gives to Aphrodite a girdle which contains all that should belong to the goddess of love :

ἔνθ' ἔνι μὲν φιλότης, ἐν δ' ἵμερος, ἐν δ' ὀαριστὺς
πάρφασις, ἥ τ' ἔκλεψε νόον πύκα περ φρονεόντων.[2]
(*Il.* XIV, 216-17)

Tasso, with a more sophisticated view of womanhood, expands this to

Teneri sdegni, e placide e tranquille
Repulse, e cari vezzi, e liete paci,
Sorrise parolette, e dolci stille
Di pianto, e sospir tronchi, e molli baci.[3]
(XVI, 25, 1-4)

Armida has all the allurements that Tasso can give to her, and it is understandable that Rinaldo is entirely in her power.

[1] Her, to command ; to serve, it pleased the knight ;
He, proud of bondage ; of her empire, she. (Fairfax)

[2] Therein was love, and desire, and discourse fond and deceitful,
Such as taketh away their wits from even the wisest.

[3] Tender denials, peaceful, gentle scorn,
Loving caresses, hours of silent bliss,
Soft smiles and words, and sweet laments that mourn,
Sighs broken midway, lips that softly kiss.

It is of course true that into his description of Armida Tasso put much of his own amorous nature and many of his own dreams. But his training had taught him that these dreams were wrong and that any realisation of them, such as an earlier age would have allowed, was wicked. So his treatment of Armida is implicitly a criticism of the liberty which the Renaissance had allowed and the Counter-Reformation denied. That Tasso himself sometimes looked back to the Renaissance with regretful longing is true enough. It was for him in some ways a Golden Age, as it was for his contemporary Guarini, who sang in the *Pastor Fido*:

> O bella età dell' oro ![1]

Tasso knew this appeal, but renounced it, and made the desire for such freedom a temptation such as the figure of Lust holds out to the rescuers of Rinaldo:

> Questo è'l il porto del mondo ; e qui il ristoro
> De le sue noie e quel piacer si sente
> Che già sentí ne' secoli de l' oro
> L' antica e senza fren libera gente.[2]

> (xv, 63, 1-4)

Nor is Tasso's renunciation merely formal or intellectual. It has an emotional justification. There is in Armida's garden, despite all its beauties and pleasures, a pervading melancholy, as if the boasted delights of love did not really content those who enjoy them. Indeed this underlying sadness gives much of their power to the incomparable lines which caught the imagination of Spenser so strongly that he translated them in his *Faerie Queene*:

> Deh, mira, egli cantò, spuntar la rosa
> Dal verde suo modesta e verginella,
> Che mezzo aperta ancora e mezzo ascosa,
> Quanto si mostra men, tanto è più bella.
> Ecco poi nudo il sen già baldanzosa
> Dispiega ; ecco poi langue, e non par quella ;
> Quella non par che desiata avanti
> Fa da mille donzelle e mille amanti.

---

[1] O lovely golden age !

[2] This is the place, wherein you may assuage
Your sorrows past ; here is that joy and bliss
That flourished in the antique golden age ;
Here needs no law, here none doth aught amiss. (Fairfax)

> Così trapassa al trapassar d' un giorno
> De la vita mortale il fiore e il verde ;
> Nè, perchè faccia indietro april ritorno,
> Si rinfiora ella mai nè si rinverde.
> Cogliam la rosa in sul mattino adorno
> Di questo dì, che tosto il seren perde ;
> Cogliam d' amor la rosa ; amiamo or quando
> Esser si puote riamati amando.[1]
>
> (XVI, 14-15)

The theme is as old as Mimnermus, but Tasso has brought a new note into it, an undertone of melancholy which is not to be found in such poems of the Renaissance as Lorenzo de' Medici's :

> Quant' è bella giovinezza
> Che si fugge tuttavia !
> Chi vuol esser lieto, sia ;
> Di doman non c' è certezza.[2]

Tasso, who felt so strongly the lure of the flesh, also felt that in the last resort it is inadequate and does not fulfil all its promises.

The situation to which Armida reduces Rinaldo is both wrong and unsatisfying. It breaks down before the appeal

---

[1] The while some one did chaunt this louely lay ;
Ah see, who so faire thing doest faine to see,
In springing flowre the image of thy day ;
Ah see the Virgin Rose, how sweetly shee
Doth first peepe forth, with bashfull modestee,
That fairer seems, the lesse ye see her may ;
Lo see soon after, how more bold and free
Her bared bosome, she doth broad display ;
Loe see soon after, how she fades and falles away.

So passeth, in the passing of a day,
Of mortall life, the leafe, the bud, the flowre,
No more doth flourish after first decay,
That earst was sought to decke both bed and bowre,
Of many a Ladie, and many a Paramowre ;
Gather therefore the Rose, whilest yet is prime,
For soon comes age, that will her pride deflowre :
Gather the Rose of loue, whilest yet is time
Whilest louing thou mayst loued be with equall crime.
(Spenser, *F.Q.* II, xii, 74-5)

[2] Ah, how sweet is youth that goes
All too swiftly in its flight !
Let him have, who will, delight ;
What to-morrow brings, who knows ?

which the rescuing knights make to his nobility. Armida faces the crisis with great force and eloquence. She becomes a second Dido and forces Rinaldo into the embarrassing position of being her Aeneas. When she finds that pitiful entreaties do not move him, she resorts to furious rage and heaps hideous threats on him. The situation which before looked so happy and harmonious has revealed its instability and the destructive and discordant elements which lay hidden in it. Since Armida cannot have what she wishes, she abandons any hopes of regaining Rinaldo and shows the fierceness of her wounded vanity by first annihilating the palace and the garden :

> Come imagin talor d' immensa mole
> Forman nubi ne l' aria, e poco dura,
> Chè il vento la disperde o solve il sole ;
> Come sogno sen va ch' egro figura ;
> Così sparver gli alberghi, e restâr sole
> L' alpi e l' orror che fece ivi natura.[1]
>
> (XVI, 69, 1-6)

The whole enchanted scene vanishes, a fitting symbol of the love which has died and turned to hatred. Armida shows how selfish her love for Rinaldo has been. Now she wishes only to revenge herself on him and goes in her dragon-drawn chariot to Syria, where she makes a resplendent appearance in the Egyptian army and seeks, not in vain, to find helpers in her task.

Tasso might have brought Armida to an ugly end. But she meant so much to him in her beauty and her feminine versatility that he must have shrunk from any such conclusion, and he surprises us by making even this illicit and perilous love finish happily. In the final battle Armida finds herself confronted by Rinaldo. She tries to kill herself, but he prevents her. He feels for her in her distress a truer and more tender love than he ever felt before :

---

[1] As oft the clouds frame shapes of castles great
Amid the air, that little time do last,
But are dissolved by wind or Titan's heat,
Or like vain dreams soon made, and sooner past :
The palace vanished so, nor in its seat
Left ought but rocks and crags by kind there placed.
(Fairfax)

E il bel volto e il bel seno a la meschina
Bagnò d' alcuna lagrima pietosa.
Quale a pioggia d' argento e mattutina
Si rabbellisce scolorita rosa ;
Tal ella, revenendo, alzò la china
Faccia, del non suo pianto or lagrimosa.[1]

(xx, 129, 1-6)

At first Armida resists Rinaldo's loving attentions. Her
vanity is still strong, and she begs him to let her die. But
Rinaldo insists and offers her his terms. If she will abandon
her paganism, he will restore her to her honours and be her
devoted servant. To such appeals at last she melts ; her
pride and revengefulness are lost in a flood of real affection
and tenderness for him :

Onde, siccome suol nevosa falda
Dov' arda il sole e tepid' aura spiri,
Così l' ira che in lei parea sì salda,
Solvesi, e restan sol gli altri desiri.
Ecco l' ancilla tua ; d' essa a tuo senno
Dispon, gli disse, e le fia legge il cenno.[2]

(xx, 136, 3-8)

The couple are reconciled. Hate has turned to love, and the
old selfish sensuality has been transformed by suffering into
real affection. Even the religious obstacles are overcome, and
we are left with the impression that Armida, converted and
reformed, will make an excellent wife to Rinaldo.

Such a solution may seem a little superficial or sentimental
to us, but it would not have appeared so to Tasso's contem-
poraries or to Tasso himself. The Counter-Reformation, in
dealing with a generation which had gone far astray both in its

---

[1] And her fair face, fair bosom he bedews
With tears, tears of remorse, of ruth, of sorrow,
As the pale rose her colour lost renews
With the fresh drops fall'n from the silver morrow,
So she revives, and cheeks empurpled shows
Moist with their own tears and with tears they borrow.
(Fairfax)

[2] That as against the warmth of Titan's fire,
Snowdrifts consume on tops of mountains tall,
So melts her wrath ; but love remains entire.
" Behold," she says, " your handmaid and your thrall :
My life, my crown, my wealth, use at your pleasure."
(Fairfax)

beliefs and its pleasures, saw that it must not ask too much of these erring spirits or impose too heavy demands upon them. It therefore laid great emphasis on the need and beauty of confession and repentance, even at the last hour. It was not for nothing that painters of the sixteenth century liked to paint St. Mary Magdalene. She embodied a whole world of sentiment concerning men and women, especially women, who combined the pleasures of youth with a decorous and devout middle age. The young woman, who in the height of her sinfulness and in the flower of her beauty, prostrates herself before Christ was dear to this amorous age which saw in her combination of beauty and holiness, of past sins and present repentance, something very near and dear to itself. It believed that she was closer to Christ because she had loved much and that her sins only made His love greater for her in the end. Armida appeals to this sentiment. The greatness of her faults adds to the glory of her repentance, and the beauty which is still hers increases the interest of her conversion.

Tasso's solution for Armida finds an interesting contrast in Spenser's treatment of a similar theme. In his " Boure of blis " and his character of Acrasie he followed Tasso's Armida closely. A gallant knight is seduced and depraved by an enchantress in circumstances of extraordinary beauty. But Spenser's conclusion is quite different from Tasso's. The good Sir Guyon comes to the magic bower and breaks its enchantment. So far from being allowed a chance to repent, Acrasie is left in bonds, and her bower is destroyed not by her but by Sir Guyon. Spenser of course wrote for an England touched by a Puritanism which felt that sexual irregularity was a grave sin and almost past forgiveness. Confession played no part in its religion, and it preferred virtue to repentance. Indeed the Catholic and the Puritan are sharply differentiated in the different importance which they attach to the spirit and the flesh. The Catholic, especially under the Counter-Reformation, felt that sins of the flesh were less grave than those of the spirit and that therefore Armida, who is capable at last of true love, can be forgiven. The Protestant, with his horror of the flesh, felt that its sins were worse than those of the spirit, which can be corrected by instruction. Tasso, with an insight beyond Spenser, makes

Armida's love for Rinaldo, base and selfish though it is at first, become the means for her salvation. He felt that love of this kind had in it something good and noble and that it could, if properly treated, get rid of its corruption and baseness.

It seems, then, that in his treatment of love Tasso follows a principle and seeks to show how the sufferings and sins of his lovers are obstacles which have to be overcome in their attainment of a fuller and more Christian character. He did not find such a scheme without a conflict with himself, and it is true that into his account of illicit pleasures he puts some of his finest poetry and warms rather more to such subjects than to the praise of virtue. But that is because he understood, perhaps too well, the fascination and the dangers of love and its extraordinary appeal even to the noblest men. He knew both sides of the question, and his imagination rose to both with poetical impartiality. From this conflict and contradiction his poetry gained. The hold which Armida has on Rinaldo is easier to understand than the hold which Dido has on Aeneas, just because it is depicted with so flaming an imagination and with so vivid an understanding of what it means. The final solution is all the more impressive not merely because of the change in Armida but because it has been preceded by so different a kind of poetry. Nor is this process psychologically false. When Tancredi derives a new strength from the vision of Clorinda and takes his place so effectively in the battlefield, he is rid of a distracting influence which has hitherto hampered his efforts. So too when Rinaldo is shriven and comes back to the camp looking a different man, he really is a different man. He has got rid of his voluptuousness and is ready to concentrate on the martial prowess which belongs to his true nature. In such changes the power which has worked for evil may also work for good. His love for Clorinda at last spurs Tancredi to show all his powers against Argante, and it is Armida's love for Rinaldo and his for her which provide the beginning of their new lives.

Tasso's introduction of such themes as magic and love raises an aesthetic as well as a moral question. His first critics, and others after them, have argued that such imaginary and romantic subjects have no place in a heroic epic. It is true that they are unusual, and that Virgil gives them only a subordinate place. In this criticism there is an element of truth. The appeal of epic, whether primary or secondary, is to our admiration for human achievements, and if too many marvels are introduced, we feel that the subject is unreal and does not touch us very closely. That is, no doubt, why Camões, with his firm hold on fact, kept his marvels in so strict control. But Tasso works differently. There is no great gap between what is real and what is unreal in his poem, between his history and his magic. The two elements are closely interwoven, and we pass easily from one to the other, from the catalogue of the Egyptian forces to Armida in a jewelled chariot drawn by unicorns. The reason for this is that in the *Gerusalemme* fact passes imperceptibly into fancy and becomes merged with it. Even when Tasso owes something to history, he sees it in relation not to the common world but to an inner, special world of his own. His battle-scenes, for all their detailed presentation, are not accounts of real battles but creations of his imagination. His characters are not copied from life but projections of his own experience and desires ; even in Erminia there is something of Tasso's own melancholy and in the Sage something of his ambition to be a philosopher. The intense emotions which sweep his characters along have a simplicity which would be simplification if Tasso did not make them convincing in his imaginary world. The many landscapes with their birds and streams and flowers belong to no countryside but come from the art of the Renaissance and its cult of gardens. Tasso combines these elements into a whole because they are all deeply impregnated with his own desires and dreams ; they are products of his meditations and projections of himself. The *Gerusalemme* is really a world of its own, with its own rules and its own atmosphere. It is wrong to test it by reality or to judge it by the practice of other epics. It arose in special circumstances, and its author was very unlike Virgil or Camões. His achievement is to have given to his dreams and fancies a solidity and persuasiveness so great that many have judged them as if they were a transcript of fact.

This dream-world of Tasso's is none the less informed by an extremely serious purpose. He has his own conceptions of glory and sacrifice and of the parts which they play in a heroic life. The sacrifice demanded of his Crusaders is not so much that they should renounce many things which men value as that they should subordinate them to a divine scheme of existence and pursue them in the right spirit. What is wrong with the loves of Tancredi and of Rinaldo is not that they are loves but that they are unsanctified ; all is changed when Clorinda is baptised and Armida repents. This view of what a man must pursue or avoid spreads beyond Tasso's love-stories to his whole conception of glory. Living in an age which had seen the collapse of many high pretensions in Italy, he felt that earthly glory was in itself of no great import-ance. When the rescuers of Rinaldo pass the site of Carthage, Tasso pauses to point a moral on the futility of earthly grandeur :

> Giace l' alta Cartago ; appena i segni
> De l' alte sue ruine il lido serba.
> Muoiono le città, muoiono i regni,
> Copre i fasti e le pompe arena ed erba ;
> E l' uom d' esser mortal par che si sdegni :
> Oh nostra mente cupida e superba ! [1]
>
> (XV, 20, 1-6)

So too when God sends a dream in the form of Ugone to Goffredo, it shows him the wonders and beauties of Heaven and then tells him how small in comparison is any achieve-ment of man :

> Quanto è vil la cagion ch' a la virtude
> Umana è colà giù premio e contrasto !
> In che picciolo cerchio e fra che nude
> Solitudini è stretto il vostro fasto ! [2]
>
> (XIV, 10, 1-4)

Against this illusory and unimportant glory Tasso sets the glory which a man gets by fighting for his faith. It is this

---

[1] Great Carthage low in ashes cold doth lie,
Her ruins poor the herbs in height scant pass,
So cities fall, so perish kingdoms high,
Their pride and pomp lies hid in sand and grass :
Then why should mortal man repine to die,
Whose life, is air ; breath, wind ; and body, glass ?
(Fairfax)

[2] How vile, how small, and of how slender price,
Compared with this is their achievement's gain ;
A narrow room our glory vain upties,
A little circle doth our pride contain.
(Fairfax)

which Goffredo attributes to Dudone who is killed in battle and which the dream promises to Goffredo himself when he dies. The glory which Homer found in remembrance by other men, Tasso finds in the Christian belief that the good are rewarded after death and that this is the only real glory. By this means he preserves some of the old respect for heroic actions and self-sacrifice but relates them to a scheme in which what counts most is the end for which they are undertaken. Even in the martial frenzy of Rinaldo we must see the doings of a Christian knight who is able to show such prowess because he has made his peace with God.

Yet though Tasso undoubtedly shapes his epic to a Christian purpose in the true spirit of the Counter-Reformation and gives a new meaning to many old ideas of heroism and chivalry, that is not his only or his chief claim. The *Gerusalemme* succeeds as poetry because it is generously and vividly alive. Its most remarkable characteristic is an intensity which shows itself not only in its sustained lyrical quality but in the characters and their actions. The atmosphere of doubt and misgiving which encompasses Aeneas is completely lacking. Goffredo is as firm in counsel as he is unflinching in fight; Clorinda is as whole-hearted in repentance as in her earlier loyalty to her old faith; Armida yields to Rinaldo with the same intensity that she showed in dominating him; Rinaldo is as single-minded in battle as in love. The characters reflect Tasso's own fervid and tense personality with its distrust of irony and humour and its capacity for treating every situation with the utmost concentration and seriousness. Tasso's seriousness and solemnity are what most of all separate him from Ariosto, and show that he lived in a different world from the high Renaissance. Though in the *Gerusalemme* we may miss the humour and the humanity of the *Orlando Furioso*, it is just because Tasso's poem is so serious that it can claim to be a real epic and not a chivalrous romance. Despite his youth, Tasso had a creative vision of life which helped him to turn his own struggles and renunciations into a poem for his age. Like Virgil and Camões, he saw that the goal which he set for mankind imposed heavy burdens on those who sought it and that glory is found only by the sacrifice of much that men usually desire and respect. And the extent of this sacrifice is shown in the wonderful poetry which Tasso sheds on the common objects of desire whether in Armida's garden or in the ambitions of Solimano and Argante. Though his own spiritual conflict exacted a heavy price from him in later years, in his great poem Tasso resolved it and brought his discordant elements to harmony and order.

Though the main plan and the dominating spirit of the *Gerusalemme* belong to the Counter-Reformation, its richness is due to the special position which Tasso holds between the Renaissance and Counter-Reformation. The Counter-Reformation had on the whole a deplorable effect on the arts, partly because in its desire to reach a public wider than the old cultivated aristocracy it encouraged a vulgar sentimentality, partly because in its insistence on external conformity to Christian beliefs it fostered a cynical perversity such as we find in Caravaggio. It is indeed remarkable that the chief poet of this age should have been the serious and eager Tasso with his sense of human achievement and his love of passionate personalities. The truth is that, though Tasso did not accept the humanistic ideals of the Renaissance, he was sufficiently close to it to preserve much of its essential seriousness and love of life. Even his reformed ideal of Christian heroism reflects an earlier age which believed that man could really be heroic. From the Renaissance come the purity of his taste, his lucent language, his pleasure in varied and vivid action, his devotion to knowledge and his interest even in its more recondite and perilous branches. If Ariosto shows the Renaissance in its gaiety and its glory, Tasso shows how some of its most typical qualities still lived for men who had disowned its ideals. In him the Renaissance makes its final appearance, tamed and ordered and even denied, but still powerful in its assertion of human worth and in the wide range of its appreciation and sensibility.

V

MILTON AND THE DESTINY
OF MAN

Far more consciously and deliberately than Camões, Milton
in his education, his early travels, his unshaken sense of a
vocation, his long delays and hesitations before beginning his
great poem, carries out Vida's prescription for an epic poet.
After deciding early in life to write an epic he gave years of
thought to finding the right subject and of self-discipline to
maturing his mind and perfecting his art. In 1628, when he
was nineteen years old, he showed in *At a Vacation Exercise*
that he was already thinking of a heroic poem,

> Such as the wise *Demodocus* once told
> In solemn songs at King *Alcinous* feast.

From this youthful ambition he moved to the idea of an
Arthuriad, an epic which, while it took King Arthur for its
central figure, would through the traditional devices of
prophecy and the like treat of the great events of English
history from its mythical dawn to his own times. This poem
was never written. If it had been, it might have been an
English counterpart to *Os Lusiadas* and have displayed with
Miltonic magnificence the splendours and struggles of our
national past. We can only imagine how Milton would have
treated it, what solidity and clarity he would have given to
the old stories,

> and what resounds
> In Fable or *Romance* of *Uthers* Son
> Begirt with *British* and *Armoric* Knights,
> (*P.L.* I, 579-81)

what charm and grace he would have put into his account

> Of Fairy Damsels met in Forest wide
> By Knights of *Logres*, or of *Lyones*,
> *Lancelot* or *Pelleas*, or *Pellenore*.
> (*P.R.* II, 359-61)

Milton nowhere says why he abandoned this project so suited

194

in many ways to his robust and bellicose temperament, and we can only guess his reasons. Some have thought that they were political. The Arthurian legend seems to have been revived by the Tudor monarchs both to provide an ancient background to their own family history and to suggest that with them the *flos regum Arthurus* had in some sense returned to England, as Merlin had foretold that he would. It was a royalist and monarchical legend, and Milton, growing more republican with every year, would at last have nothing to do with it. This may be so, but it is likely that other reasons affected Milton's decision. The *Arthuriad* would have been a patriotic poem, and when Milton ceased to believe that God had chosen England for special divine dispensation, he seems to have lost his old love for his country and to have turned his attention to the individual soul as it stands alone before God. Moreover, the Arthurian legends were not certainly true. In his *History of Britain*, written in the first years of the Civil War, Milton shows his doubts : " Who Arthur was, and whether ever any such reigned in Britain, hath been doubted heretofore, and may again with good reason ". Milton was too convinced that epic must tell the truth to use so doubtful a legend as this, and he abandoned his plan of an *Arthuriad*. For some years he flung himself into politics and active life ; then after 1655, when his blindness forced him to give up many of his public duties and to accept a pension, he began to compose a very different poem and in 1667 published *Paradise Lost*.

Paradise Lost is by common consent an epic poem, and Milton himself calls it heroic :

> Since first this subject for Heroic Song
> Pleas'd me long choosing, and beginning late.
>
> (IX, 25-6)

It was intended to resemble preceding epics in its manner and to surpass them in its subject. Milton knew what he was doing. He had studied the ancients like Homer and Virgil, the Italians like Boiardo, Ariosto and Tasso, and he knew Camões, if not in the original, at least in the translation of Sir Richard Fanshawe, who was a public figure of the time and published his *Lusiad* in 1655. Milton's indebtedness to his predecessors is clear on every page of his poem in episodes and phrases taken from them. He had mastered the epic poetry available to him and sought to convey in a new setting what was best in the tradition. In *Paradise Lost* we find all the familiar features of the epic such as war, single combats, perilous journeys, beautiful gardens, marvellous buildings, visions of the world and of the future, expositions of the structure of the universe, and scenes in Heaven and in Hell. Yet all these are so transformed that their significance and even their aesthetic appeal are new. The reason is that Milton has grafted his epic manner onto a subject which lies outside the main epic tradition. By finding his subject in the Bible he had to make the machinery of epic conform to a spirit and to a tradition far removed from Virgil. Before him the best literary epic had been predominantly secular ; he made it theological, and the change of approach meant a great change of temper and of atmosphere. The old themes are introduced in all their traditional dignity, but in Milton's hands they take on a different significance and contribute to a different end.

Milton, who owes so much to his predecessors, is at pains to explain that his subject is better than any of theirs. In the first place he claims that it is true. Of this he seems to have had no doubt. Despite his refusal to submit to any Church and his difficulty in finding any satisfactory creed, he clung devotedly to the Bible as the Word of God, and since his subject was largely based on it, he believed that his position was unassailable. He even goes further than this and claims divine inspiration. When he calls on Urania to inspire him, he explains that she is no classical invention but a divine power:

> Thou with Eternal wisdom didst converse,
> Wisdom thy Sister, and with her didst play
> In presence of th' Almightie Father, pleas'd
> With thy Celestial Song.   (VII, 9-12)

This power not only helps him to compose but actually gives him his words ; it is she

>   who deignes
> Her nightly visitation unimplor'd,
> And dictates to me slumbring, or inspires
> Easie my unpremeditated Verse.
>   (IX, 21-3)

Milton's Heavenly Muse is a divine voice, close to the Holy

196

Spirit, whom in his opening lines he invokes immediately after her and calls to illumine and support him ; she is the Voice of God that spoke to Moses from Oreb and Sinai. Coming from such a source Milton's poem demands special respect. No Christian writer of epic had made comparable claims. It is true that Tasso's Muse may be the Virgin, but he is discreet in his appeal to her and certainly does not claim that she gives him either his subject or his words, while Camões, who lays emphasis on the truth of his story, appeals simply to the Nymphs of the Tagus who have little more than a conventional or allegorical existence. At the outset Milton claims to be heard with a peculiar attention because he repeats what the Voice of God has told him.

Milton also claims that his subject is more heroic than that of any other epic and explicitly singles out Homer and Virgil for invidious comparison :

> Sad task, yet argument
> Not less but more Heroic than the wrauth
> Of stern *Achilles* on his Foe pursu'd
> Thrice fugitive about *Troy* Wall ; or rage
> Of *Turnus* for *Lavinia* disespous'd,
> Or *Neptun's* ire or *Juno's*, that so long
> Perplex'd the *Greek* and *Cytherea's* son.
>
> (IX, 13-19)

His objection to Homer and Virgil is that they treat of war, and Milton rejects war as not a truly heroic subject. He introduces it on a noble scale into *Paradise Lost*, but his war is of a very special kind, unlike human war and far more important in its issues and its results. His fuller feelings about the old ideal of military prowess can be seen in his words on the Giants who were born to the Sons of God from the daughters of men :

> For in those dayes Might onely shall be admir'd,
> And Valour and Heroic Vertu call'd ;
> To overcome in Battel, and subdue
> Nations, and bring home spoils with infinite
> Man-slaughter, shall be held the greatest pitch
> Of human Glorie, and for Glorie done
> Of triumph, to be styl'd great Conquerours,
> Patrons of Mankind, Gods, and Sons of Gods,
> Destroyers rightlier call'd and Plagues of men.
>
> (XI, 685-93)

197

There is not much justification in *Genesis* for this view of the
Giants, and Milton's outburst shows that he felt a need to say
what he really thought of the old heroic ideal. He is equally
uncompromising in his rejection of chivalrous epic with its
tournaments, armour and feasts, on the ground that it relies
for its appeal on external circumstances instead of on truly
heroic qualities. He suggests that patience and martyrdom
are more suitable subjects, though no one has yet attempted
them, and though he himself can hardly be said to deal with
them. He indicates that he has his own idea of a heroic
poem, but he does not say what it is ; he leaves us to find
it out from his story. It is, however, clear that the qualities
which he thinks heroic are not those which win power and
glory but those which concern the relations of man to God
and are good in the ethical sense of the word.

The august character of Milton's subject is matched by
his style. Of all grand styles it is the grandest, and that not
merely in its sustained sonority and its distance from the
speech of every day. It has a more than Latin solidity ; in
comparison with the language of Camões or of Tasso it is
cold and even inhuman. No concessions are made to human
weakness ; all topics are raised to the same sublime level.
But it is easy to misunderstand and to under-estimate this
style. *Paradise Lost* was composed by a blind man, much of
it in the sleepless hours of the night. In it Milton created out
of his memories a second world to replace the visible world
which he had lost. His poem must have its own independence
and its own strength ; it must live for the ear and for the mind
as other poetry lives for the eye and for the sensibility. This
solidity may blind us to the great emotional reserves and
hidden powers which *Paradise Lost* contains ; the classicism
of the form and the grandeur of the language may prevent us
from seeing how deeply informed with emotion it is. But
slowly we feel the imaginative power which lies in these
marmoreal lines, the vivid personal experience that has gone
to their making, and the life which still stirs in this stiff dress
when other poetry, superficially more attractive, ceases to
move us. The poem was written after a great crisis in
Milton's life. He, who had believed that the Commonwealth
would establish the Rule of the Saints on earth, and had looked
forward to " a universal and mild monarchy " in England,

had seen all his hopes founder. He turned from the stricken political scene to his poem and hoped to create in it the order which he had failed to find in the common world. His love of order, his classical taste for words, his dominating and uncompromising intellect, shaped the poem that we know, but behind its swelling harmonies we can detect the sufferings and the disillusion through which Milton had passed and over which he had, in himself at least, triumphed. *Paradise Lost* gradually reveals the range of Milton's emotional experience. Its apparent coldness is, after all, only apparent, the solid form which Milton gave to this, his greatest message about human life. In style, as in subject, Milton withdrew from active life in the hope of finding something more durable and more satisfying.

Milton's subject, as he says at the start, is the Fall of Man ; Adam is his central figure and, in the literary sense, his hero. We may well wonder how such a subject and such a hero can be raised to the level of epic ; for Adam's fall does not normally awaken admiration for human achievement or a sense of man's grandeur in the universe. But Milton's poem is heroic because of the great issues with which it deals. He counts these the most important of all issues ; for they concern the goodness and the baseness of man. Whereas other epics display a struggle for what is in the last analysis a temporal or worldly end, like the foundation of Rome or even the capture of Jerusalem, Milton displays a struggle between good and evil, both in the special case of Adam and in the more general cases of the fallen Angels and of Adam's descendants. To him this seems much more important than any struggle yet told in epic, and, granted that his premisses are right, it is impossible to confute him. Moreover, the greatness of the struggle calls for qualities equally great. *Paradise Lost* sets forth the noblest virtues and the darkest sins. On one side is the Son, on the other Satan. By displaying these extremes of conduct Milton may seriously claim that his persons are, by his standards, more heroic than Achilles or Aeneas. For him the question of right and wrong was more important than any other question ; he recognised almost no kind of good except the good in conduct. Other poets had valued other, more worldly goods such as power and success, and though they had related these to some sort of divine scheme and justified them morally, their concept of the good was wider and much less strictly ethical than Milton's. For him heroism is goodness, and he sets out to show what he means by this. It is this

> which justly gives Heroic name
> To Person or to Poem,   (IX, 40-41)

and which guides Milton in the construction of his epic.

Adam is the central figure of *Paradise Lost*; his actions give unity to it, his fate is its chief subject. He takes the place of Aeneas. Like him he is not perfect, and like him, when he errs, his errors lead to grave results. In creating him Milton attempted a very peculiar task. Adam, the father of mankind, is almost without human experience. He cannot therefore have even so much personality as Aeneas. Milton has to present a figure who appeals imaginatively and poetically and has a natural magnificence that fits him to be the hero of an epic. In Milton's time Adam was still a powerful figure in the popular imagination and kept some of the impressive dignity which he had for the Fathers of the Church and for the Middle Ages. As the only man ever created entirely free from sin, he was unique ; as the ancestor of all mankind, he had a special importance ; as the chosen companion of God, he possessed knowledge denied to his descendants. Adam, who meant so much to St. Ambrose, to Dante and to the sculptor who set his image high on the cathedral at Chartres, meant nearly as much to Milton. But Milton has to place him in epic surroundings and contrast him implicitly with other epic heroes. He does so without flinching, and often to his advantage. Other heroes might have a noble appearance ; Adam is nobler still,

> *Adam* the goodliest man of men since born
> His Sons.   (IV, 323-4)

He is indeed the lord of creation, which exists entirely for him and for Eve ; he has named the animals, and they sport for his entertainment ; his dwelling is rich with all the beauty that flowers and trees can give. His very lack of external splendour only enhances his natural dignity, as when he goes to meet Raphael :

.without more train
. Accompani'd then with his own compleat
· Perfections, in himself was all his state,
More solemn then the tedious pomp that waits
On Princes, when thir rich Retinue long
Of Horses led, and Grooms besmeard with Gold
Dazles the croud, and sets them all agape.

(v, 351-7)

He greets Raphael with a high natural courtesy, which the Archangel appreciates and acknowledges. Within his limited experience Adam is well informed, and there is no point which he does not take and understand at its proper worth. He is not natural man, as Rousseau was later to imagine him; still less is he the primitive savage of anthropology. He is man in the original splendour of innocence, man as he might have been if sin had not come into the world. An age which accepted the Bible as a record of truth would understand what Milton meant by him.

This impressive figure has two devoted loyalties, to his Maker and to his wife. These constitute his *pietas* and show a nobility of character worthy of so noble an appearance. In them he finds satisfying and exalting objects for his thoughts and actions. Both devotions appear in the first words that he speaks, when he begins with a declaration of his love for Eve and proceeds to show his love for God. For God he feels, above all, gratitude for having set him in such bliss. He gladly gives praise and gladly keeps the single prohibition that he must not eat of the Tree of Knowledge. The joy which he takes in his existence and the gratitude which he feels for it find noble expression in the morning hymn, the *Benedicite*, which he and Eve offer to God before setting out on their daily tasks. In calling on the powers of nature to celebrate their Maker Adam shows his own delight at living in so beautiful and so harmonious a world. In nature he sees the manifestation of God's goodness, and his language suggests that for him all this splendid natural frame is a kind of dance or symphony in which he takes his own delighted part. The imagery of music is dear to Milton, and he makes Adam in his unfallen state participate in the divine joy of those who submit to the will of God and find in this submission a pleasure comparable to that of hearing or playing music.

Adam hears angelic voices singing about him day and night, and this is almost an emblem of his state. He is entirely contented. Therefore he does not question God's command not to eat of the Tree and cannot conceive that he should ever wish to do so. When Raphael suggests that there is a danger of this, Adam dismisses it as impossible :

> can wee want obedience then
> To him, or possibly his love desert
> Who formd us from the dust, and plac'd us here
> Full to the utmost measure of what bliss
> Human desires can seek or apprehend ?
>
> (v, 514-18)

Adam lives in the eye of God, and is entirely happy to do so. He asks for nothing else and cannot imagine that he should.

Adam's other devotion is to Eve. The mother of mankind is as pre-eminent in female beauty as her husband is in male. This beauty Milton, true to his early and lasting love for ancient poetry, suggests by comparisons with figures from Greek and Roman legend. Eve is like Pandora, like Juno when Jupiter smiles on her, like Flora when Zephyrus breathes on her, like all the young goddesses of field and orchard :

> To *Pales*, or *Pomona*, thus adornd,
> Likest she seemd, *Pomona* when she fled
> *Vertumnus*, or to *Ceres* in her Prime,
> Yet Virgin of *Proserpina* from *Jove*.
>
> (IX, 393-6)

Eve is the only human being that Adam knows. To her he gives all his human affection, and he loves her with a complete, unquestioning love. Their love is both spiritual and physical. Milton does not shrink from showing how in their state of innocence their love for each other is fully and beautifully satisfied. It is the ideal marriage,

> Uninterrupted joy, unrivald love; (III, 68)

and because it is innocent, because Adam and Eve know that what they do is right, it has a special sanctity. Milton contrasts their sleep in the leafy bower, lulled by the music of nightingales, with the wanton loves of modern life. He insists that the marriage of Adam and Eve was a real marriage and contradicts St. Augustine who denies that they could have had sexual relations. Milton maintains that since Adam and Eve are to bear children and people the earth, they must know each other physically, and he makes this knowledge as innocent and as beautiful as he can. This love is innocent because God commands and approves it, and Milton leaves no doubt about his own feelings towards it :

> Sleep on,
> Blest pair ; and O yet happiest if ye seek
> No happier state, and know to know no more.
>
> (IV, 773-5)

The harmony of Adam and Eve is the earthly counterpart of the harmony that reigns in Heaven ; it is complete and satisfying because it is based on love.

Into Eve Milton has thrown much of his own deep admiration for womanhood. She is not only beautiful, but until Satan tempts her, she is almost all that a wife ought to be. She loves Adam as much as he loves her, and has always loved him since she first saw him and realised that she needed him. In his company she finds everything a delight :

> With thee conversing I forget all time,
> All seasons and thir change, all please alike,
>
> (IV, 639-40)

and she says that without him even the most beautiful sights mean nothing to her. After the frightening dream which Satan has sent her, she finds strength and comfort in Adam. She shares with him the cheerful, daily task of gardening in Eden. She is even, in her special circumstances, a good housewife ; she prepares their dinner of " savourie fruits ", and when Raphael joins them at it, she ministers to his and to Adam's wants and fills their cups. When Raphael discourses to Adam, she listens in respectful silence to the story of the war in Heaven and of the Creation, but when the talk turns to more disputable topics like the awkward comparison of the Ptolemaic and Copernican systems, she sees the studious look on her husband's face and retires

> With lowliness Majestic from her seat,
> And Grace that won who saw to wish her stay.
>
> (VIII, 42-3)

This perfect union excites the envy of Satan when he sees it and knows that he is shut out for ever from anything like it. It is Milton's idea of a perfect marriage, of something which hardly exists in the world as he knows it but is a type of what the relations between man and woman ought to be.

Adam's devotion to God and his devotion to Eve seem to involve no conflict. Yet even before Satan takes advantage of such a possibility, there are signs that Adam may find himself torn between his two loyalties and make a wrong choice between them. In his love for Eve he is in danger of losing his reasonable control of himself. He tells Raphael of his deep admiration for her, and especially he hints that she disarms his judgment :

> All higher knowledge in her presence falls
> Degraded, Wisdom in discourse with her
> Looses discount'nanc't, and like folly shewes.
>
> (VIII, 551-3)

Raphael listens to this eager confession " with contracted brow " and discourages Adam from allowing his love for Eve to rule his reason. He admits that she is beautiful, but he denies that beauty is everything and tells Adam that he should not submit to her :

> fair no doubt, and worthy well
> Thy cherishing, thy honouring, and thy love,
> Not thy subjection,   (VIII, 568-70)

and his farewell words warn Adam against allowing passion to sway his judgment. There is, Milton hints, a chance that if Adam has to choose between his two devotions, he will make the wrong choice. So far this is only a warning. The crisis is still remote, and Adam has been forewarned and should be forearmed. In the meanwhile the first couple of mankind show how delightful and complete life can be in a state of innocence.

This perfect harmony is broken, and in showing how this happens Milton follows a scheme that recalls Greek tragedy. The material from which the tragic crisis arises is the conflict of Adam's loyalties to God and to Eve. The power that starts the crisis comes from outside in Satan, but this power makes use of the potential weakness which it finds in Adam and drives him to choose wrongly, to break the harmony of existence by disobeying God, and so to precipitate a tragic

situation in which life has lost all its charm and death seems
desirable. Milton uses the ancient device of the Warner in
Raphael, and treats Adam's fault in the Greek manner as
the excess of what is in moderation a virtue. Satan works
upon Eve, no doubt because she is the weaker member of the
human pair. First he puts doubts into her head by sending
her a dream ; then he finds her alone and plays upon her
credulous vanity. He is lucky to find her away from Adam,
but even this has its reason. Eve, from some female whim,
has wished to assert her independence and to work alone.
Her desire is harmless enough, but she insists obstinately on
it despite her husband's wish to the contrary, and shows that
she is good material for Satan to work upon, while by giving
in to her petulance Adam shows that his love for her sways his
judgment and is not without its dangers. Once Eve goes off
by herself, she is ruined :

> O much deceav'd, much failing, hapless *Eve*,
> Of thy presum'd return ! event perverse !
> Thou never from that houre in Paradise
> Foundst either sweet repast, or sound repose.
> (IX, 404-7)

Eve's fall is not the Fall of Man. Adam could and should
reject her request to share the forbidden fruit with her, but
when he hears what she has done, the weakness and unreason
against which Raphael has warned him rise and dominate his
nature. He knows quite well what Eve's action means and
that she has acted wrongly :

> How art thou lost, how on a sudden lost,
> Defac't, deflourd, and now to Death devote ?
> (IX, 900-901)

Nor does he deceive himself about his own decision to share
Eve's guilt. He finds himself torn between his love of God
and his love of Eve, and he decides to follow the second. He
cannot endure to live without Eve, and since he believes that
she is now doomed to die, he prefers to die with her :

> How can I live without thee, how forgoe
> Thy sweet Converse and Love so dearly joyn'd,
> To live again in these wilde Woods forlorn ?
> (IX, 908-10)

In this state of mind, knowing well how wrongly he is acting, Adam gives in to his love for Eve, and the irreparable evil is done. Like other tragic heroes, he has been faced by a choice between two conflicting desires, and he follows the wrong one. Milton marks the tragic crisis by nature's response to it:

> Earth trembl'd from her entrails, as again
> In pangs, and Nature gave a second groan,
> Skie lowr'd, and muttering Thunder, some sad drops
> Wept at compleating of the mortal Sin
> Original.   (IX, 1000-1004)

The harmony which existed between Heaven and Earth is now broken, and disaster will follow.

The sin of Adam and Eve is disobedience to God. Milton says so in the first line of *Paradise Lost*, and there is no need to stress it further. They have been told that all in Eden is theirs to enjoy but that they must not eat of the Tree of Knowledge. They disobey this command, and so break the conditions which govern their life. For Milton disobedience to God is the fundamental sin, the root of all evil, and in committing it Adam and Eve display what sin really means in human life. But Milton had not thought about such matters for years without finding an explanation for them. In his system disobedience to God is wrong because in it man denies his rational nature and so cuts himself off from God who is known through reason. The lesson is given later by Michael, when, after telling Adam of Babel, he says:

> Reason in man obscur'd, or not obeyd,
> Immediately inordinate desires
> And upstart Passions catch the Government
> From Reason, and to servitude reduce
> Man till then free.   •   (XII, 86-90)

Against this Raphael has warned Adam, and when the Son delivers his judgment, he partly repeats Raphael's words. Adam has sinned with his eyes open, knowing what he does. He has no defence and no excuse better than

> Shee gave me of the Tree, and I did eate.   (X, 144)

Adam's sin is therefore typical of all sins. In it he disobeys God and allows his passion to conquer his reason. It does not matter that the actual eating of the fruit may seem in itself a trivial thing. It is considered not in isolation but in relation to God's command against it. The prohibition imposed a test on Adam, and in the test he fails.

The sin of Adam has also its psychological significance. It affects him and Eve in a special way which shows what sin is. The Tree, of which they eat, gives knowledge of good and evil. Adam himself, as God later, explains what this means : they have lost good and found evil ; if they had not eaten, they would have continued to know good alone. In other words, whereas before they knew that all their actions were good, now they feel that they are evil, and they are right in feeling this, for they themselves are full of evil desires and appetites. After eating the apple they become like drunkards :

> They swim in mirth, and fansie that they feel
> Divinitie within them breeding wings
> Wherewith to scorn the Earth,
>
> (IX, 1009-11)

and their love which before was unashamed becomes carnal and lascivious. From it Adam rises with shame and a sense of guilt ; he wishes to hide himself from the heavenly powers upon whom he used to look with such a happy confidence :

> Cover me ye Pines,
> Ye Cedars, with innumerable boughs
> Hide me, where I may never see them more.
>
> (IX, 1088-90)

The sign of this shame is that Adam and Eve now cover their nakedness with aprons. Milton marks the change with one of his most significant similes. They who before had all the majesty of naked innocence and were the lords of the world are now like savages :

> O how unlike
> To that first naked glorie. Such of late
> *Columbus* found th' *American* so girt
> With featherd cincture, naked else and wilde
> Among the Trees on Iles and woodie Shores.
>
> (IX, 1114-18)

The simile shows the degree of the Fall. From their old dignity Adam and Eve have become like the lowest of mankind, conscious only of their human shame.

The tragic crisis of the Fall leads to tragic results. The old harmony has been destroyed, and discord follows. Adam and Eve, who have lived in perfect concord, quarrel and recriminate each other. Each tries to put the blame on the other. Once their passions have begun to take command, there seems to be no end to the disorder in their souls :

> They sate them down to weep, nor onely Teares
> Raind at thir Eyes, but high Winds worse within
> Began to rise, high Passions, Anger, Hate,
> Mistrust, Suspicion, Discord, and shook sore
> Thir inward State of Mind, calme Region once
> And full of Peace, now tost and turbulent.
>
> (IX, 1121-6)

This discord in them is matched by discord in the world. Sin and Death find their way into it, and the animal creation, which has hitherto lived at peace with itself, turns to mutual slaughter. God no longer regards the earth with his old tenderness now that it has falsified his hopes of it, and he gives orders for its delights to be diminished. The sun and moon are regulated to prove more noxious; the axis of the earth is set askew, and the old temperate climate is replaced by one of extremes, while fierce winds blow from all quarters of the compass. The change in nature corresponds to the change in man and rises from the same cause. The old harmony no longer exists between God and man; God no longer delights in what He has made, and shows His displeasure by spoiling its perfection. Adam sees what happens and is filled with despair. All his old glory is lost. He is like those figures of Greek tragedy who feel in their fall that life has no longer any value for them and that it would be better for them not to have been born :

> On the ground
> Outstrecht he lay, on the cold ground, and oft
> Curs't his Creation. (X, 850-51)

The old full life is replaced by a feeling of emptiness and futility; the old dignity is lost in despair.

Again like heroes of Greek tragedy who are struck by some appalling disaster, Adam and Eve think of death. Adam welcomes the idea of it :

> how gladly would I meet
> Mortalitie my sentence, and be Earth
> Insensible, how glad would lay me down
> As in my Mothers lap ?   (x, 775-8)

Eve interprets this wish by suggesting that they should even seek death at their own hands. From this despair they recover. Adam, who has spurned Eve as his temptress, is touched by her pity for him, and this gives him a new sense of something worth living for :

> But rise, let us no more contend, nor blame
> Each other, blam'd enough elsewhere, but strive
> To offices of Love, how we may light'n
> Each others burden in our share of woe.
>
> (x, 958-61)

Eve is slow to respond, but in the end she is persuaded that life may still hold something for them if they humble themselves before God. Despite the Christian setting Milton concludes his crisis in the Greek spirit. The disaster which has befallen Adam and Eve creates in them a true modesty and sense of their insignificance before God. Just as Sophocles makes his tragic events teach in different ways this lesson and find in it their solution, so Milton ends his tragic presentation of Adam and Eve by making them offer prayers of sorrow and humility and find an end to their present misery and a hope of a new, different life. To this result their human affections contribute. Adam's love for Eve, which has been the cause of his fall, is also the cause of his recovery. Reawakened by her pity for him, it enables him to master his emotions and to take the initiative in restoring their broken lives.

The Greek tragedians seldom take their tragic story beyond such a point, but in the vast frame of his epic Milton shows what this recovery means and what good comes of it for mankind. Though God's plan for Eden has failed, yet out of this failure He will create something good, and with this Milton is earnestly concerned. The last two books of *Paradise Lost* display the need for nobility in a fallen and disordered world. This is the new heroism which Milton offers to our attention ; this is his reformed heroic outlook. The evil doings of Adam's breed are beyond doubt. In vision and from prophecy Adam learns what his descendants will be and is allowed no illusion or false hopes :

> so shall the World goe on,
> To good malignant, to bad men benigne,
> Under her own waight groaning.
>
> (XII, 537-9)

But this inherent badness of the world is a challenge to human
virtue. Michael shows contrasted scenes of war and peace,
of pleasure and pain, only to point out that each has its own
faults and may be equally wrong. He instructs Adam in the
nature of each case and forms his mind to judge it rightly.
By so doing he awakes a real sense of good and evil in Adam
and leads him to draw his own conclusion :

> Henceforth I learne, that to obey is best,
> And love with feare the onely God, to walk
> As in his presence, ever to observe
> His providence, and on him sole depend.
>
> (XII, 561-4)

Michael approves this, and tells Adam that if he follows his
knowledge with the right deeds, he will be amply rewarded :

> add Faith,
> Add Vertue, Patience, Temperance, add Love,
> By name to come call'd Charitie, the soul
> Of all the rest : then wilt thou not be loath
> To leave this Paradise, but shalt possess
> A Paradise within thee, happier farr.
>
> (XII, 582-7)

Milton's solution to the Fall of Man is that out of it a new
kind of goodness is born and that man can show heroic
qualities by doing his duty in the face of great obstacles. The
old poet, who had himself hoped that a new Heaven would be
built in England, and had seen his hopes shattered by the
corrupt doings of men, found a solace in the thought that a
man's nobility lies in his own grasp and is his to command.
In this Milton believed true heroism to lie, and it was this
that he offered as an alternative to the old belief that heroism
was to be won in battle or magnificent display. The incom-
parable end of *Paradise Lost* shows the spirit of confidence
and of courage in which men should set out on the undoubted
perils of life. Adam and Eve go, knowing well all that it means
for them in effort and sacrifice :

> The World was all before them, where to choose
> Thir place of rest, and Providence thir guide :
> They hand in hand with wandring steps and slow,
> Through *Eden* took their solitarie way.
>
> (xii, 646-9).

Paradise Lost ends with an entry into a new world where man can redeem his fault by hard effort and show a new kind of heroism in endurance and in devotion to what he knows to be right.

This is not the whole of Milton's solution, though it is all that concerns his heroic ideal. So far as this world is concerned, man must act like this, but beyond human history lies something else. Believing as he did in the end of the world and in the Last Judgment, Milton did not exclude them from his poem. God foretells that at some point of time the Archangels will proclaim the " dread Tribunal " ; then Hell will be closed for ever, the world will burn and a new heaven and earth spring from its ashes,

> wherein the just shall dwell
> And after all thir tribulations long
> See golden days, fruitful of golden deeds,
> With Joy and Love triumphing, and fair Truth.
>
> (iii, 335-8)

Michael repeats the promise to Adam at the end of his account of human history. Such a conclusion agrees with Milton's conception of divine justice. Just as Adam must be punished for his disobedience, so the good must be rewarded for their constancy. Yet even this fits into the epic frame. As Virgil sets the heroes of Rome in Elysium, so Milton promises that the heroes of Christianity shall win a somewhat similar reward. This prospect gives an end and a direction to Milton's concept of virtue and does for it what Virgil's vision of Elysium does for his *virtus*. But it is kept in the background and is less important in the narrative than the duties which man must carry out while the world lasts. The heroic ideal still envisages life as a long struggle in every stage of which a man must be in full command of himself and ready to sacrifice all that he has.

Just as the tragic episodes of Dido and Turnus are enclosed in the wide frame of the *Aeneid* and find their full meaning from it, so Milton's Fall of Man, with its tragic structure and implications, is enclosed in a wider setting which illustrates and explains it. Milton follows epic precedent in giving an important part to divine persons. With his Puritan convictions he could not resort to the allegorical divinities of Camões, and he boldly presented the God of his own faith. He could hardly have done otherwise ; for God is an essential character in his story and must appear in His own person. Milton's God and Devil are far from what Dryden calls " machining persons ". They are as near to current theological conceptions of them as his own views and the conditions of poetry allowed Milton to make them. Since he set out to " justify the ways of God to man ", his theology is of central importance and directs his story. It does more than illustrate what happens ; it explains why it happens and what it means. If the episode of the Fall is the centre of Milton's narrative, his conception of God is the centre of the doctrine which the Fall illustrates. For this reason the theology of *Paradise Lost* is much more explicit, exact and controversial than that of the *Aeneid* or *Os Lusiadas*. To bring home his pondered conclusions on God, Milton clothes them in an epic form and gives them an epic interest. The conflict between God and Satan, between good and evil, becomes an enthralling and thrilling struggle. This struggle is so closely interwoven with the Fall of Man that it cannot be divorced from it, and nothing is more characteristic of Milton's architectonic skill than the way in which his views on vexed questions of theology are worked into a coherent and well developed plot. From the Fall of Man he reaches out to questions of even greater import and never shrinks from producing an emphatic answer to them. No doubt he felt that he must do what poets like Du Bartas had done in a different kind of poetry, but he always weaves his theological disquisitions into his epic fabric.

Adam and Eve, and their descendants after them, stand in a middle position between God and Satan. The conflict which begins in Eden and ends only with the end of the world takes place in man because God and Satan contend for him. Our human condition is thus the battlefield of supernatural powers whose nature is hard to express in any language and whose character seems almost inconceivable in the narrative of an epic. In attempting to give them an important place in

Paradise Lost Milton was faced by a great difficulty. The spiritual issues which were fundamental to his theme had to be displayed mythologically and dramatically. We might apply to his own method the words of his Raphael:

> what surmounts the reach
> Of human sense, I shall delineate so,
> By lik'ning spiritual to corporal forms,
> As may express them best, though what if Earth
> Be but the shaddow of Heav'n, and things therein
> Each to other like, more then on earth is thought ?
>
> (v, 571-6)

For the moment Milton suggests that his war in Heaven is symbolical or allegorical, only to add that it need not be so allegorical as we think. No doubt in his own mind he believed that divine things were ultimately not to be portrayed in human language and imagery, but so visual and so plastic was his imagination, so firm its hold on the world that he knew, that we hardly ever look for a secondary meaning in *Paradise Lost* and accept Milton's myth as he presents it without such questions or reservations as we make with the divinities of Virgil. Nor is there any need to interpret Milton's divine episodes allegorically. Allegory is a way of conveying a general lesson through a particular story, but Milton conveys his lessons directly through the speeches of his characters and his own comments. What happens illustrates the universal truths which he proclaims and may be treated as something complete in itself.

Milton lived in an age of religious change and dispute. He himself never remained for very long in any single set of beliefs, and when he wrote *Paradise Regained*, he was an Arian who denied the divinity of Christ ; but in *Paradise Lost* he had not taken up this extreme position and shows no traces of it. In spite of his changes, he was always opposed to institutional religion and strongly condemned the Roman church. He speaks scornfully of

> Embryos, and Idiots, Eremits and Friers
> White, Black, and Grey, with all thir trumperie.
>
> (III, 474-5)

He tilts at the belief that buildings can be sanctified, when he says that Eden will be destroyed

To teach thee that God attributes to place
No sanctitie, if none be thither brought
By Men who there frequent, or therein dwell.
(XI, 832-4)

He does not believe that any kind of ritual or service is necessary to the proper offering of prayer, and shows how simply Adam and Eve perform their orisons :

This said unanimous, and other Rites
Observing none, but adoration pure
Which God likes best.   (IV, 736-8)

He implicitly compares Satan to the " lewd hirelings " who come into the Church, and he is as hostile to Anglican as he is to Roman priests. Indeed in Book XII Michael discourses at length on the harm wrought by ecclesiastical institutions and the wrongful emphasis given to outward forms. Milton was a Protestant with all a Protestant's dislike of priests, ritual and the magical elements in religion. Though he would never deny the power of performing miracles to God, he would emphatically deny it to priests. Theologically, his epic is the epic of Protestantism. Allowing no intermediary between God and man, Milton dispenses with all the elaborate machinery which the Church has built to bring the two closer together and confronts man in his naked soul with the unreckonable power of God.

But though he was so emphatically Protestant, Milton was not in *Paradise Lost* a sectarian. No doubt he held many views not shared by large numbers of his countrymen and was in his private beliefs a special kind of heretic. Of these views there are perhaps traces in his poem. He is neither clear nor consistent about the relations of the Son to the Father ; he seems to assume that both God and man die in the whole of their natures ; in one remarkable passage it is hard not to think that God creates the world out of His own substance. But these hints are incidental and do not affect the main action of the poem. They are indeed hardly perceptible except to professed theologians and heresy-hunters. Milton thought that such disagreements with common belief were mere " neighbouring differences ". The main theology of *Paradise Lost* is almost that of the Apostles' Creed, though it is hardly that of the Athanasian.

214

It is sufficiently orthodox for the ordinary pious reader, but that is not its chief interest. What really matters is the use that Milton made of it. In presenting his myth he could not fail to set a strong personal imprint on some accepted beliefs and to give them a special significance. That is what counts for his poetry.

At the outset Milton was faced with the almost impossible task of representing the Trinity in speech and action. He followed the obvious solution of presenting three persons rather than one God, but highly differentiated as his three persons are, their total effect must be treated as single. In so far as they supplement or even correct each other's actions, that is only because the conditions of the story demand it; in so far the Father seems to have a certain superiority, that was because such a superiority was traditional and enabled Milton to ascribe to him what ordinarily would be ascribed just to God. A second difficulty in Milton's theology is that his intellectual convictions did not always correspond with his emotional and imaginative powers. Conceptions of Godhead which his mind accepted did not always touch his heart or mean very much to him as a poet. There are times, as in his explanation of the compatibility of omniscience with free will, when he seems to force himself to expound a difficult matter without being deeply concerned about it. However much he felt the logical cogency of such beliefs, they were not the most vivid or most intimate part of his faith; they were forced on him when he tried to justify his beliefs by argument. Milton's more truly religious convictions lie elsewhere and call out other powers in him.

The Father in *Paradise Lost* stands in the first place for order. This order does not reign throughout the whole universe and is, for instance, noticeably absent from Chaos:

> a dark
> Illimitable Ocean, without bound,
> Without dimension, where length breadth, and highth,
> And time and place are lost. (II, 891-4)

From such disorder the Father creates, when he chooses, order, as he creates the earth from the darkness of the abyss. In the moral world he creates a similar order. It exists among the Angels, and mankind is created that in the end earth and heaven may be united and produce

> One Kingdom, Joy and Union without end. (VII, 161)

This order is symbolised in Heaven by the songs sung there and by the devotion and service which the angels give to God. For a time it reigns in Eden and in the souls of Adam and Eve. Even after the Fall such an order may still be found in those who obey God and will be found again after the Last Judgment. Milton's belief in this divine order lay at the root of his religion. His own experience taught him that it was not to be found in politics, but he found it in the spirit and never ceased to believe that it was divine. When he saw disorder rampant, he felt that man had lost his harmony with God and even that God had withdrawn Himself from man. This is what happens to Adam and Eve after their disobedience and is reflected in the ensuing disorder of the physical world. To such an order man must make his own contribution by obeying the will of God. Such a belief does not imply a dualism in the nature of things. God might of course impose a compulsory or mechanical order on everything and on everybody, but Milton thinks that such an order would be worthless. Because the acceptance of order demands the exercise of his reason by man, it has a profound moral importance. The denial of it means that man surrenders his reason to his passions and so ceases to follow the divine element in his nature.

Since the Father stands for order, he also stands for law and for justice, but to this conception Milton gives his own peculiar turn, and associates his conception of divine justice with his own belief in human liberty. At no point has he more fully emancipated himself from his earlier Calvinism than in his belief in free will. This belief he justifies by argument, when he makes the Father explain the whole matter in a formal, even academic manner :

> Such I created all th' Ethereal Powers
> And Spirits, both them who stood and them who faild ;
> Freely they stood who stood, and fell who fell.
> Not free, what proof could they have givn sincere
> Of true allegiance, constant Faith or Love,
> Where onely what they needs must do, appeard,
> Not what they would ? what praise could they receive ?
> (III, 100-106)

As Milton states it, the argument for man's freedom sounds like a tribute to the vanity of God. It is not, and only Milton's anthropomorphic presentation of God suggests that it is. Milton means that the only actions worth doing are those which are done voluntarily, because their real value lies in the choice which prompts them and the best choice is the desire to please God. When he makes God speak about this from His own point of view, it sounds a little unreal. But the statement that God wishes to be pleased by men's actions is only another way of saying that men should wish to please Him. Milton agrees with common morality in thinking that the worth of an action depends on its motive and that if there is no free will, no actions have any worth because they are then automatic. Therefore man must be free. But this freedom is of a special kind. Though Milton had championed various kinds of personal and political freedom in his time, it is not of them that he thinks here. This freedom is that which man finds when he acts reasonably and does what God demands; it lies above all in the service of God. Therefore when man acts unreasonably, it is impaired, as Michael tells Adam :

> Since thy original Lapse, true Libertie
> Is lost, which alwayes with right Reason dwells
> Twinn'd, and from her hath no dividual being.
>
> (XII, 83-5)

Adam and Eve enjoyed such a freedom before the Fall ; after it they have to struggle for it and enjoy it only partially. It follows that man is truly free only when he is in perfect harmony with the order that God demands of him. Such a conception of freedom was no doubt different from the conceptions which Milton held in his old regicide and republican days, but it is based on an important fact in moral experience. By following what his reason knows to be right, man is free from the forces in his own nature which enslave and debase him. God leaves man free to choose that he may find this harmonious existence and really know what goodness is.

Since man is free and God is just, it follows that man must be punished for his disobedience to God. The logic is faultless if we admit that justice lies in giving their deserts to those who have done wrong. Milton follows orthodox

tradition in explaining the Crucifixion in this way : the fall
of man must be atoned for by death, and the Son makes the
atonement for man by dying in his place. Milton's presenta-
tion of this may seem a little too legalistic, but behind it lies
something of great importance, his conception of God's love
for man. Adam knows of this love and in his unfallen state
believes that he can never desert it, but its fullest expression
is in the Son's speech when he offers to give himself in atone-
ment for man's sin. The sacrifice which he will make is the
supreme example of God's love for man, and Milton pays it
a special tribute :

> O unexampl'd love,
> Love no where to be found less then Divine !
> (III, 410-11)

This love is bound to the divine order and is an important
part of it. Without it man would be lost for ever and God's
work undone. The Father sums the situation up when he
says

> So Heav'nly love shall outdoo Hellish hate. (III, 298)

Just as man must play his part by following his reason, so
God plays His by exercising His love. It is true that Milton
is forced by the conditions of narrative to display this love
almost exclusively in the Son, but of course his apparent
anthropomorphism must not delude us into thinking that
love does not belong to God as such.

Though Milton's conception of God has its logical basis
and is fortified by argument, it is informed by a spirit which
suggests that his own personal experience was based neither
on logic nor on argument but drew its strength from a belief
in a divine reality which appealed to some of his inmost
needs, his desire for order, reason and love. These are the
qualities which differentiate man from the beasts and which,
in Milton's faith, imply the existence of God. Milton
accepted the doctrine that man was made in the image of God
but interpreted it in his own way. In his account of the
creation he says ;

> There wanted yet the Master work, the end
> Of all yet don ; a Creature who not prone
> And Brute as other Creatures, but endu'd
> With Sanctitie of Reason, might erect

His Stature, and upright with Front serene
Govern the rest, self-knowing, and from thence
Magnanimous to correspond with Heav'n.

(VII, 505-11)

When Adam and Eve disobey God and cut themselves off
from Him, they lose all these things. They break the order
in which they live ; they cease to be reasonable beings ; their
love turns to lust. No doubt Milton had once imagined that
the Rule of the Saints would bring to England and to earth
the divine gifts which man had in common with God. He
had been grievously disappointed, but he still felt that these
gifts could be won by the individual man and that in the
struggle to maintain them he could find a new kind of heroism.
His theology, despite its formality and its logic, was built on
his own spiritual experience and reflects his own sufferings
and distress.

Milton's theology is mainly based on his desire for the
good life and on his conviction that goodness is divine. How
deeply he felt this may be seen from the part which he gives
to the Holy Spirit. In his *De Doctrina Christiana* he displays
serious doubts about the Third Person of the Trinity, but in
Paradise Lost he not only says that God will send a Comforter
to men, but speaks of what this means to him personally,
especially at the beginning of his poem :

And chiefly Thou O Spirit, that dost prefer
Before all Temples th' upright heart and pure,
Instruct me, for Thou know'st ; Thou from the first
Wast present, and with mighty wings outspread
Dove-like satst brooding on the vast Abyss
And mad'st it pregnant : What in me is dark
Illumine, what is low raise and support.   (I, 17-23)

At the very centre of his life, in the creative activity which
meant more than anything to him, Milton found something
which he could not but believe to be God. This spirit is
certainly much more than what he or we would mean by
conscience. It is a sustaining and creating power and is
indeed what Milton would call wisdom. Just as in the moral
life he lays great stress on reason, so in his inner spiritual life
he lays stress on wisdom and assumes that it is a direct
manifestation of God. The voice which spoke to him in so

special terms and in so special a way was no doubt heard by others in a different way and was

> The Spirit of God promisd alike and giv'n
> To all Beleevers. (XII, 519-20)

Though Milton's religious experience, as he presents it, is not in the least like the mystical vision which Dante presents in the *Paradiso* and though it seems to lack that intimate and passionate love for God which gives so special a sanctity to the poetry of St. John of the Cross, it has at its centre a real sense of a personal relation, of a spiritual communion with the Divine, especially in those moments when Milton, alone with his inspiration, was most fully and most truly himself.

Against God who stands for order, wisdom and love, Milton sets Satan who stands for disorder, passion and hatred. Tradition told that pride was the cause of Satan's fall; Milton accepted this and made full use of it. He knew well what pride was, what illusions it can breed and what havoc it can create. So he sets the beginning of his whole story in Heaven, when Satan, incensed with envy and injured vanity at the elevation of the Son to share the Father's glory, prefers revolt to submission. The first result of this is that the order of Heaven is turned to disorder and though the celestial day is spent

> In song and dance about the sacred Hill, (v, 619)

the song and dance no longer reflect the old concord and harmony, and before long Heaven becomes a battlefield. The desire for disorder rules Satan's actions; he seeks it in the hope of inflicting pain upon God. For this reason he decides to promote ruin on the newly created earth and accepts Beelzebub's plan to corrupt man as a means to revenge himself upon God:

> This would surpass
> Common revenge, and interrupt his joy
> In our Confusion, and our Joy upraise
> In his disturbance. (II, 370-73)

Satan succeeds in his enterprise and breaks the harmony and order which exist between God and man. The disorder which Satan creates leads to nothing but greater disorder; it does not even give him any satisfaction except to boast of what he has done. His position is in no way improved by it.

Milton marks this almost symbolically when Satan returns triumphant to Hell and tells what he has done. Before he can hear the applause, his companions are turned to snakes, and

> he hears
> On all sides, from innumerable tongues
> A dismal universal hiss.   (x, 506-8)

The disorder which he creates follows him to Hell and deprives him of the dignity and approbation which are necessary to his pride.

Satan's pride darkens his reason. Persuasive as his words usually are, they are based on false assumptions and show that he lives with lies and delusions. He begins with a feeling of injured merit because the Son has been exalted above him. He soon justifies this with invented reasons and tells Abdiel that there is no evidence that the Son was created by God, for no one remembers it happening. In the battle he has already advanced to other reasons and denies not merely the exaltation of the Son but the omnipotence of God on the principle that he can allow omnipotence to nobody. He, who began by fighting for his own honour, is soon fighting for

> Honour, Dominion, Glorie, and renowne. (VI, 422)

This he believes, and it shows that what prompts him is pride. So in Hell after his defeat his pride prevents him from seeing things as they have really happened and from judging the facts correctly. There is a kind of heroic defiance in his attempt to make himself at home in Hell :

> Farewel happy Fields
> Where Joy for ever dwells : Hail horrours, hail
> Infernal world, and thou profoundest Hell
> Recive thy new Possessor : One who brings
> A mind not be chang'd by Place or Time.
> The mind is its own place, and in it self
> Can make a Heav'n of Hell, a Hell of Heav'n.
>   (I, 249-55)

It sounds splendid, but it is not true. The difference between Heaven and Hell is absolute and cannot be transcended in this way, as Satan himself admits later when he soliloquises in Eden :

> Me miserable ! which way shall I flie
> Infinite wrauth, and infinite despaire ?
> Which way I flie is Hell ; my self am Hell.
>
> (IV, 73-5)

He no longer thinks that he can make his own Heaven in himself, and the Hell which he finds there gives no pleasure to him. Satan has no real or reasonable principle even in his malice. He changes his opinions and justifies himself by different arguments, most of which he seems for the moment to believe. With him the passion of envy counts much more than any correct assessment of facts. Conscious of what he has lost, he is flung from one false theory to another until he is suitably punished by being transformed into a snake.

Satan's dominating passion is hatred. After his expulsion from Heaven his sense of injured pride turns into hatred for those who, as he thinks, have humbled him and for all connected with them. It becomes his driving motive and takes on heroic airs when it strengthens his will in defeat and makes him insist on carrying on the war. It appears in his defiant words to Beelzebub :

> What though the field be lost ?
> All is not lost ; the unconquerable Will,
> And study of revenge, immortal hate.
>
> (I, 105-7)

His plan for the corruption of man rises from his " deep malice ", and this grows greater when he sees the happiness of Adam and Eve and finds in it a " sight hateful, sight tormenting ". When he returns to Eden on his second visit, hatred is still strong in him. He knows that revenge recoils on him, but he is prepared to face it, provided that he can vent his spite :

> Let it ; I reck not, so it light well aim'd,
> Since higher I fall short, on him who next
> Provokes my envie, this new Favorite
> Of Heav'n, this Man of Clay, Son of despite,
> Whom us the more to spite his Maker rais'd
> From dust : spite then with spite is best repaid.
>
> (IX, 173-8)

Such spite carries him through his temptation of Eve and shows itself in the cold-blooded, calculating spirit in which he plays with her. It resounds in the speech which he makes on his return to Hell when he glories in the enmity which he has set between God and man. In making Satan the victim and the advocate of hatred Milton develops the old theme of envy in a powerful and convincing way. So strong is it in Satan that it can only be satisfied by exacting revenge from those who cause it. Just as in God love sustains and creates an order which might otherwise perish, so in Satan hatred creates an ever greater disorder and leads to no satisfying results even for himself.

Milton thus plans Satan as an antithesis to God and shows how the powers of evil, of disorder, unreason and hatred, work in him. But these powers, however odious they may be, are not contemptible ; they are formidable, and in certain settings they look impressive. In the first four books of *Paradise Lost* Satan almost cuts a heroic figure in the high style of epic. This Milton must have meant him to do. He stresses his enormous stature, his courage in defeat, his panoply and armaments and the music of his army. In this company Satan is a commanding and eminent figure. When he holds his " great consult ", he sits like an oriental potentate on his royal throne and controls the proceedings with masterful ability. Milton admits that he deserves his position :

> Satan exalted sat, by merit rais'd,
> To that bad eminence, (II, 5-6)

and we confirm this when Satan sets out alone on his voyage across the vast abyss. He triumphs over the appalling obstacles of his journey and never complains of them :

> So eagerly the fiend
> Ore bog or steep, through strait, rough, dense, or rare,
> With head, hands, wings, or feet pursues his way,
> And swims or sinks, or wades, or creeps, or flyes.
> (II, 947-50)

His deception of Uriel is in the best manner of Odysseus, and it is hard not to enjoy his adroit management of the watchful angel. Even when he comes to earth, despite the hideous emotions which assail him, he keeps some of his heroic stature. He may lose it when he turns himself into a toad and whispers into Eve's sleeping ear, but he regains it when the patrolling Angels catch him and he resumes his proper shape and defies them :

223

> On th' other side *Satan* allarm'd
> Collecting all his might dilated stood,
> Like *Teneriff* or *Atlas* unremov'd :
> His stature reacht the Skie and on his Crest
> Sat horror Plum'd ; nor wanted in his graspe
> What seemd both Spear and Shield.
>
> (IV, 985-90)

Even after the check which he here receives he holds to his purpose and journeys round the earth for seven days and nights while he waits for a chance to return to Eden. Then, when he turns himself into a serpent and might be expected to excite horror and disgust, he is given an unexpected magnificence :

> His Head
> Crested aloft, and Carbuncle his Eyes ;
> With burnisht Neck of verdant Gold, erect
> Amidst his circling Spires, that on the grass
> Floted redundant ; pleasing was his shape,
> And lovely, never since of Serpent kind
> Lovelier.   (IX, 499-505)

Satan certainly has an extraordinary appeal, and Milton must have intended him to have it. It is no wonder that for many readers he is the most impressive and most interesting figure in *Paradise Lost*.

Satan's impressiveness is only half the picture. Against it we must set his evil motives and his evil actions. There is an apparent contradiction between his heroic spirit and his corrupt motives, between his courageous acts and the end to which they are directed. But Milton takes care to solve this contradiction. His Satan is a fallen archangel, and his decay is gradual. He keeps, both in appearance and in character, some of his old qualities, until gradually they are corrupted and lost. In the first scene in Hell

> his form had not yet lost
> All her Original brightness, nor appear'd
> Less than Arch Angel ruind. (I, 591-3)

Care and the desire for revenge have begun to mark his appearance, but it keeps some of its old splendour, and is like the sun shining through mist or the moon in eclipse. He is still able to disguise himself enough to deceive Uriel into thinking that he is one of the faithful angels. But when he reaches earth, anger and envy have begun to mark his face, and though he smoothes them with outward calm, he no longer deceives Uriel who knows that he is one of the rebels. When Gabriel sees him coming with Ithuriel and Zephon, he remarks on his changed appearance :

> And with them comes a third of Regal port,
> But faded splendour wan ; who by his gate
> And fierce demeanour seems the Prince of Hell.
>
> (IV, 869-71)

Later, when he returns to Hell, he loses all his old magnificence ; he is turned into a serpent, and we hear no more of him.

This change of appearance is matched by a change in character. The heroic leader of the first scenes and of the journey to earth has in him violent elements of hate and disorder which are bound to show themselves in greater discord before long. Satan suffers from an internal conflict, and when he comes to earth, he shows what it means. His address to the sun in Book IV reveals his sense of guilt. He knows that pride and ambition have cast him down and that God deserved no such treatment as he gave to Him. He examines his conscience with some care and is at first quite candid with himself. He even thinks of repentance, but rejects it as impossible, and then his pride reasserts itself :

> and that word
> *Disdain* forbids me, and my dread of shame
> Among the spirits beneath.   (IV, 81-3)

Since he believes that no reconciliation with God is possible, he decides to pursue the only alternative course and to follow evil :

> Evil be thou my Good ; by thee at least
> Divided Empire with Heav'n's King I hold.
>
> (IV, 110-11)

Even when he sees Adam and Eve and knows that they are his victims, he feels some pity for them and admits that they are not to be blamed for the fate that awaits them. When he returns to Eden, he again communes with himself, but now he feels no such hesitations as before. His bad conscience only makes him more eager to cause havoc :

> For onely in destroying I finde ease
> To my relentless thoughts.
>
> (IX, 129-30)

He has now set himself on his desperate path and cares for nothing but to destroy. His heroic spirit has finally disappeared and never again shows itself. He has even lost his old effrontery ; for after his successful corruption of Eve

> Back to the Thicket sunk
> The guiltie Serpent.   (IX, 784-5)

Just as his appearance decays, so does his character, until he becomes wholly loathsome and even contemptible. In him Milton has shown the corruption of a spirit through pride and envy and the destructive illusions which they breed.

The decay of Satan from his original brightness may be illustrated by a remarkable scene in Book II which tells what the fallen angels do while they wait for their chief's return from his voyage. Milton dwells at some length on their activities, and makes them resemble those of the angels who have not rebelled. Some, for instance, hold races

> As at th' Olympian Games or *Pythian* fields,   (II, 530)

and this is just what " th' unarmed Youth of Heav'n " does while, under Gabriel's command, it watches over Eden. Others retire to a silent valley and sing songs of heavenly beauty :

> Thir song was partial, but the harmony
> (What could it less when Spirits immortal sing ?)
> Suspended Hell, and took with ravishment
> The thronging audience,   (II, 552-5)

and we are at once reminded of the songs which are sung in Heaven to celebrate the Father's doings or the Son's return from his victory over Satan. Still others discourse philosophically :

> Of Providence, Foreknowledge, Will, and Fate,
> Fixt Fate, free will, foreknowledge absolute,
> And found no end, in wandring mazes lost.
>
> (II, 559-61)

And this is just what the Father, on more than one occasion, does, though perhaps His arguments are intended to be more impressive and more cogent than those of the fallen angels. In all these respects the fallen angels are like their lost comrades in Heaven, and there is no reason to think that Milton disapproves of these activities as intrinsically wrong. But he moves on from them to something different. The explorers who go out to search the nether regions find nothing but the rivers of Hell and a frozen continent where the air " performs th' effect of Fire ". They are appalled by what they find and realise what their lot really is, that theirs is

> A Universe of death, which God by curse
> Created evil, for evil only good.
>
> (II, 622-3)

In this universe life dies and death flourishes, and its only creatures are monsters. So the fallen angels pass from their old celestial habits to a place of doom and disorder. Like Satan they keep for a while traces of what they once were, but they soon lose them and in due course, like him, they are turned into serpents and mocked by a tree whose fruit becomes ashes in their mouths.

There can be no serious doubt about the main lines of the scheme in which Milton presents Satan. Beginning as a celestial being he gradually decays until he becomes loathsome and abhorrent. Yet we may still ask why Milton adopted a plan which might well create misunderstanding and is responsible for the acceptance by many of Blake's view that Milton was " of the Devil's party ". Such he certainly never was, and he would have been appalled by such a suggestion. There is undeniably a problem, and various answers, with different degrees of truth and importance, have been given to it. First, Milton took a bold step by giving Satan a leading part in the first books. This would in any case give him a special place and claim on our interest. But circumstances made this importance even greater than Milton can have intended. When he wrote these books, his powers were at their highest, no doubt because they were written before the Restoration had finally broken all his hopes of a better world. The second half of the poem, as the beginning of Book VII shows, was written when he was

> In darkness, and with dangers compast round,   (VII, 27)

At this date something went out of him. The later books have many magnificent merits, but in them Milton seldom rises to quite his earlier heights or displays the same sweep and energy in creation. By this accident of history Satan benefited. His most important scenes were created by Milton in the full onrush of energy after years of silence and are poetically the finest things that he ever wrote. The result is that we credit Satan with qualities which really belong to Milton. Secondly, it is tenable that, despite all his efforts to the contrary, Milton put much of himself into Satan. He had himself been a rebel against a tyrannous king and had known the excitements of war in a proud cause. He too was an uncompromising character and had a peculiar gift for turning his own personal problems into causes of universal importance, as we see in his treatment of divorce. It may be the case that despite all his watchfulness he put into the Prince of Darkness qualities which were so deeply ingrained in himself that he could not but portray them sympathetically. There is much to be said for both these explanations, but they do not completely solve the problem. In the first place, the greatness of Milton's creative powers in the first books need not necessarily have been directed to making Satan appear like a great hero, and in the second place, if Milton felt some unconscious sympathy for Satan, it is surprising that he should also have felt horror for his hatefulness. It looks as if the real explanation lay elsewhere.

When Milton decided to write a heroic epic in the traditional manner with a new purpose, he could hardly avoid altogether the old type of hero. It is true that he disparaged him, but none the less he must find some kind of place for him. It was part of the tradition and could not well be excluded. It might even be argued that such a hero was necessary as a contrast and a preliminary to the new type of hero whom Milton proclaims. In Satan Milton displays various qualities that belong to the old type. He is a great leader in war, especially in defeat; he does alone what none of his comrades dares to do; he keeps royal state on his throne; he is full of resource, as when he invents gunpowder for the war in Heaven; he is unfailingly eloquent; he hides his own despair from his comrades as Aeneas hides his when he thinks that his ships are all wrecked. Even in

incidental effects Milton compares Satan with the heroes of
classical epic. For instance, the magnificent simile which
describes Satan when he meets Death :

> Incenc't with indignation *Satan* stood
> Unterrifi'd, and like a Comet burn'd,
> That fires the length of *Ophiucus* huge
> In th' Artick sky, and from his horrid hair
> Shakes Pestilence and Warr,   (II, 707-11)

can be traced back, by way of Tasso, to the simile by which
Virgil conveys the menacing appearance of Aeneas ;

> non secus ac liquida si quando nocte cometae
> sanguinei lugubre rubent, aut Sirius ardor
> ille sitim morbosque ferens mortalibus aegris
> nascitur et laevo contristat lumine caelum.[1]
>
> (x, 272-5)

For the moment Satan takes on the grandeur of Aeneas in
one of his most formidable moments, and though we may
not think of Virgil when we read Milton, there is no doubt
that Milton knew what precedent he was using and intended
to create a similar effect. It is clear that Milton quite deliber-
ately fashioned Satan on heroic models, because he rejected
the old heroic standards and wished to show that they were
wicked. He had his own ideal of heroism, which he displays
in other ways, and his Satan prepares us for it by showing that
pride, on which the old ideal was based, is not only inadequate
but dangerously wrong. No doubt when he wrote the first
books of *Paradise Lost* Milton's renewed powers enabled
him to display this type in all its splendour ; no doubt, too,
he had enough of it in himself to portray Satan at least with
understanding. But in his main scheme Satan provides a
contrast to something quite different and infinitely more
admirable.

In rejecting Satan Milton rejects the heroic ideal in more
than one form. In the first place, he rejects the authentic
hero who lives for his glory and is moved by personal pride.
Satan shows this type at its worst. Pride is the root of his

---

[1] As in the liquid night great comets glow
Blood-red and gloomy, or bright Sirius,
Bringer of thirst and plague to luckless men,
Rises and grieves the sky with cruel light.

being, and glory is his aim ; both are denied and displayed as worthless. Milton may still keep his old love for the poems which told of Achilles or Roland, but he denies the ideals which they embody. He finds that the old heroic type is no better than the Giants of *Genesis* and that it gets the glory deserved by a very different type :

> This Fame shall be achiev'd, renown on Earth,
> And what most merits fame in silence hid.
>
> (XI, 694-5)

Just as Virgil implicitly criticises the heroic ideal in Turnus, so does Milton, more hostilely and destructively, in Satan. But he is not content to criticise only this type. In Satan he even criticises the more civilised types of heroism which Virgil and others had created. When Satan is indirectly compared with Aeneas, the comparison harms Aeneas. For what Milton rejects is the whole notion that heroism lies in deeds which bring earthly glory or are concerned with human power. In their different ways Virgil, Camões and Tasso, even Boiardo and Ariosto, had made this assumption, but Milton thinks that heroism lies in suffering for the good and that the only true glory belongs to this. A view of this kind ran counter to much in his own nature, and perhaps he did not quite realise all that followed from it or how much he must sacrifice that he valued. But he made a valiant effort to be consistent and to show in Satan a false ideal with all its disastrous consequences. If we allow his assumptions, his presentation of Satan is consistent and clear.

Though Milton thus rejects the old heroic ideal, he has a substitute for it not merely in the noble souls of whom Michael speaks,

> What Man can do against them, not affraid,
> Though to the death, against such cruelties
> With inward consolations recompenc't,
>
> (XII, 494-6)

but in the figure of Abdiel. Abdiel is what Satan ought to be. He alone of Satan's entourage has the courage to rebut his claims and to refuse to follow him. Milton's poetry rises as easily and as nobly to describe Abdiel as to any of Satan's feats and leaves no doubt that he is a real hero :

> Among the faithless, faithful only hee ;
> Among innumerable false, unmov'd,
> Unshak'n, unseduc'd, unterrifi'd
> His Loyaltie he kept, his Love, his Zeale.
>
> (v, 894-7)

Abdiel's bearing and behaviour are worthy of the bravest hero in the old style. He stands up to Satan and defends his own master with unflinching devotion. But his heroism is of a special kind. Brave though he is in battle, he has the highest kind of courage in that he defends what he knows to be right. Milton gives this a special significance and makes Abdiel the champion of truth against error, as God tells him when he returns from his defiance of Satan :

> Servant of God, well done, well hast thou fought
> The better fight, who single hast maintaind
> Against revolted multitudes the Cause
> Of Truth, in word mightier then they in Armes.
>
> (VI, 29-32)

By defending the truth Abdiel has almost been ready to endure that " heroic martyrdom " which Milton thought a proper subject for epic. And Abdiel is really a champion of truth. When Satan complains that God has treated him and his fellows unjustly, Abdiel replies that Satan has no right to deny such a power to God who has made him and defined his being. Through Abdiel Milton conveys his own belief that liberty lies in the exercise of reason while servitude lies in following the passions. He states the case in language suited to his myth, but his meaning is clear when Abdiel in the course of battle tells Satan that it is servitude to serve the unwise :

> Reign thou in Hell thy Kingdom, let mee serve
> In Heav'n God ever blest, and his Divine
> Behests obey, worthiest to be obey'd.
>
> (VI, 183-5)

On this note he begins the battle with a stroke against Satan, and shows that he is a true hero ready to fight for what he knows to be true and right.

What Abdiel shows in his special circumstances, all the loyal angels show in theirs. They serve God because they are glad to do so and recognise that it is right. As Raphael tells

231

Adam, this service is based on love :

> Freely we serve.
> Because wee freely love, as in our will
> To love or not ; in this we stand or fall.
>
> (v, 538-40)

Milton, who believes so strongly in the freedom of the will
and in its fundamental importance for morality, makes even
the angels' love for God deliberate. They choose to love Him,
and therefore their service is what He desires. This love is
closely allied to faith and shows itself in allegiance (III, 104) ;
acts of zeal and love are emblazoned on the banners of the
celestial army (v, 592) ; love is the spirit which inspires the
concourse of angels in heaven (VI, 94). Milton symbolises
this love, and the harmony which it brings, in his favourite
figure of music. Against it he sets the discord which grows in
Satan when he cuts himself off from God, and the hideous
frozen world where the fallen angels are condemned to dwell.
What he means can be seen from the Father's words about the
Son :

> him who disobeyes
> Mee disobeyes, breaks union, and that day
> Cast out from God and blessed vision, falls,
> Into utter darkness, deep ingulft, his place
> Ordaind without redemption, without end.
>
> (v, 611-15)

The loyal angels are loyal because they love the service of
God, and for this they are rewarded with complete happiness ;
the fallen angels, who love themselves, have no reward and
no happiness. The issue is absolute and no compromise is
possible. It is a war which lasts for ever :

> Whence in perpetual fight they needs must last
> Endless, and no solution will be found,
>
> (VI, 693-4)

and therefore it is a perpetual challenge to true heroism. In
his intermediate position between God and Devil man too
must take his part in the struggle, and in the degree of his
constancy and courage lies his claim to glory. Milton carries
his concept of heroism beyond his story until it is relevant to
the whole of human life.

Milton, then, differs from his epic predecessors both in

his biblical subject, with its particular theology and its strange setting, and in the new view of heroism which he propounds from it. But he had decided that his epic was to resemble other epics and to take its place in the tradition by containing many of their characteristic features. The dangers of such an assumption can be seen from Vida's *Christiad* where the events of the Gospel are fitted into a Virgilian frame which makes them curiously unreal and unsatisfying. Milton avoided the greater dangers by presenting his theology without making any concessions to his epic models. It is candidly and unashamedly Protestant. But his story is so largely theological that it might almost have led him into rejecting many honoured devices of epic. If he had done this, he might have satisfied his conscience on the ground that such elements are mere external decoration, but he was too good a poet and too devoted a lover of poetry to adopt such a plan. His head was full of the old masterpieces and he felt that he must do honour to them by giving a new place in his poem to their themes and phrases. What Virgil felt about Homer, Milton felt about Virgil, Ariosto, Tasso and Camões. His many verbal reminiscences show his admiration for them and his skill at changing their words to suit his own style and his own need. So too his larger adaptations show how he remoulds the old themes and gives them a new significance. His poem has the traditional accoutrements of epic, but they have been refashioned by a master hand.

An initial difficulty lay in Milton's love of Greek and Latin poets. No poet has known them better or loved them more. Yet he was convinced that what they said was usually untrue and in some cases pernicious. When he wrote *Paradise Regained*, he rejected the ancient world and most of what it had once meant to him, but in *Paradise Lost* he had not reached this ultimate austerity and he abounds in classical allusions. It is true that some of these are not very friendly. He places in his Limbo of Vanity both Empedocles, who thought himself a god, and Cleombrotus, who drowned himself to find Plato's Elysium. His comparison of the Serpent's address to Eve with that of " som Oratour renound " in Athens or Rome is hardly a compliment to Demosthenes or Cicero. Even his comparison of Satan voyaging through space with Ulysses sailing between Scylla and Charybdis might be thought to cast a slur on Ulysses, though it probably refers only to the dangers which encompass both travellers. More important and more characteristic is Milton's treatment of the ancient gods. For him they must have been either fictions or devils, and he hesitates between the two views. While he considers the Muse an empty dream and throws doubt on the existence of the Hesperian Gardens, there were other creations of Greek fancy which he could not quite dismiss in this way. He had to recruit the ranks of his fallen angels somewhere, and the gods of the heathen, as the Bible presented them, were insufficient in number and variety. So he reinforced them with figures from Greece, but with an unexpected slyness. All that he actually names are the Titans, the older generation of gods whom even classical myth agreed to have been thrown out of Heaven. These provided excellent reinforcements for Milton's hellish army, but though he goes on to speak of such Greek sanctuaries as Ida, Olympus, Delphi and Dodona, he seems to consider them only as the seats of the Titans. If we press Milton's text, the real Olympian gods are not in Satan's army. Perhaps he would for the moment like us to think that they are; for his language is obscure, if not ambiguous. It looks as if he felt that Hell was really their right place, but could not quite bring himself to say so. There is indeed one important exception. Mulciber, the Greek Hephaestus and Roman Vulcan, is an Olympian figure, not of the highest order but still important. Milton sets him in Hell and makes him build Pandemonium. Yet even so he is treated with a special indulgence. Milton may disclaim the importance of good buildings, but he lets his fancy roam on this which Mulciber builds :

> Anon out of the earth a Fabrick huge
> Rose like an Exhalation, with the sound
> Of Dulcet Symphonies and voices sweet,
> Built like a Temple, where *Pilasters* round
> Were set, and Doric pillars overlaid
> With Golden Architrave.   (I, 710-15)

The stern Puritan in Milton might condemn the frivolity of Doric architecture but the scholar warms to the description of it, and warms still more a little later to Mulciber's fall from Heaven. Following a hint from Homer he pours out his

234

finest poetry, and for a moment we forget that we are in Hell and that Mulciber is a fallen angel :

> from Morn
> To Noon he fell, from Noon to dewy Eve,
> A Summers day ; and with the setting Sun
> Dropt from the Zenith like a falling Star,
> On *Lemnos* th' *Ægean* Ile.   (I, 742-6)

No doubt the Greeks related this " erring ", but that did not prevent Milton from bringing it into his poem.

With such small ambiguities and exceptions Milton uses classical myths for decoration when he wishes to suggest the visible beauty of a person or a scene. Though these myths might be false, he still seems to have felt that they set a standard of beauty which was the highest known to him. When he describes the beauty of Eve, neither the Bible nor other epic poetry provide him with his parallels ; he takes them from Greek and Latin poetry and especially from accounts of goddesses. When he speaks of the bower in which Adam and Eve sleep, he draws on the rustic deities of Greece and Rome :

> In shadier Bower
> More sacred and sequesterd, though but feignd,
> *Pan* or *Silvanus* never slept, nor Nymph,
> Nor *Faunus* haunted.   (IV, 705-8)

The words " though but feignd " are a concession to his Puritan passion for truth, but the vision loses nothing by them. In his incomparable description of Eden classical parallels come first to Milton's mind. From the Graces and the Hours, who may legitimately be classed as allegorical, he moves to something that is purely classical, to Ceres in search for Proserpine, and makes one of his most enchanting comparisons :

> Not that faire field
> Of *Enna*, where *Proserpin* gathring flours
> Her self a fairer Floure by gloomie *Dis*
> Was gatherd, which cost *Ceres* all that pain
> To seek her through the world. . . .
>   (IV, 268-72)

The pathos that echoes in the concluding monosyllables shows how deeply Milton felt this story and how real it was to him. For all his disbelief in the truth of Greek legends, there were moments in his poem which called for their assistance. When he felt a need to make his story attractive, he often resorted to the enchanted creations of ancient fancy.

His epic precedents demanded more of Milton than incidental decoration, and especially they demanded scenes of battle. Milton must have been in two minds about this. He felt strongly that military prowess was no real heroism, and no doubt after the Restoration, if not earlier, he was thoroughly disillusioned of any hopes that an army could reform society. At the same time, both as a scholar and as a man, he had known the excitement and the glamour of war and felt a genuine admiration for generals of the Commonwealth. His interest in war shows itself even when he speaks in disapproval, as in his account of Cain's descendants with its Homeric battle-scenes :

> On each hand slaughter and gigantic deeds. (xi, 655)

To solve this discord in himself he had to find a war which really contented his conscience and into which he could put more than the old heroic fury. He did so by a full-length picture of war in Heaven. Constructed almost on a Homeric plan, it begins with an interchange of defiant speeches between leading antagonists and proceeds through single combat to general carnage. Milton understands the fury of battle better than Virgil does, and on his vast celestial landscape he conveys an unlimited havoc :

> all the ground
> With shiverd armour strow'n, and on a heap
> Chariot and charioter lay overturnd
> And fierie foaming steeds.   (vi, 388-91)

But since this is unlike any other war, it demands more than the traditional details. To emphasise its hideous and infernal character Milton introduces cannons and gunpowder on the rebel side and makes what are for Camões legitimate means to defeat the heathen literally inventions of the Devil. Nor was he content with this. His love of grandiose effects led him to an even more surprising result when the loyal angels, who lack cannons, tear up hills and throw them :

> So Hills amid the Air encountered Hills
> Hurl'd to and fro with jaculation dire.
> (vi, 663-4)

236

Virgil's warriors may aim at each other with " no small fragment of a mountain ", but Milton's show their celestial superiority by hurling whole hills. The final stroke is delivered when the Son drives the rebels over the edge of Heaven :

> headlong themselvs they threw
> Down from the verge of Heav'n, Eternal wrauth
> Burnt after them to the bottomless pit.
>
> (VI, 864-6)

In this unique battle Milton uses some traditional themes, but so enlarges their scope and changes their significance that it bears little resemblance to other epic encounters.

War was a subject which belonged to nearly all previous epic, but there were other themes of a more special kind which Milton also adopted and refashioned. A notable case may be seen in his Limbo of Vanity in Book III. Behind this lies a passage of Ariosto's *Orlando Furioso*, where Astolfo is shown a valley in the moon,

> Ove mirabilmente era ridutto
> Ciò che si perde o per nostro difetto,
> O per colpa di tempo o di Fortuna :
> Ciò che si perde qui, là si raguna.[1]
>
> (XXXIV, 73, 5-8)

In this place there is a remarkable collection of lost property, — fame, prayers, lovers' tears, vain ambitions, courtiers' gifts, and presents made to favourites. Under its gay exterior it hides a note of seriousness, and what must have caught Milton's interest is that here too are the charity which men order to be distributed after their deaths and the famous donation of Constantine to Pope Sylvester. That Milton knew and admired these lines is clear from his translation of some of them in *Of Reformation in England*. Where Ariosto slips in a few words of anti-ecclesiastical feeling, Milton creates a whole scene. He is not interested in most of Ariosto's vanities, and his Limbo is almost exclusively peopled with persons whom he disliked for ecclesiastical

---

[1] A place wherein is wonderfully stored
Whatever on our earth below we lose,
Collected there are all things whatsoe'er
Lost through time, chance, or our own folly here.
(W. S. Rose)

reasons, from the builders of Babel to the friars and pilgrims of his own time. His dislike of them inspires him to a burst of sardonic humour, and he tells with gusto how a wind comes and blows all these impostors and their trumpery away :

> then might ye see·
> Cowles, Hoods and Habits with thir wearers tost
> And flutterd into Raggs, then Reliques, Beads,
> Indulgences, Dispenses, Pardons, Bulls,
> The sport of Winds. (III, 489-93)

Ariosto provides Milton with a chance to release his feelings on some matters far removed from his main subject, and he seizes the occasion with avidity.

' Milton's respect for his predecessors has not always been properly understood. When, for instance, Michael takes Adam to the top of a high hill

> To shew him all Earths Kingdomes and thir Glory, (XI, 384)

the resounding list of proper names that follows has caused T. S. Eliot to say that Milton is only playing " rather a solemn game ". Nothing could be further from the truth. Milton follows a good epic precedent, in this case Camões, who in Canto X of *Os Lusiadas* makes Venus show Gama the whole world and tell him that he has opened it up for future generations. The geography that follows would be appreciated in an age which not only felt the romance of strange regions recently made known to it but expected poetry to give information on most matters of importance. In his own way Milton does something of the kind. His debt to Camões is obvious, not merely in the main idea of the scene but in many of its place-names and in such a line as

> *Mombaza*, and *Quiloa*, and *Melind* (XI, 399)

which betrays its descent from

> De Quiloa, de Mombaça, e de Sofala.[1] (I, 54, 4)

But even here Milton changes the significance of the device which he borrows. The world which Venus shows to Gama is to be in some sense the heritage of the Portuguese; it is at least the scene of many of their glorious exploits. The world which Adam sees belongs to all mankind, and while the rolling

---

[1] Of Quiloa, Mombasa and Sofala.

names show how great a possession it is, they are only a preliminary to the dismal history that follows. For Milton, as for Camões, geography has its romance, but, so far from finding satisfaction in the great world which lies before him, Adam is called to see what havoc his descendants will make of it and what a need there is for real devotion and courage.

It was not always easy for Milton to adapt the devices of epic into his poem and one of his greatest obstructions was his own respect for the truth. An epic, for instance, was expected to say something about the structure of the universe. Virgil had given a sketch of a cosmology, and the place of man in the universe was hardly intelligible if the poet did not say what the universe was. So Camões' Venus shows Gama a model of it, in which, as we might expect in 1572, the system is that of Ptolemy. Milton adopts this arrangement in the main narrative of his poem. His world is a system of concentric globes, at the middle of which is the actual earth. Through these Satan travels from the outside to the centre. It is an easy and useful plan for Satan's voyage, and it gives to the earth the importance which the story demands for it. But Milton knew of Copernicus and had met Galileo ; he may even have used the great inventor's telescope to look more closely at

> the Moon, whose Orb
> Through Optic Glass the *Tuscan* Artist views
> At Ev'ning from the top of *Fesole*,
> Or in *Valdarno*, to descry new Lands,
> Rivers or Mountains in her spotty Globe.
>
> (1, 287-91)

Milton might have left the Ptolemaic system to look after itself and have said nothing about the new discoveries which certainly upset the plan of Satan's journey and might seem to detract from the dignity of the earth. But his conscience and his desire to cover his field prevented him from taking such a course. He makes Adam question Raphael about the structure of the universe and raise an awkward problem. As the Argument says, " Adam inquires concerning Celestial Motions, is doubtfully answer'd, and exhorted to search rather things more worthy of knowing ". What happens is that Raphael sets out with commendable fairness the competing cosmologies and seems to decide against the Ptolemaic by saying that it is the kind of thing that makes God laugh. But he fails to draw a definite conclusion and leaves Adam with a warning not to ask too much about Heaven. Milton saves his story and points his moral, but the main difficulty remains unresolved.

Examples like these show how Milton uses the traditional devices of epic. His devotion to the tradition makes *Paradise Lost* a European poem when it might have been insular or sectarian. Its roots go down to Homer; it often presents themes handled by many poets, but it gives them a new life and freshness. How deep his roots were even Milton did not always know. Describing the number of the fallen angels, he says that they lie

> Thick as Autumnal Leaves that strow the Brooks
> In *Vallombrosa*, where th' *Etrurian* shades
> High overarch't imbowr.   (I, 302-4)

The comparison of spirits in the underworld to fallen leaves is of great antiquity. It may first have appeared in some lost Orphic poem about a descent into Hades. From this Bacchylides, in the fifth century B.C., probably took it when he told how Heracles visited Hades :

> ἔνθα δυστάνων βροτῶν
> ψυχὰς ἐδάη παρὰ Κωκυτοῦ ῥεέθροις,
> οἷά τε φύλλ' ἄνεμος
> Ἴδας ἀνὰ μηλοβότους
> πρῶνας ἀργηστὰς δονεῖ.[1]
>   (v, 63-7)

Virgil took up the idea for the ghosts of the unburied dead :

> quam multa in silvis autumni frigore primo
> lapsa cadunt folia,[2]   (VI, 309-10)

and after him Dante told of the ghosts pressing to cross Acheron :

[1] There he saw the ghosts
Of unlucky men by Cocytus' streams,
Like leaves that the wind flutters
On Ida's glittering headlands
Where the flocks graze.

Thick as in forests at first autumn frost
Leaves drift and fall.

Come d' autunno si levan le foglie
L' una appresso dell' altra, fin che 'l ramo
Vede alla terra tutte le sue spoglie.[1]

(*Inf.* III, 112-14)

Tasso gave a new turn to the comparison when he made the routed devils go back to Hell:

Nè tante vede mai l' autunno al suolo
Cader co' primi freddi aride foglie.[2]

(IX, 66, 5-6)

Marlowe picked it up to describe a vast army in *Tamerlane*:

In number more than are the quivering leaves
Of Ida's forest.

At the end of the succession comes Milton who knew Virgil, Dante, Tasso and Marlowe but not Bacchylides or his unknown predecessor. He picks up the old simile and uses it of the hosts of fallen angels, thus showing some indebtedness to Tasso, who used it of devils, to Marlowe, who used it of an army, and to Virgil and Dante, who used it of spirits in the underworld. Moreover his instinctive genius shows his affinity to classical art when he gives a real place to the fallen leaves. His Vallombrosa is as exact as Bacchylides' Ida and has the immediacy of Greek poetry.

Just as this simile shows how deep the roots of Milton's poetry are, so his other similes show the range of his reading and of his intellectual curiosity. Like Camões, he understands what a simile ought to be and goes far beyond the subjects canonised by Virgil. Indeed just as Homer takes his similes from many parts of life which were excluded from his narrative by its heroic subject, so Milton takes his from the rich world which aroused his intellectual and imaginative interest but had come into existence since the time of Adam and Eve and could not be brought directly into their story. Naturally enough he sometimes uses familiar comparisons

[1] And as the late leaves of November fall
One after one till on the earthen floor
The ruined bough looks on their funeral.
(L. Binyon)

[2] Nor leaves in so great numbers fall away
When winter nips them with his new-come frosts.
(Fairfax)

like bees crowding their "straw-built citadel" or winds echoing through rocks, or draws on his beloved biblical or classical literature for Jacob's Ladder or Hercules at Oechalia. These show his background and his sense of the past. But others, even more characteristic, show his sense of the present, especially when he turns to stories of travel or to folklore or to contemporary life. Though circumstances kept him for all his mature years in England, he fed his imagination with tales of strange adventures in distant lands and seas, and introduces the Leviathan, on which a sailor anchors his ship in the belief that it is an island, the fleet hanging in the clouds as it sails from Tidor or Ternate, the winds in conflict over the Caspian Sea, the vulture that swoops down from the Himalayas to devour the flocks of nomad Tartars, the scent of spices which greets sailors as they round the Cape of Good Hope, the aboriginal Americans found by Columbus, the Polar winds that drive blocks of ice on the eastern sea, the Tartar retreating before the Russians or the Persian before the Turks. Quite different from the sense of space and adventure which these similes give is the quaint or sinister charm which Milton finds in beliefs of folklore, like the "Faerie elves" which a peasant sees by moonlight by a forest or a fountain, or the Night-Hag who rides through the air, lured by the smell of infant blood, to dance with Lapland witches. Nearer home and his own times are the thief who breaks into the house "of some rich Burgher" and the man who "long in populous city pent" goes out on a summer morning into the country to enjoy its sweet scents and be delighted by the sight of a charming girl. The austere limits of Milton's story are widened and enriched by his similes which make his subject more vivid and more universal.

By such means Milton enlarged the scope of his biblical story with its obvious limitations until his epic could really take its place in the succession to Virgil. He shows his creative vitality in the range and variety of experience which he puts into *Paradise Lost*. It is of course true that not all of it is as interesting to us as it was to him or even to our grandfathers. His theology has not worn so well as he assumed that it would, partly because it has lost many adherents to its tenets, partly because its poetry seems to have aged despite its uniformly majestic presentation. But though Milton evidently believed that his first task was to explain and to expound, he was also a poet who used a poet's means to make his message inspire and delight. The poet in him was not the same as the theologian and the Puritan, and in *Paradise Lost* we feel the tug between them. By his own strictest standards he should have admitted nothing that was not true, but the war in Heaven is almost his own invention ; he should have paid no attention to the false legends of antiquity or to the equally false stories of modern romance, but he gave his own story much of their beauty and attractiveness ; he should probably not have written a poem at all, for poetry is notoriously deceitful, but he believed that a great poem was one of the noblest works of man, and nothing could deter him from writing one ; he was convinced that the only real goodness lay in obedience to God, but he could not altogether control or conceal his admiration for other forms of distinction. It is well that these contradictions existed in Milton. They add greatly to the variety and richness of his poem and show on how wide an appreciation of life it is built.

The contradictions in Milton are perhaps greater than those in Virgil, Camões or Tasso. These poets at least harmonised their conflicts in the main scheme of their poems and found solutions to the doubts and difficulties which beset them. But though the main scheme of *Paradise Lost* seems to settle everything to Milton's satisfaction, we cannot but feel that it is based on a compromise between ultimately discordant aims. The real conflict in Milton was between the Puritan and the Humanist. As a Puritan he believed that nothing was good except in so far as it carried out the will of God ; his conception of goodness was strictly ethical. But as a Humanist he felt that many things are good in themselves without reference to theology or morals. In his love of reason, of nature, of music, of physical beauty, of poetry, of knowledge, of all the intellectual delights which he found in books or in the world, he showed himself a true Humanist. Though he was deeply impressed by the fallen state of men and the wickedness of the world, he refused to believe that man was absolutely corrupt and that all his activities were wrong. Just as Erasmus and his fellow Humanists believed that many ordinary human instincts and desires might well be good in themselves, so Milton could not in practice keep himself from feeling that there was much good in men which bore little relation to the service of God. His position was quite different from that held by the stricter Puritans like Richard Baxter, who said, " Nor have I ever been much tempted to any of the sins which go under the name of pastime ". When he wrote *Paradise Lost*, Milton still believed in noble pastimes and was far from thinking that man's duty and dignity were alien to them. It is true that later in *Paradise Regained* and *Samson Agonistes* he was far more consistent in his Puritanism and rejected much that he had previously accepted. Just as Jansenism drove Racine to give up the writing of tragedy except on religious subjects, and then only in *Esther* and *Athalie*, so Puritanism drove Milton to write his last works on subjects about which he could have no conscientious qualms. But before that he wrote *Paradise Lost* and put into it the two sides of his nature, the Puritan and the Humanist, and the combination is responsible for some of its best qualities and for much of its fame.

The balance or tension which Milton keeps between his Humanism and his Puritanism is typically English. While French logic tended to keep the two apart, with the Humanist Montaigne on the one side and the Jansenist Pascal on the other, English compromise found no difficulty in keeping the two together. The English Humanists of the sixteenth century, Linacre, Latimer and Grocyn, were all men of profound religious convictions, and Colet came back from Italy to lecture on the Epistles of St. Paul. Protestantism in its early stages had a great respect for learning and especially for classical learning. From Greek and Latin literature it derived not only the evidences of its faith but a genial corrective to its austerity. The religious quarrels of the seventeenth century upset this happy balance and created a new kind of religious fanatic who broke images and church windows and saw nothing but the Devil's work in polite letters. Partly because it was a proletarian movement, Puritanism lacked respect for a culture and refinement which its own class had never enjoyed, and it fortified this ignorance with moral arguments. But Milton never quite yielded to these extreme claims. He felt their force, and perhaps gave more weight to them than they really deserved. But as a scholar and a poet he preferred on the whole to maintain the old compromise and to combine his respect for God with his respect for the finer achievements of man. In this he resembled the men of the sixteenth century rather than his own contemporaries. Fashion hardly touched his independent mind, and he went his own way, confident that his poetry was beyond the reach of moral disapprobation.

The chief strength of Protestantism is its belief in the intellect and in its capacity to solve all problems. For this reason, though it produces few works of art, what it produces has a special quality and even distinction. The "umpire Conscience" may perhaps be deceived into approving matters that it should not, but at least it exacts high standards and gives in return a strength and nobility which may be lacking when standards are more lax. Indeed Milton's classical form is in some respects as much the result of his Protestantism as of his education in Greek and Latin. The order which he sets on his experiences and the impression which he conveys of having meditated and judged them, are typical of a man who would pass nothing that did not conform to strict conceptions of nobility and propriety. Even his occasional primness is a kind of elegance, a rejection of the coarse and the vulgar. And all this discipline and selection are imposed by a mind which was intensely serious about human life and its worth. Milton conforms to the highest epic traditions in his conviction that a man can, if he chooses, find an impressive nobility. Though he subordinated his sense of beauty to his sense of goodness, that does not mean that his sense of beauty is impaired. Of course he lacks the wayward charm and sensuous fancy of Ariosto and even of Tasso, but his appreciation of human worth and dignity is as great as theirs. His trained, controlled, critical taste is as true a reflection of real sensibility as are many more riotous imaginations. Behind the discipline and the selection, behind the bursts of disapproval and disgust, we can see the sensitive poet who grew to manhood before the Civil War and was in more than one way the legitimate successor of Spenser. Just as Milton's language gives permanence to his emotions while it seems to hide them, so his critical judgment sifts out the false from the true in his experience and presents only what he himself believed to be of unquestionable worth.

In *Paradise Lost* Milton gave form and order to his own troubles and to the disappointments which he found in an age of confusion and failure. It is therefore not surprising that at times it shows an illiberal and even a rancorous spirit. But these moments are rare and relatively unimportant. They are the cries of a proud and sensitive soul when it finds that the misdeeds of men are almost more than it can bear. What really matters is the temper in which Milton surmounted his troubles and the spiritual exaltation which he found. He sees life as an unending battle and has the temperament of a heroic fighter. But though he enjoys the battle and deals resounding blows, he is inspired by an ideal which really means more to him than anything else and amply compensates for his defeats and disappointments. In the intellectual love of God Milton found a peace and a satisfaction which even he found hard to describe. He comes nearest to doing so when he speaks of music in Heaven or of the divine voice which dictates his poetry or of the celestial light which he summons to irradiate his mind. It was to this ideal of harmony, strength and beauty that he gave his devotion and his service, and in it he found the central point of his creative life. It enabled him not only to surmount his defeats and to keep his courage high in evil times but to look from a lofty eminence upon the spectacle of human life and to consider it without despair and even at times with hope.

Milton is the last great practitioner of literary epic. With him it found a finality which forbade any extension of its scope. No poem can include more than the whole of history or be set on a stage wider than the whole of space. It may even be doubted whether the grand style can be grander than Milton's or the heroic temper more sublime than his. The great features of *Paradise Lost*, its language, its temper, its scope, its theology, its ornaments, are all natural developments of Virgil's art, but they are applied with a rigour and a consistency which lie far beyond their original uses. While Milton developed the art of literary epic in some directions, he simplified it in others. *Paradise Lost* has not the rich humanity or the creative exuberance of its predecessors. It looks as if Milton had formed from his study of other poets the idea of an essential epic in which all the emphasis should be on the fundamental issues and on the truly epic task. Since the epic deals with the destiny of man, Milton was determined to show this in its full range and significance, to rid it of extraneous'considerations, and to shape the old devices until each fitted into his main plan. This simplification adds to his sublimity. Our attention is inevitably fixed on the great issues which he presents and forced to grasp them in their stark power. Milton keeps more faithfully to his task than any of his forerunners. For not only does he set out the extremes of good and evil and show what they mean and what results they produce, but at the same time he gives so sublime a setting to his human beings that they too, despite their failures and their imperfections, gain in majesty from their circumstances and are not unworthy to take their parts in the vast scene

> from Eastern Point
> Of *Libra* to the fleecie Starr that bears
> *Andromeda* farr off *Atlantick* Seas
> Beyond th' *Horizon*.

INDEX

PRINTED BY R. & R. CLARK, LIMITED, EDINBURGH

extraneous considerations, and to shape the old devices until each fitted into his main plan. This simplification adds to his sublimity. Our attention is inevitably fixed on the great issues which he presents and forced to grasp them in their stark power. Milton keeps more faithfully to his task than any of his forerunners. For not only does he set out the extremes of good and evil and show what they mean and what results they produce, but at the same time he gives so sublime a setting to his human beings that they too, despite their failures and their imperfections, gain in majesty from their circumstances and are not unworthy to take their parts in the vast scene

> from Eastern Point
> Of *Libra* to the fleecie Starr that bears
> *Andromeda* farr off *Atlantick* Seas
> Beyond th' *Horizon*.

INDEX

Apollonius Rhodius, 18
Ariosto, L., 19 ff., 30, 99, 121, 122, 123, 126 ff., 131, 133, 134, 139, 141, 143 ff., 154, 162, 168, 174, 192 ff., 230, 236 ff., 244
Aristotle, 67
Arnaut de Marueil, 108
Augustine, St., 33, 49, 51, 58, 65, 84, 202

Bacchylides, 240, 241
Battle of Maldon, 41, 42
Baxter, R., 244
Beowulf, 2, 3, 5, 18
Blake, W., 227
Boiardo, M., 18 ff., 121, 127, 139, 141, 143, 154, 163, 195, 230
Boileau, N., 110

Camões, L. de, 5, 11, 14, 15 ff., Ch. III *passim*, 139, 140, 141, 142, 148, 154, 174, 190, 192, 195, 198, 212, 230, 236, 238 ff., 243
Castiglione, B., 157
Chaucer, G., 33
Cicero, 52, 60, 63, 64, 79, 233
Claudian, 150
Corneille, P., 110

Dante, 14, 33, 150, 220, 240
Demosthenes, 233
Donatus, 33, 67
Dryden, J., 109

Eliot, T. S., 238
Empedocles, 70, 233
Ennius, 34, 40
Epicurus, 59
Erasmus, 243
Euripides, 49

Fanshawe, Sir R., 195
Ferreira, A., 88

Guarini, G. B., 184

Homer, 2, 3, 4, 5, 7 ff., 18, 24, 26, 35, 36, 37, 38, 39, 42 ff., 46, 56 ff., 70, 83, 84, 88, 102, 106, 109, 138, 148, 155, 168, 183, 195, 197, 234, 241
Horace, 51, 52, 58, 75

John of the Cross, St., 220
Jugoslavian epic, 2, 5, 26

Kalevala, 4

Livy, 52, 75, 154
Longinus, 18
Lucretius, 40, 70, 80

Macrobius, 33
Marcus Aurelius, 67, 84
Marlowe, C., 241
Medici, L. de', 185
Melinno, 75
Milton, J., 2, 3, 5, 6 ff., 14 ff., 25 ff., 30 ff., 150, 183, Ch. V *passim*
Mimnermus, 185
Montaigne, M. de, 244

Naevius, 34

Ovid, 50, 113

Pascal, B., 244
Petronius, 33, 36, 109
Plato, 71
Polybius, 75

Racine, J., 244
Roland, Song of, 2, 3, 5, 6 ff., 18, 41

Seneca, 59, 63, 67
Servius, 33
Simonides, 153
Sophocles, 47, 209
Spenser, E., 23, 25, 184, 185, 188, 244
Statius, 112

Tasso, T., 5, 11, 14, 15, 17 ff., 27 ff., Ch. IV *passim*, 195, 197, 198, 230, 241, 243, 244

Valla, L., 88
Verlaine, P., 1
Vida, 11, 14, 89, 150, 194, 233
Virgil, 2, 3, 4 ff., 7 ff., 12 ff., 28 ff., Ch. II *passim*, 88, 89, 90, 96, 98, 102, 104, 105, 106, 109, 111, 112, 115, 120, 129, 135, 138, 139, 140, 148, 151, 152, 153, 155, 161, 192, 195, 196, 197, 211, 212, 213, 229, 230, 236, 240, 241, 243, 246

Zeno, 66

PRINTED BY R. & R. CLARK, LIMITED, EDINBURGH

Date Due

JUL 2 6 '49		JA 24 '66
AUG 1 '53	OCT 1 '61	JAN 17 '66
SEP 1 8 '53		JA 26 '66
SEP '54	NOV '61	FE 7 '66
OCT 2 3 '54		
	OCT 29 '61	MY 20 '66
SEP 2 9 '55	JAN 4 - '62	DE 3 '66
NOV 2 1 '55	JAN 2 '62	JA 14 '67
DEC 3 '55	APR 6 '62	MY 21 '68
DEC 1 7 '55	AUG 15 '62	FE 19 '70
OCT 1 4 '57	SEP 1 0 '62	OC 29 '70
NOV 1 0 '57		NO 4 '70
AUG 1 0 '58	OC 1 '63	NO 19 '70
DEC 1 9 '58	NOV 1 '63	MR 10 '71
APR 8 '59	RESERVE	NO 28 '72
SEP 2 1 '59	SE 14 '64	'72
	RESERVE	
	ONE WEEK	
APR '60	JAN 13 '66	
	⊕ FE 5 70	

CPSIA information can be obtained
at www.ICGtesting.com
Printed in the USA
BVHW052350080223
658190BV00005B/117